The Seventeenth Generation
The Lifework of Rabbi Walter Jacob

Best wishes,

Walter Jacob

The Seventeenth Generation
The Lifework of Rabbi Walter Jacob

By Eric Lidji

Rodef Shalom Press
Pittsburgh

4905 Fifth Avenue
Pittsburgh, PA 15213
USA

ISBN 978-0-692-08844-9

Inside cover: In his retirement, Walter returned to his native Germany to start the Abraham Geiger College, reviving a spirit of Jewish religious scholarship that had been vital to his ancestors and destroyed during his youth.

Contents

Foreword

Those of us who know Walter Jacob as our rabbi have long appreciated his wisdom and sagacity, his perspective on life's unfolding, and his equanimity in the face of challenge and loss. But, perhaps, most of all, we are grateful for Rabbi Jacob's tireless dedication to the families of Rodef Shalom Congregation, whom he has tended for some 60 years; the wider Pittsburgh community, to which he and his late wife, Irene, contributed many labors of love; and world Jewry, which, over and above serving in national and international positions of leadership, he has strengthened most significantly by founding the Abraham Geiger College, therein reconstituting rabbinic education in the heart of Germany following the decimation of European Jewry in the Holocaust.

Rabbi Jacob's biography is one most of us know only in snippets or sound bites and, perhaps, from the occasional news article detailing his experiences and accomplishments. This is due, surely, to Rabbi Jacob's simple yet prodigious work ethic coupled with his unfailing modesty. Thus, to date, any information we may have about Walter Jacob — his youth and family of origin, his memories of growing up in Germany and later as an adolescent immigrant in America's heartland, his service as a chaplain in the Pacific theatre, as well as his family life and private concerns — is a result of personal interactions where perchance he may have referred to his own experiences, or of observing him in situ as he quietly goes about his work on the pulpit, in the boardroom, or tending to his gardens. Beyond these all but bygone opportunities, however, Rabbi Walter Jacob's remarkable life story is little known outside a coterie of devoted congregants and rabbinic colleagues. Hence, this book.

It is our hope that, through the pages of this biography, readers far and wide will gain not only a greater understanding of the man, but will grow in appreciation for that which has informed, motivated, and compelled Walter's indefatigable and inspiring efforts to bring the wisdom of Judaism to Jews and the wider world.

Pittsburgh, Pennsylvania, is Walter Jacob's home; the entire world is his pulpit; and all who have benefited from his care in the moment and his commitment to the future are his students.

We, his congregants and colleagues at Rodef Shalom Congregation, feel privileged to share his story with you.

Rabbi Aaron Benjamin Bisno
Frances F. and David R. Levin Senior Rabbinic Pulpit
Rodef Shalom Congregation
Pittsburgh, Pennsylvania

March 2018

Acknowledgments

Ruth Westerman conceived of the idea of honoring Rabbi Walter Jacob by commissioning a book about his life. She was the driving force behind this project throughout the years of planning, research, writing and production. Early on, she assembled a devoted project committee including Rabbi Aaron Bisno, former Rodef Shalom Librarian Anne Molloy, Rodef Shalom archivist Martha Berg and congregants Marcia Frumerman, Hanna Gruen and J. Robert Myers. Their professional expertise and personal insights made this biography both a scholarly endeavor and a human one.

Martha Berg provided access to the large collection of historic materials held at the Rodef Shalom congregational archives. She also created the index and the bibliography for this book. Susan Melnick edited the original manuscript. Her keen eye and her insistence on clarity and accuracy turned rough text into palatable prose.

Rodef Shalom Congregation generously provided the necessary financial support for this project and supported it under the tenures of two presidents: Eric Schaffer and Harlan Stone. Curt Krasik provided legal counsel. Hope Nearhood arranged the many project meetings. Lauren Wolcott advised on marketing matters. Nancy Berkowitz was the final proofreader. JoAnn Ruffing greeted everyone with a smile. A grant from the Fine Foundation helped bring this book into existence.

The administration, students and alumni of Abraham Geiger College offered their hospitality during a research trip to Germany in December 2015. Without their assistance, the sections of this biography focusing on Europe would be greatly diminished. Tobias Berniske graciously provided some of his many photographs of life at the college. In addition to their expertise as designers, the team at Landesberg Design provided crucial guidance on the process of turning a stack of manuscript pages into a published book. Rick Landesberg was a calm, wise presence throughout the process.

It would be impractical and perhaps even impossible to list all the people who offered insights and anecdotes about Walter along the way. Even those whose stories do not appear in this book nevertheless influenced its direction. That being said, this is a book about rabbis, and Walter is a "rabbi's rabbi," and so it seems appropriate to name the rabbis who shared their perspectives: Rabbi Andrew Busch, Rabbi Antje Yael Deusel, Rabbi Jason Edelstein, Rabbi Joan Friedman, Rabbi Walter Homolka, Rabbi Samuel Karff, Rabbi Tom Kucera, Rabbi Ruth Langer, Rabbi Debbie Pine, Rabbi Frederick Pomerantz, Rabbi Danny Schiff, Rabbi Jona Simon, Rabbi Alan Sokobin, Rabbi Mark Staitman, Rabbi Alina Traiger, Rabbi Mark Washofsky and Rabbi Sheldon Zimmerman.

Finally, any official biography is improved by the willing cooperation of its subject. Rabbi Jacob graciously opened his life to examination, giving life to dry facts.

Sixteen Generations

The family of Rabbi Walter Jacob has been in the rabbinate for sixteen generations. Sixteen generations is a long time for a family to remain in any profession, let alone one without any tangible assets to pass along to successors. But while Walter is proud of this long lineage, he is also self-conscious and perhaps even cautious about the awe it can inspire. "Anything that makes the rabbi more distant from the congregation is, to my mind, wrong," he once said,[1] when asked to explain why he preferred to wear a suit on the pulpit, rather than the austere black robes favored by some Reform rabbis of his generation. Along similar lines, at the first ordination ceremony of the Abraham Geiger College, the rabbinic seminary he helped establish in Germany, Walter was introduced as "Rabbi Prof. Walter Jacob B.A., M.H.L., D.H.L., D. Litt." But he generally answers the phone, "Walter Jacob here," without any title at all.[2] A rabbi who is reluctant to introduce himself as a rabbi is also unlikely to make a big deal about belonging to a long line of them.

In the years before his accomplishments matched his potential, Walter was clever enough to deploy his rabbinic lineage in situations where it helped his cause. He mentioned it, privately, to the board of trustees of Rodef Shalom in early 1966, when he was campaigning to become the senior rabbi of the Pittsburgh congregation.[3] He was trying to reassure those trustees who were worried about hiring someone so young and so modest to oversee one of the most storied Jewish congregations in the world and to succeed its famous and distinguished leader, Dr. Solomon B. Freehof. By citing his pedigree, Walter was practicing the ancient Jewish art of calling upon one's ancestors as character witnesses. Just as the morning prayers appeal to the God of "Abraham, Isaac and Jacob," Walter was adding his name to an auspicious chain of tradition.

Walter freely acknowledges the limits of his ancestry. At a speaking engagement in 1993, the master of ceremonies introduced Walter as a sixteenth-generation rabbi and noted, "That must be a record somewhere." In retort, Walter quipped, "All those generations don't really help. You have to learn Hebrew like everybody else." While the transcript does not describe his timing or delivery, it notes that the line got a laugh.[4] Anyone who knows Walter personally will be able to hear his amused, deliberate and self-effacing voice as they read his words and will likely chuckle at his punch line, too.

Walter is quiet and unassuming. He has a tendency to disappear in crowds. Even though his complete bibliography stretches beyond thirteen hundred listings, he is just as likely to be found leaning on a shovel as buried in a book, and he has undoubtedly spent more time cleaning gutters and hauling soil than all of his rabbinic predecessors combined. He rarely peppers his speech with scripture, and he generally avoids philosophy and theology. He appreciates any opportunity to discuss subjects other than being a rabbi. His interests extend far beyond religion and include art, theater, classical music, gardening, history, travel and a general curiosity about people and cultures. After listening to a colleague describe a sabbatical spent touring synagogues around the world, Walter privately mused, "Not my idea of a sabbatical."[5]

And yet, the way Walter conducts his daily affairs carries a rabbinic aura — something ancient and true. His polite modesty suggests great depths of feeling. His folksy wit contains surprisingly practical wisdom. His easy-going manner is certainly what Maimonides had in mind when he advised, "Avoid both hysterical gaiety and somber dejection, and instead be calmly joyful always."[6]

Walter developed this aura by combining "scholarship and *menschlichkeit*," as the late Central Conference of American Rabbis Executive Director Rabbi Joseph Glaser explained to members of the rabbinic body in 1993, using a Yiddish word that evokes a combination of humanity and integrity. By the early 1990s, Walter's scholarly achievements were well known to his contemporaries and his younger colleagues within the Reform movement. "But," as Glaser continued, "scholarship is more than knowing a lot. Scholarship is also accessing and applying knowledge with discernment. Scholarship is an unerring sense of right and of what is true, and the character and devotion to principle combined with that, equals real genuine leadership. That is what we have had along with the *menschlichkeit* of Walter Jacob."[7]

Walter credits his family with helping him develop his even temperament. He credits families, generally, with performing this task. In several sermons, he described the Torah as a family story, rather than a story of tribes or nations. The final chapters of Genesis, he noted, primarily focus on the quarrels and reconciliations of the children of Jacob, and push the more historically relevant proceedings of the Egyptian court into the background. "It is the family which has given us inner strength from the beginning and it is the family which has kept us strong ever since," he explained.[8] Even though most people can provide a rational explanation for their beliefs and behavior, he noted, "our ethics and morality are generally based on emotion, mood and feeling. Much of this comes to us as a heritage from the previous generation, not through anything overt, but through the presence of that generation."[9] One reason why Walter has generally been more conservative on family matters than in other areas of Jewish law is because of this idea that heritage inspires belief.

Walter has jokingly described the process of acquiring acumen through proximity as "osmosis," and the metaphor works. He absorbed many of his most deeply held values from his immediate family, especially as political persecution forced an already tight-knit family even closer together. As he trained for the rabbinate in America and came of age in the profession, he borrowed many skills and techniques from mentors and from admired colleagues. He has the rare ability to grow within the shadow of greatness, to chart a new path within the footsteps of his predecessors. His greatest accomplishments can most accurately be categorized as feats of resourcefulness and adaptation. He solved immediate problems with available tools and made ancient ideas relevant under new circumstances.

Walter even borrowed his attitude toward his long rabbinic ancestry. When his father, Rabbi Ernest Jacob, was being installed as the rabbi of a small Reform congregation in Missouri, after more than three years of Nazi-imposed exile from the pulpit, he told his new flock, "The rabbinate is a tradition in my family. I am the fifteenth generation in the service of God and our people. The tradition does not count for much in itself, but it is always good if a man can look at life from a past and if it can point out his assets to him. It provides him with a challenge and he must live up to it."[10] Walter was expressing a similar sentiment, five decades later, when he joked about having to learn Hebrew like everyone else. But where his father had been reflective and eloquent, he was irreverent and self-deprecating. That is the nature of progress within an ancient tradition: the message stays the same, but the voice must change in order to be heard anew.

Tradition was subtle but ever-present
in the Jacob home. In this photograph,
Walter gives a toast in honor of his
father's 50th birthday as his mother,
Annette, watches with pleasure. A portrait
of her father, Jakob Loewenberg, watches
over them both. In the background is a
seder plate given to the Jacobs by their
first congregation in Germany.

DIE NEVE SYNAGOGE ZV AVGSBVRG .

DIPL ING·FRITZ·LANDAVER ·v· D? ING· HEINRICH LÖMPEL
·ARCHITEKTEN MÜNCHEN

The Jewish Community of Augsburg
dedicated a new synagogue in 1917,
after seven centuries of documented
Jewish life in the city. The design of the
building embodied the aspirations of
the community by blending modern
German architecture with details drawn
from Jewish antiquity. On this postcard,
Ernst Jacob marked the location of an
apartment on the synagogue grounds
set aside for the rabbi and his family.

CHAPTER I

Influenced By
Their Surroundings

"We are an extraordinarily fortunate group," Walter told a crowd of rabbinic colleagues in 1993, in a presidential address to the Central Conference of American Rabbis, "especially when I think of the fifteen generations of rabbis in my family who preceded me. I know little about most of them, but I know that they moved from one place to another in Central Europe, and it was not because they were advancing from one pulpit to another, they were withdrawing from one persecution after another."[11]

Although he grouped himself among those extraordinarily fortunate American rabbis, Walter had also withdrawn from persecution. He was the last generation in his family born in Europe and the first to be ordained in the United States. As is his general inclination, he expresses more gratitude for the latter than regret for the former. He freely discusses his experiences in Germany but worries about the psychic cost of focusing on those years and others like them in Jewish history. To Walter, those moments are not the story of Judaism. They are interruptions of a larger story. "When sad events occurred, and we have survived many tragedies, we have tried to forget them as quickly as possible," he once said in a sermon,[12] confidently defying a view of Judaism as a faith obsessed with its misfortunes.

In an interview with the Survivors of the Shoah Visual History Foundation, Walter made a point to mourn not only the loss of life that occurred after his family fled Germany but also the loss of a way of life. He felt it was important to retain, as he described it, "some memory of what German Jewry was like." He recalled a great nation with many large, knowledgeable and enthusiastic Jewish communities, all of them eager to further ancient traditions in a modern way. Honoring their lives, their values and their accomplishments was "possibly even as important" as remembering their deaths, he said, tactfully, then noted, "We tend to focus on the negative, the destruction at the end."[13]

Walter rarely focuses on destruction. He prefers restoration to commemoration, and he prioritizes the future over the past. But, he also listens to what previous generations have to say. He often refers to the "development" of history.[14] It is a way of turning the past into a story, of identifying the general direction of human events by connecting seemingly unrelated incidents occurring in disparate places over long periods of time. His picture of Jewish life in Germany before World War II is one of those developments, and his ancestors played a part in developing it. His family joined the rabbinate in the decades before the Thirty Years' War began in 1618 and continued in the profession through the Middle Ages, the Renaissance, the Reformation, the Enlightenment, the Industrial Revolution, World War I and World War II. The shifting of national and cultural boundaries brought periods of peace for the Jews and also periods of persecution. At the time Walter was born, in 1930, the arc of those centuries was moving toward greater opportunities for Jews throughout much of Central Europe. Secular societies were increasingly accommodating Jewish people. As a result, the Jewish religion faced new pressures. Some shielded their traditions from outside influence by pulling away from society altogether. Others rejected their traditions by assimilating into society to whatever degree their neighboring citizens allowed. The Jacob family took a middle path. They were part of a wider liberalizing trend that was trying to adapt Judaism to the needs of the time and the place.

If history had proceeded in a more merciful direction, Walter and his contemporaries would have shepherded Judaism through another century of change across the European continent. Instead, every Jewish child of his generation in Germany was hidden, exiled or murdered. Walter is part of a small group that was fortunate enough to make it safely to America and was committed enough to continue their religious task in a new country.

Walter never lost the essence of his European upbringing. Rabbi Yael Deusel, an Abraham Geiger College alumna who now leads a liberal Jewish congregation in Bamberg, Germany, says she can hear an alternative history of Europe whenever Walter uses his native tongue. Without the benefit of hearing the German language evolve over the 20th century, Walter still occasionally uses bits and pieces of an older, more formal style common during the final days of the Weimar Republic. "We see, just a glimpse, how it could have been, if there wouldn't have been that gap," she said.[15] America was the beneficiary of "that gap." Walter adapted the religious culture of his European ancestors to fit the opportunities he discovered in his new home. To fully appreciate the accomplishments of his rabbinate, it is necessary to understand how his European ancestors practiced their faith, or, more precisely, his understanding of how they practiced it.

Walter has often presented Judaism as an ongoing compromise between high standards and practical decisions. "Our historic past has been marked by idealism mixed with realism," he said in February 1966, during a lecture at Rodef Shalom about the Vietnam War. The purpose of the lecture was to remind the congregation that the societal obligation to be realistic about world affairs was not an excuse to set aside the demands of idealism, particularly the ideal of peace. "Fads come and go; cars, food and clothing change according to the whim of public response. Fads vanish, so do ideals. It is our task as Jews to keep this ideal alive," he explained. "It is not a mere fancy for us; it is the grandest ideal of our ancient religion. We must assure that it is never viewed as an eccentricity or … relegated to the outer perimeter of our conscience."[16]

Walter was keeping a different ideal alive when he described German Jewry as committed, integrated and growing. He witnessed only a brief glimpse of that community before it disappeared forever. He was born in 1930, which made him three when Adolf Hitler was elected chancellor of Germany, five when the Nuremberg Laws halted more than a century of social advances for Jews, eight when the Nazis destroyed almost every synagogue in Germany in a single night and nine when his family was forced to flee the country or risk death by staying. His warm image of Jewish culture thriving within a German milieu is not a snapshot, but a collage. It brings together the best memories he and his surviving peers have from their childhoods, the stories he heard from his elders and the examples their lives presented to him, and a deeper understanding of the past acquired through heritage, tradition and years of loving study into the world of his ancestors. His portrayal of a Jewish community fully committed to its religion and also fully at home in its modern setting is as much an heirloom as a personal reminiscence. It is one of the ideals he has mixed with reality throughout his life.

By the time the Jacob family entered the rabbinate, the institution was mature, established and widespread. It had emerged during the 1st century, after Roman conquerors destroyed the second Holy Temple in Jerusalem. The end of the Jewish monarchy and its associated orbits of priests, sages and prophets left only scholars to keep the faith alive and adapt it to a perpetual state of exile.

The rabbinate assumed different forms in different eras and different parts of the world. The first rabbi in the Jacob family line was Rabbi Aharon Moshe Teomin, who led a congregation in Prague during the late 16th century. It was early in the era of the professional rabbinate in Europe. A class of strong lay leaders was taking over the civic responsibilities of the rabbinate, such as acting as a liaison between Jewish communities and the governments of states where Jews resided. The daily work of the rabbi was turning inward to focus on religious, spiritual and communal affairs.[17]

The first thirteen rabbis in the Jacob family line oversaw these responsibilities for relatively isolated Jewish communities living within a predominately Christian context. As the influence of religion over civic life waned in the 19th century, Jews were emancipated and given the full rights of citizenship throughout much of Central Europe. These emancipated Jews entered society and became acquainted with new professions, new social and religious customs, and new schools of thought.[18]

Jewish laity felt the impact of emancipation before Jewish clergy. Walter's maternal great-great-grandfather Nathan Löwenberg was the father of one of eight Jewish families living in a Catholic village in Westphalia. In that region, Jews were restricted to rural areas and thereby kept at a distance from the economic and cultural opportunities available in cities. Even before emancipation, though, Jews were engaging with their neighbors, as can be seen by a pair of simple bureaucratic facts. When Nathan married, he signed the government registry in Hebrew. When Nathan died, his son signed the death certificate in German.

His son Levi Löwenberg was a peddler, and knowing the local language was therefore a commercial imperative. But he showed little interest in participating in the wider culture outside of his work. He left home early on Monday morning and returned early on Friday afternoon to welcome the Sabbath with his wife, Friederike. A different kind of literacy became important to their youngest child, Jakob Loewenberg. His desire for inclusion was cultural rather than economic. He was born in 1856, making him a teenager in 1871, when the German states united into an empire and the rights granted to Jews in regional kingdoms became a national law.

Emancipation was a legal designation. It allowed Jews to live where they wanted to live and to pursue careers they wanted to pursue. But many cultural restrictions persisted and many private prejudices remained. Jakob was a writer, and his art was permeated with a yearning to join German society without having to abandon his Jewish culture. In one of his autobiographical novels, he longingly wrote, "Even the stream that flows from two sources tranquilly joins its water to the great ocean."[19]

Jakob started his career as a *melamed*, an educator responsible for overseeing religious life in a community too small to support a rabbi. He and his siblings struggled to fit the closed religion of their youths into an ever-opening world. Some of his siblings moved to America. Others went into business. Jakob loved "the fatherland" too much to leave it and was too sensitive for commerce.[20] He wandered for a time, learning English and French in London and Paris and later attended the World's Columbian Exposition in Chicago in 1893. "If he had been a little bolder, and stayed here, it would have saved me a lot of trouble," Walter joked.[21]

Jakob eventually entered the German university system. Academia provided a pathway of social improvement for many, but not for him. Although he passed his examinations after only two years, he struggled to find a teaching position. The limited educational opportunities available to him in his village had failed to provide a certain certificate required for advancement.[22] An understanding of that sort of systemic injustice rings through a lecture Walter delivered at Rodef Shalom, in early 1968, about the frustrations facing black communities. "In a bureaucracy," Walter noted, "the inner workings are considered correct and the recipient in error."[23]

Excluded from the academy, Jakob moved to Hamburg in 1886 to teach at a Protestant school. He bought a small private school in the city in 1892 and became its director. The *Anerkannte Höhere Mädchenschule Lyzeum von Dr. J. Loewenberg*, (The Accredited Girls' Grammar School of Dr. J. Loewenberg), as it eventually became known, was officially non-sectarian but drew its student body from a largely Jewish part of Hamburg, allowing Jakob to pursue the melding of national and religious identity he had described in his writings.

Small details of student life speak to the orderliness of German education. After recess, older students would stand at each half-landing on the main stairwell to escort the younger students to their classes. Jakob would emerge from his office to greet the students and make sure none of them had hair covering their brows. But he also introduced progressive reforms and added a Jewish bent to the typical rigors of the German system. Preferring enthusiasm to discipline, he created a curriculum to help his girls develop the "moral courage and spiritual energy" to enter adulthood—either in the home or in a professional field. He moved the school to larger quarters within walking distance of a botanical garden, an art gallery and a historical museum, and he made the new accommodations as welcoming as he could by installing central heating, electric lighting and the first gymnastics bars of any school in the city. Girls were taken on tours of great architecture and on hikes through nearby forests.

In those days, all accredited schools in Hamburg were required to offer religious classes, tailored to the faith of their student bodies. Jakob introduced a Sabbath curriculum of scripture, Jewish poetry and Hebrew language studies.[24] Students and teachers lived close to the school and often walked to class together each morning. Walter once described this close-knit Jewish world as an "elegant ghetto."[25]

Jakob turned his school into one of the jewels of the Hamburg educational system, admired by educators and beloved by students. When the Hamburg Senate issued a tribute to him in honor of his seventieth birthday, in 1926, more than two hundred alumni came to the city to celebrate. Jakob died in 1929, and the school closed two years later, as a worsening economic depression forced families to move their children into public schools. At the time, Jakob's son and successor Ernst Loewenberg described the closing of the school as a culmination of its cultural mission to integrate Jewish students into German life. But any hope for a German-Jewish amalgamation disappeared in 1940, when the Nazi Party moved into the old school building.[26]

The experience and promise of the school stayed with its alumni. Former students who met Walter in later years always fondly recalled their time at the school and their memories of his grandfather. And as Walter visited Germany with growing frequency in the decades after the war, he often came upon laudatory mentions of his grandfather in retrospectives about education and art in the country before World

Benno Jacob was a leading rabbi of
his day in Germany, a respected pulpit
rabbi and a leading Biblical scholar.
In this photograph, he sits at a desk in
his son Ernst Jacob's study in Augsburg.
Walter Jacob now uses the desk in his
study in Pittsburgh.

War II. Those encounters recalled a time when German Jews still felt hopeful about their prospects for acceptance.

The reformation of Judaism started not with rabbis but with lay people who wanted to adjust the religion to fit modern times. By the 1840s, a group of Jewish intellectuals was agitating for change outside of the official structure of German religious communities.[27] Their numbers grew as more Jews entered German society. Within a few decades, rabbis could accept or reject their ideas, in whole or in part, but they increasingly could not ignore them.

The first rabbi in the Jacob family line to encounter these changes directly was Walter's paternal grandfather, Rabbi Benno Jacob. Benno was born in a village outside Breslau in 1862. He was the son of a rabbi in a long line of rabbis, and he was only a boy when the North German Confederation and later the German Empire emancipated Jewish citizens. His education was a mixture of old religion and the new secular subjects just becoming available to Jewish children of his generation. He studied traditional biblical and Talmudic texts, and he also attended the gymnasium in Breslau, where he learned Greek, Latin and classical fields. The only break in his studies was a voluntary yearlong stint in the Prussian army.[28]

Benno continued to pursue his religious and secular training into early adulthood. He simultaneously attended the University of Breslau and the nearby *Jüdisch-Theologische Seminar*, or Jewish Theological Seminary. The former was a public institution of higher education where Benno was able to further his study of antiquities. The latter was the first liberal rabbinic academy. The Jewish Theological Seminary brought the intellectual ferment of the reformation into the curriculum for training rabbis. It was part of a "positive-historical" movement that combined faith and scholarship. Students were expected to honor the traditional foundations of Judaism, but they were given the freedom to enhance their faith using the emerging scientific system known as *Wissenschaft*. They studied the development of Judaism historically to understand the ways in which it had evolved over time.[29] By applying the rigorous methods of the German academy to their religion, these Jewish scholars invented a field called *Wissenschaft des Judentums*, or the Science of Judaism. For modern Jewry, the turn toward these methods was "the intellectual equivalent of its political emancipation," according to Rabbi Ismar Schorsch, who led the Jewish Theological Seminary in America, a descendant of the European school.[30]

The Jewish Theological Seminary and the other major liberal rabbinic seminary in Europe, the *Hochschule für die Wissenschaft des Judentums*, or Higher Institute for Jewish Studies, in Berlin, were trying to restore rabbinic authority in an emancipated age. As the closed system of the Jewish ghettos came to an end, rabbis no longer had any practical mechanism for enforcing their rulings on matters of Jewish law. The early reformers, especially the 19th century rabbi and scholar Abraham Geiger, believed that rabbinic authority could only be re-established through learnedness. If the curriculum of a rabbinic seminary was sufficiently rigorous, the seminary would produce community rabbis who were also theologians.[31]

Benno encountered obstacles at both of the institutes of higher education he attended. Some of these obstacles he placed before himself. He was opinionated and outspoken, and he greatly annoyed the dean of the Jewish Theological Seminary in Breslau, who in turn refused to sign his ordination papers. Benno and a group of like-minded students were undaunted. They convinced a special committee of leading German rabbis to ordain them.

At the University of Breslau, Benno discovered the limits of emancipation. Growing nationalism and economic instability fostered a wave of anti-Semitism in the 1880s. Some public figures openly called for a reversal of rights, and the hostility was especially strong at universities. "Tired of insults," as Walter put it, Benno and eleven Jewish medical students formed the *Viadrina*. It was the first Jewish dueling fraternity in the country.[32] Such fraternities were ubiquitous among non-Jewish students at German universities. Members wore matching caps and sashes, drank strong beer, sang boisterous songs and defended their brothers' honor through "academic fencing."[33] The motto of the *Viadrina* was "No one attacks me with impunity."[34] Benno took it to heart, and once dueled and disabled a classmate who refused to recognize the *Viadrina*.[35]

Other notorious stories followed. Benno ducked crossfire to conduct a funeral during a battle in the November Revolution. He forced an apology from a soldier who had muttered a derogatory taunt about Jews. He violated the Nazi boycott of Jewish businesses—and also the Sabbath, so great was his verve—by going door to door through the Jewish business district of Hamburg to patronize every store in spite of a large, angry, picketing mob.

Most famously, he interrupted a meeting where a notorious German statesman was delivering a disparaging lecture on the subject "Is the Moral Teaching of the Talmud Compatible with the Civil Law?" Before an audience of hundreds, Benno held aloft a volume of the Talmud and asked the speaker to indicate exactly which passages in it contradicted German law. When the statesman balked, Benno turned to the crowd and said, "This gentleman who has himself admitted that he does not understand one Hebrew letter has the temerity to talk about the moral teaching of the Talmud for two and a half hours without being able to read a single line in this volume." Adding to the audacity of this act was the fact that Benno's porter had accidentally brought the wrong Talmudic volume to the assembly hall.[36]

Walter reviewed the early years of the *Viadrina* at a centennial celebration for the fraternity in Princeton, N.J. in 1986, and he discovered much more than a turf war. The brothers had been taking part in the much grander effort to inject the ethical imperatives of Judaism into the wider culture. Like the 12th-century Tosafists who saw Christianity as the fulfillment of the universal covenant between God and the "children of Noah," or the 15th-century mystic Isaac Luria who issued the call for Jews to "repair the world," Walter credited the *Viadrina* as being an agent of prophetic Judaism. Its members not only believed Judaism could flow through the world without becoming polluted by it but also believed that the world could be cleansed by the encounter. Their matching hats and ribbons were a statement of identity. "This was a clear indication to everyone that the wearer was a proud Jew, as striking as wearing a *kippah*," Walter said. "It meant that thoughts of assimilation were rejected and identification with Judaism was stressed."[37]

By pushing Judaism into direct contact with a central institution of German culture, Benno was also advancing a mission of the Jewish reformation going back to Moses Mendelssohn, whom Walter once called the "first modern Jew." Mendelssohn gained widespread cultural acceptance in his day while still adhering to his traditional faith.[38] Walter was greatly inspired by the idea of this "symbiosis," by the ways religion can be merged with national culture without sacrificing the integrity of either.

In a sermon about the positive influence of hospitable societies on Judaism throughout history, he contrasted the great advances in Jewish scholarship in Germany after emancipation with the inward-looking scholarship produced during previous eras, when Jewish communities in the country were isolated. "When we think of German Jewry, it is hard to imagine how much at home they felt at the end of the last century and early in this century. They developed Jewish life in accordance with the German spirit. This led to their scientific approach to scholarship...Their critical work was thorough, as precise as anything done by Germans in other fields. The scientific study of Judaism which developed in Germany owes a debt of gratitude to that German spirit. Compare this approach with German Jews four centuries earlier who did not feel at home. They produced legal codes and compendia, which are supposed to help us understand Judaism better. Those books... are so confused that only those who know the law well can benefit from them. There is chaos and no system. They had not been influenced by their surroundings."[39] Feeling at home in Germany was one reason why Benno was staunchly opposed to Zionism. As a colleague explained, "His conviction was that Jerusalem must not be built in the physical world if it is to continue as a messianic symbol."[40]

A s Benno was challenging his fellow citizens to accept Jews, he was also making demands on coreligionists. He was critical of the direction of Jewish scholarship as the scientific approach to the religion neared its first centennial. He accused practitioners in the field of being aimless, sluggish and passive. He thought Jewish academics were too eager to mollify their Christian contemporaries, which made their scholarship tepid and apologetic.[41]

This was the opinion of an intellectual who was also a congregational rabbi. Benno held a pulpit for nearly forty years. His practical rabbinate shows how the occupation was once again taking a central role in larger communal affairs, as well as in religious matters. He gave weekly sermons and conducted weddings and funerals, but he also taught religion in public schools and oversaw charities and other communal organizations. He participated in the wider religious life in the region. During World War I, he delivered gifts to German soldiers, conducted citywide interfaith services and worked with government officials to ensure that his congregants could follow religious dietary laws despite food shortages. After the war, he provided care and classes to Jewish refugees from Eastern Europe, and he even conducted religious services according to their customs. To ease the intellectual loneliness of rabbinic colleagues from small communities, he organized a fellowship that met in a different town each month to discuss professional and personal problems. He advocated for legislative changes that granted rabbis more authority in determining the ritual practices of congregations.

Benno was part of a movement known as liberal Judaism. ("Conservative in practice, Reform in theology," as Walter once deftly described it.[42]) In its early years in the 19th century, the movement struggled for acceptance from traditional authorities and also from the German government officials who oversaw religious communities in the country. By the dawn of the 20th century, though, it had become the dominant form of the religion in Central Europe.

Even as liberal Judaism gained stability, it remained a dynamic force. It took different forms in synagogues than it did in journals. Benno observed the Sabbath and the dietary laws, but he rejected religious dogma, which for him included the stiffness he found in the Orthodox position as well as the shortsightedness he criticized in the ideas of the most radical reformers. He valued tradition as well as the freedom to reinterpret it. "I am a liberal rabbi," he said, "but not a rabbi of the Liberals."[43]

His scholarly field was the Hebrew Bible, and his criticism of the scientific approach to Judaism strengthened his enthusiasm for the central text of Judaism.[44] He built his historical analysis upon a religious foundation to create a wholly modern approach to traditional Torah study. He used new archaeological, philological, linguistic and literary techniques to uncover the original meaning of the text. He went straight at the most difficult material, mining genealogies, census counts, architectural plans, sacrificial descriptions and unusual word choices for ethical insights. One of his most famous interpretations proved that "an eye for an eye" referred to exclusively to monetary compensation.

These methods were explicitly opposed to the burgeoning use of the "documentary hypothesis," which treated textual variations in the Hebrew Bible as proof that the text represented a patchwork of writings by numerous authors, each with a distinct agenda to consider. Benno considered the Torah to be a unified text. If these "contradictions" were so obvious to present-day scholars, he argued, they would have been just as obvious to the original author of the text, whoever it might be. The stakes of the debate were high. Protestant scholars were using the documentary hypothesis to discredit Judaism and to present Christianity as its corrective.

Benno's particular combination of scholarship, faith and fighting spirit culminated in a crowning, albeit unfinished, achievement. He spent the final decades of his life collecting his ideas into a single Torah commentary. His volume on Genesis was the most comprehensive ever written. Across more than one thousand pages, he summarized every existing commentary, refuted each claim of the documentary hypothesis one by one and provided his conclusions about the nature and the intention of the holy text.[45]

One of the most essential insights in his commentary illuminates the enigmatic story of Jacob wrestling the angel and being given the new name "Israel." Why did God send a heavenly opponent to fight Jacob? In previous verses, Benno explained, Jacob had prayed for assistance. He was preparing to meet his older brother Esau for the first time since stealing Esau's birthright and worried about what his brother might do. The angel was sent as a protector. Why would the wealthy and powerful Esau need to seek revenge against his brother if his brother was already weakened? "The salvation of Jacob is his lameness. As he cannot yet recognize this, his confidence is restored by the promise of a new name. No man thus designated for greatness can perish," Benno wrote. "The name contained a vocation and a future for him and for all his descendants. The Bible intends the name Israel to mean: fight with God and God's fight." Benno found guidance in both meanings. "God answers a man if he prays by searching himself, becoming his own opponent; this self-searching must be relentless, even if it lessens some of the buoyancy of his native, earthly being," he wrote. "The more joyfully will the soul breathe the light of a new life."[46]

The story held great personal significance for Benno. His bookplate was a woodcut based on Rembrandt's "Jacob Wrestling with the Angel" over the verse "You will be called Jacob no longer, your name will be Israel." It is easy to see why a battle-hardened man of faith would admire a wounded fighter—named Jacob, no less—who discovered his earthly purpose through a divine struggle. And it is also easy to see how this heritage of resilience would later inspire Benno's progeny when they, too, were forced to wrestle with harsh opponents.

B enno had three children, and he actively discouraged the eldest, Ernst, from becoming a rabbi. He understood the challenges of the occupation too intimately to recommend them to his son, especially in an age when Jews could enter almost any profession they desired. Ernst briefly studied law as a courtesy to his father before pursuing the rabbinate. Like most liberal rabbinical students of his generation, Ernst studied at both of the liberal seminaries in Germany—the Jewish

Ernst Jacob was the first generation of
his family born after the emancipation
of Jewish citizens in Germany and came
of age at a time when liberal rabbinic
students were expected to pursue
general university studies alongside
their religious training.

Theological Seminary in Breslau and the Higher Institute for Jewish Studies in Berlin. He also attended a public university, where he studied ancient languages and joined the *Viadrina*. Ernst was ordained as a rabbi in 1921, earned his doctorate in 1924 and soon accepted a pulpit in Saarbrücken, a capital city in southwest Germany.[47]

Ernst became a pulpit rabbi and a scholar, like his father. In terms of temperament, though, he took after his mother. Helen Stein Jacob was the daughter of a seminary president and, like her husband, an intellectual. She continued her university studies through the early, childless years of their marriage. Unlike her husband, she was a born peacemaker who used gentleness and humor to keep her husband from making too many enemies.[48]

Ernst also preferred mediation to fighting. He started his rabbinate in the aftermath of World War I, when Germany was reckoning with its military and moral defeat. He dealt with these challenges in an immediate way in Saarbrücken, which was under French occupation in the years after the war. The influence of his mother can be seen in the way he handled a delicate moment early in his career. At the millennial celebration of Saarbrücken, with nationalist fervor running high, he avoided the combative approach his father might have taken and instead delivered a sermon on a unifying verse from Jeremiah: "Seek the welfare of the city to which I have caused you to go in exile and pray to God on its behalf; for your welfare is bound up in its welfare."[49]

While attending a lecture in Hamburg, Ernst met Annette Loewenberg, the youngest child and only daughter of Jakob Loewenberg. Annette was an inquisitive, enthusiastic and caring young woman and, like Ernst, had also followed the professional path of her father, becoming a teacher at his school.[50]

Ernst and Annette married in 1929. A few months later, he was elected to become the rabbi of the Jewish community of Augsburg, the administrative seat of the Swabia region of Bavaria, in the south of the country. In his installation address, he praised the Jewish community for its "living faith," in addition to its erudition. He was referring to its ability to persist through centuries of great change by adapting religious observance.[51]

The Jewish community of Augsburg was among the oldest in Central Europe, with surviving documentation dating to 1217 and anecdotal claims going back even further. By the time Augsburg became a free imperial city in 1276, its Jewish quarter included all the features of an organized community—a synagogue, a cemetery, a bathhouse, a wedding hall and a rabbi overseeing a twelve-member community council. The city of Augsburg enshrined rights for its Jewish residents within its charter and even protected its Jews from a regional massacre in 1298. In gratitude, the Jews financed a section of a new wall being built around the city.

The seal of the Jewish community of Augsburg was a two-headed eagle with a hat covering both heads. Any expression of religious-civic unity intended by the image was periodically undermined by murder and persecution. Augsburg incinerated Jewish moneylenders with their promissory notes during the Black Plague in 1348. It expelled the Jews again in 1440 and used their cemetery stones to build City Hall. It allowed Jews into the city during the Thirty Years' War in 1618, the War of Spanish Succession in 1701, the War of Austrian Succession in 1741 and the French War of 1796—and expelled them after each conflict was resolved.

The rise of the modern nation-state and the legal emancipation of Jews eased this cycle of persecution. Encouraged by new political freedoms, Jews came to Augsburg in great numbers over the second half of the 19th century. They numbered less than one hundred in 1840 and more than one thousand by 1880. At the start of the 20th century, Augsburg had Jewish doctors, Jewish lawyers, Jewish bankers and Jewish factory owners, and even the director of the local theater and the conductor of the local orchestra were Jewish.[52]

Acceptance influenced observance. The medieval Jewish community of Augsburg had been pious and rational but was focused inward. Its famed yeshiva pioneered a scholarly method known as the "Augsburger *hillukim*." It was a way of determining why the Talmud had cited large passages of earlier texts when only a small portion of the citation was immediately relevant to the discussion. It was a perfect example of the brilliant but aloof scholarship that Walter later attributed to cultural isolation. Over the latter half of the 19th century, the Jewish community of Augsburg enthusiastically liberalized. It adopted a "moderately reformed" worship service in 1858, installed the first synagogue organ in Bavaria in 1865, and, in 1871, hosted the second Israelite Reform Synod, where progressive Jewish leaders from across the country boldly resolved: "While fully appreciating and venerating the past, Judaism strives, in accord with earnest scientific research, to set aside what is obsolete and antiquated, so that it may unfold itself in the spirit of the new age."[53]

Filled with that spirit, the Jewish community of Augsburg commissioned a new synagogue on a prominent lot near the center of the city. While the building now appears timeworn and dignified amid blocks of modern office buildings, its stucco facade would have fit seamlessly among the apartments, offices and shops along the street at the time of its dedication in 1917. Beyond the front gates, though, modernity yields to antiquity. A secluded forecourt of iron and stone introduces the grand ivy-covered dome of the sanctuary. Inside the sanctuary, scalloped patterns of golden tiles stud the black interior of the dome, providing the sense of eternal vastness that comes from staring into a starry sky.

Only a community committed to honoring its heritage would undertake the cost and effort of building such a beautiful house of worship, and only a striving minority eager for acceptance would put that building on a main street of its city. Those twin desires are neatly expressed in a mosaic embedded in a wall of the forecourt. It is a pinecone inside a Star of David—the civic symbol of Augsburg at the center of the ancient symbol of Jewish peoplehood.

One of the two street-level wings of the Augsburg synagogue was a "community house" with apartments for various congregational employees, including the rabbi. When Ernst and Annette Jacob entered their apartment for the first time, they found a bouquet of red roses waiting on a table.[54] It was a welcome gift from their new congregation, as well as an unintentional reminder that the door to their home could never be completely closed. The spheres of work and home often overlapped. The rabbinic study was located inside the apartment, meaning that congregants seeking rabbinic counsel had to enter the Jacob residence to find it. A passageway connecting the apartment to the sanctuary turned religious services into an event occurring just down the hall.[55]

Walter was born six months after his parents arrived in Augsburg. His birth coincided with the start of the holiday of Purim, when the Jewish people wear festive costumes and listen to a melodic reading of the Book of Esther to remember their deliverance from a genocidal plot in ancient Persia. That evening, Ernst rushed back from the maternity ward to find a sanctuary full of merry congregants who were celebrating his good fortune as well as the good fortune of their ancestors. "So my life started on a happy note," Walter noted.[56]

Walter and his younger brother, Herbert, who was born three years later, spent most of their days within the walls of the synagogue. They lived there, attended secular and religious school there, and wandered freely through the building and its grounds. Young friends were often close at hand, and, after the school day ended, the religious school playground became their private family gym.[57]

Adding to this already insulated childhood was a distinctively inclusive communal structure. All religious communities in Germany were organized geographically, rather than ideologically, as they are in America. Every co-religionist living within a given area automatically belonged to the same publicly owned *gemeinde,* or "local community," regardless of any nuances of personal belief. It was hard for a dissenting group to establish a new religious congregation outside of this governmental structure, but individuals were free to ignore religion entirely. Growing up inside a synagogue, Walter would have only had regular contact with those Jewish families who chose to participate in communal functions, which certainly encouraged his later portrayal of Germany as a country full of devoted and enthusiastic Jewish communities.

As the leader of this community, Ernst was responsible for creating a program to serve every Jew in Augsburg who wanted to be served. He reorganized youth services to integrate children into the routines of the congregation, rather than separating them from adults. He started a popular parents' evening where mothers and fathers could learn about the religious school curriculum and also hear the latest findings in the field of child psychology. Ernst and Annette took long walks through the city to visit the homebound elderly. "As they called on them, they often added their ages until they could say that they had visited a thousand years in an afternoon," Walter recalled. Ernst was also admired by less religious Jews, who elected him president of the local B'nai B'rith lodge.[58]

Within the well-organized hierarchy of the German rabbinate, Ernst was a *bezirksrabbiner*, or district rabbi, over the entire Swabia region of southwest Bavaria. Ernst regularly visited small Jewish communities in towns where non-professional religious teachers were responsible for leading prayer and study in the absence of full-time rabbis. He hosted conferences where these teachers could improve their skills and also ease their intellectual loneliness through fellowship.[59] A good district rabbi needed to be both responsive and flexible. Each community had specific traditions and preferences to consider. When Ernst visited a traditional community in nearby Kriegshaber, he was expected to conduct services according to their customs, regardless of his personal convictions.[60]

Scholarship was an expectation within the German rabbinate. Ernst pursued serious studies throughout his life, including an unfinished book about Psalms and essays about sexuality within Jewish tradition. But he was more interested in communal work and found ways to direct his intellectual pursuits toward pragmatic ends. One of his primary fields of study was Christianity. He wrote essays about the religion for the German edition of the *Jewish Encyclopedia* and other publications, and Christian writers admired and frequently cited his work. This expertise allowed him to foster equal-footed relationships with Catholic and Protestant clergy throughout Swabia.[61]

Among his other written works was a popular introductory volume to Jewish observance titled *Israelitische Religionslehre,* or "Israelite Religious Doctrine."[62] His overview included a revealing description of the responsibilities of his profession, as he saw them: "The rabbi is not a priest. His task is rather to teach Judaism (*rav*), decide on religious questions (*dayan*), supervise the community's religious institutions and guide its members, both collectively and individually, towards piousness and Jewish living. He leads religious activities and ministers to his congregation."[63] By "priest," Ernst was referring partly to the ancient priests who had performed animal sacrifices on behalf of the Israelites in the days of the Holy Temple. A rabbi was not an intermediary between the Jewish people and God. Rather, he was a learned guide who could help his congregants lead more religious lives and, when questions about observance arose, could determine what actions were appropriate. Walter sought a similar combination of restraint and freedom when he became a rabbi. He set forth clear boundaries, and then he actively encouraged his congregants to innovate within those boundaries.

For all its liberalizing changes in the late 19th century, the Jewish community of Augsburg remained a formal institution. Women and young children sat in an upper balcony. The men seated below were expected to be discreet, no schmoozing allowed. The president of the congregation wore a ceremonial top hat during services and sat on a high pulpit, facing the pews. Anyone betraying decorum — "which really just meant someone talking to his neighbor," as Walter recalled — would be given a card printed with a stern warning. When the sexton carried this card down the aisle, everyone slowly turned in his or her seat to see who was being admonished. "As a rabbi's child, I received that card a number of times," Walter said with a laugh.[64]

Walter was one of the young children being shepherded into the life of the congregation. His earliest memory is walking down the central aisle of the synagogue as a three-year-old boy, climbing one set of steps to the pulpit and another set to the high lectern and handing a *Tora*

By the time Walter was born in 1930,
his family felt at home in German
society — even as great political changes
were underway for Jewish citizens.
The family left Germany so quickly, and
under such impoverished circumstances,
that Walter continued wearing his
traditional Bavarian wardrobe for a
time after moving to Missouri.

wimpel to his father.[65] A *Tora wimpel* is a sash used to tie the columns of a Torah scroll together between readings. In a tradition going back to the dawn of the Renaissance, Jewish families throughout Germany would slice strips from the swaddling clothes of infant boys, stitch these strips end-to-end to create long sashes, and embroider the name and genealogy of their sons down the length of these sashes in the form of a blessing: *May this child have a good marriage, live a long life and be useful to the community.* When the young boy began attending services, he would deliver this sash to the pulpit, where the sexton of the congregation would hold it in safekeeping. It would be retrieved at special occasions. The boy would wrap it around the Torah at his bar mitzvah and again at his wedding. If the groom fathered a son, he would create a new sash with new embroidery stitched along its length. In this way, each child was ushered into adulthood and each new generation was symbolically bound to the Torah.[66]

Walter can recall other traditions across the Jewish calendar. Every spring, boys and girls would dress as characters from the Purim story and stand as their namesakes arrived in the reading. Every summer, to decorate for the Shavuot holiday, congregants would fill the sanctuary with broad palm branches and other verdant plants. In the fall, the community would build a huge sukkah on the grounds of the synagogue. The Augsburg community was blessed with an unusually large number of Torah scrolls, as many as seventy, each festooned with crowns, breastplates, pointers and other fineries produced by famed silversmiths of Augsburg. At the culmination of the High Holidays on Simchat Torah, congregants would parade these scrolls up and down the aisles of the sanctuary.

Even though the Jacobs lived within their synagogue, they maintained a private life. They held lively Friday night dinners, beginning with a traditional meal and ending with songs. They filled their table with family and visitors every Passover, using a seder plate Ernst and Annette had received as a wedding present from the community in Saarbrücken.[67] Walter still uses it at Passover today.

The Jacob family regularly attended concerts and visited nearby museums and gardens. They hiked through the parks and forests of Augsburg and took daytrips into the nearby Alps. Walter remembers how his parents would tell him and his brother exciting stories to keep them going if their legs grew weary on these excursions. The family left Augsburg every summer for an extended vacation, usually to a secluded alpine lake. Walter recalled one year when it rained throughout the entire vacation, and his family spent the days inside, comfortably and quietly huddled together, each of them perfectly satisfied to read away the hours.

Walter loved books from a young age. His early tastes tended toward ancient subjects like Bible stories, Greek mythology and Roman history. His interest in books was a facet of his innate curiosity about the world. He greatly enjoyed wandering around Augsburg, either alone or with friends. He explored his neighborhood, or daydreamed, or carefully arranged gunpowder caps on the rails of the streetcar lines and watched with delight as they sparked under the heavy wheels of passing trams.

He was a shy and quiet boy who could also be mischievous, and occasionally even naughty. He once slid a mirror under a locked door to catch a glimpse at the birthday presents being kept on the other side. Another time, he yanked away a chair from his aunt just as she was about to sit, sending her toppling backward. He regularly exploited one of the few design flaws in the synagogue. A balcony at the back of the apartment was also the roof of the weekday synagogue. "Of course, being a rabbi's child, I often misbehaved and did exactly what I was not supposed to do," he said, "which was to play on top of that when they were having services."[68]

Walter often sounds gleeful when he recounts these incidents of mild youthful insubordination, perhaps because they represent a feature that few would expect to find in the biography of man who is descended from fifteen generations of rabbis and who was raised on the grounds of a magnificent synagogue at the precipice of a vast and historic destruction. They are signs of a normal childhood.

As a boy, reading about the beginnings of Western civilization, Walter often wondered how the vigorous Roman Empire could have simply disappeared.[69] Just a few years later, first-hand experiences provided him with a vivid illustration of the way a great nation could collapse. His peaceful world dissolved little by little and then all at once. The warning signs were ominous. Areas of the forests where he had once freely hiked were suddenly made off-limits, as the government built new Messerschmitt factories. Warplanes started swooping over the synagogue, using its prominent dome as a target for practice runs. If other children in the neighborhood identified Walter's religion during his walks through the city, he could expect to be called a "dirty Jew" and attacked. If his aggressor was alone, Walter occasionally followed the example of his grandfather and fought back. "If there were more than one child, I usually chose to run," he later said, with a smile. "Seemed safer."[70]

By 1937, some two hundred Jews had left the city.[71] A similar situation was unfolding throughout the country. Every so often, friends and family from out of town would pass through Augsburg to say goodbye to the Jacob family on their way out of the country. Among these callers was Martin Buber, on his way to Palestine. "I sat on his lap," Walter recalled. "But it made no difference: I still have no great interest in philosophy."[72] Ernst and Annette were reluctant to leave while hundreds of their congregants remained in danger, but the president of the Jewish community finally convinced them to consider their own welfare. And so, in the summer of 1938, the Jacobs started the sad, bureaucratic process of leaving a beloved yet hostile country.[73]

As circumstances worsened, the synagogue became a literal sanctuary. The Jacobs increasingly limited their lives to its expansive and beautiful grounds. Ernst and Annette took pains to keep the outside world at a distance from their boys. Only later did Walter learn about the stamps on Jewish passports, or the compulsory reporting of assets, or more personal acts of persecution, such as the suppression of Benno's Genesis commentary after years of hard work. When it became mandatory to listen to Nazi broadcasts, Ernst and Annette sold their radio. When Nazi parades came blaring down the street outside, including one with Hitler in attendance, Ernst and Annette told their sons to play out back. Walter can recall mornings when he sensed disquiet at the breakfast table. Only years later did he learn that the Gestapo had been regularly raiding the apartment at night, convinced that his father was undertaking subversive activities through his involvement in B'nai B'rith. Walter knew at the time that something was wrong, but his parents never indulged his curiosity. "If I asked," he said, "I never received a political answer."[74]

When these confrontations were impossible to sidestep, Ernst and Annette showed their children how to adjust gracefully. In 1937, the family embarked on its annual vacation to the Alps. "We packed as if we were coming to America. We took enormous amounts of equipment. We went with all this baggage," Walter said. "We got there. We found a big sign that said, 'Jews not wanted here.' And we carried all the baggage to the other platform and went back home. And that meant that the next year, we took our vacation in Denmark."[75]

The Jewish community of Augsburg also found sanctuary within the synagogue. Attendance spiked in those years. Ernst crafted optimistic sermons studded with sly, metaphorical critiques of the Nazi party. The synagogue also became the center of social activities. The Jewish community organized lectures and concerts, started a tennis club and opened a nursing home. It offered professional training for those who had lost their livelihoods to boycotts and provided emigration assistance and foreign language classes for those who were ready to leave.[76] When it became impossible to purchase kosher meat legally in Germany, community leaders located a new supplier in Argentina.[77]

Throughout his life, Walter has approached other hardships with the same resolve that his parents and his community showed in the face of political oppression. Anytime he describes his experiences in Germany, he always presents them in the best possible light, and not only in the overarching sense of feeling grateful for having survived while so many others perished. He insists he knew little about the state of affairs at the time, and he describes the inconveniences he did face as lucky turns of good fortune. For example, when Jews were no longer allowed to attend German schools, the Jewish community started a secular day school on a shoestring budget. Nearly ninety students were crudely divided by age into two large classes and crowded into spare rooms at the synagogue. "It had a great advantage," Walter later said, "because that meant that, although I was only in the first grade, I could listen to everything that was happening up to the fifth grade. You could get an advanced education, if you were so inclined."[78]

As the streets became more dangerous, Walter indulged his wanderlust by drifting through the synagogue. He was playing in the assembly hall with some classmates on November 9, 1938, when he decided to duck into the sanctuary to peek at the dome.[79] This would be the last time anyone saw the sanctuary intact and at peace. That night, Walter woke to the smell of smoke and the clatter of fire trucks. A short while earlier, Nazi officers had cut the telephone lines, forced the janitor to open the sanctuary, doused the pews in gasoline and set fire to the synagogue.[80] And then, in a perverse display of caution, they immediately alerted the fire department to prevent the flames from spreading to neighboring properties along the crowded block.[81]

After the fire was under control, officers raided the rabbinic apartment. They accused Ernst of setting the fire and advised him to accept responsibility for it by jumping from the third-floor windows. "Which he declined," Walter drolly noted.[82] The officers arrested Ernst. As Ernst was getting his coat, one of the officers noticed a framed Hebrew phrase hanging on the wall and asked what it meant. It was a page from an illustrated Passover haggadah that read "*sfoch hamatcha al hagoyim asher lo yaducha*," commonly translated as "Pour out your wrath upon the nations that do not recognize you." Ernst vaguely explained that it was a verse from the Bible. "Well, it *is* a Biblical verse," Walter noted. "But they picked the right one."[83] The officers took Ernst to the city jail without allowing him to say goodbye to his wife and his two sons, and later transferred him to the concentration camp at Dachau, where most of the working-age Jewish men of Bavaria spent the next few months.[84]

The morning after the attack, Walter watched from the window of the apartment as Nazi officers oversaw an ersatz "cleanup" of the synagogue. They looted the community archives, stole the silver Torah decorations and even took a Hebrew typewriter Ernst had been using to bypass German censors in letters to his father.[85] ("What the Gestapo did with that Hebrew typewriter is a mystery," Walter said.[86]) The officers forced all the elderly men of the community to haul the charred pews, prayers books and Torah scrolls into dump trucks idling in the yard of the synagogue. A crowd amassed to enjoy the sight of the officers shoving and prodding anyone who worked too slowly. "We watched that," Walter later recalled. "We also watched one minor gesture of defiance: the milkman brought milk anyway. No one was supposed to go anywhere near our apartment house. But he did."[87]

Citing the naivety of childhood, Walter often downplays the trauma of these events and others over the next few years. But their influence on his development is undeniable. "As a little boy I, of course, did not understand everything which I saw but even as an eight year old I realized that my childhood had come to an end," he once said.[88]

Annette told her sons to be ready to leave on short notice — Walter prepared by packing his stamp collection — and she spent the next two days buying basic supplies and arguing with government officials. In a bureaucratic oversight, she continued to receive the *New York Times*, which was how she learned that the attack on the synagogue in Augsburg was part of a larger, coordinated effort throughout the country, now known as Kristallnacht. That Friday night, she shut the blinds and served the Sabbath meal by candlelight. Raids continued over the coming days and became increasingly invasive. The president of the Jewish community worried about Annette and the boys, and he invited them to his house at the outskirts of the city. Walter recalled being on his best behavior during their extended stay at the spacious home of the retired colonel, but his mother later noted that the curious boy accidentally fell into a pond while trying to get a closer look at a school of goldfish.[89]

With the children safe, Annette took a three-hour train ride to the American consulate in Stuttgart and spent a day waiting to receive her visa quota number. Upon returning to Augsburg with her boys, she inventoried all the family belongings "from the furniture to the duster," pawned the family silver, paid new taxes levied against Jewish-owned possessions and loaded everything else into giant shipping crates. As she was packing, the Nazis forced her to take lodgers. To free up their rooms for their guests, she and the boys slept on borrowed beds crammed into the rabbinic study.[90] But Walter has made those weeks sound fun: "For kids, all these things are an adventure: now I have playmates in the apartment. And we had a rather pleasant time."[91]

In late December 1938, Ernst returned to Augsburg with a crew cut, a clean-shaven face and a thinner waistline. He also had a souvenir. The Nazis had given all the Jewish men in the camp the middle name "Israel."[92] Ernst kept this extra name for the rest of his life, as a point of pride. Like his Biblical patriarch, he was a Jacob who had been given the name Israel after a struggle. Just as Benno Jacob had written in his Genesis commentary, "No man thus designated for greatness can perish."

Soon after the family was reunited, they were separated again. The Chief Rabbi of England had secured visas for many German rabbis. Ernst felt he should be the last Jew to leave Augsburg, but a rabbinic colleague convinced him to leave the country while he had the chance. Ernst departed for London, and Annette and the boys remained in Augsburg to wait for their emigration papers. Even after they had received permission to leave Germany, Annette made a calculated decision to stay in the country as long as she could. Access to their bank accounts was restricted inside Germany but would be entirely prohibited once they left.[93]

As tensions rose in Czechoslovakia in March 1939, Annette decided to leave, rather than risk being trapped inside Germany if war broke out. She spent the week of Walter's ninth birthday going from one administrative office to another to collect all the paperwork they needed for their trip.[94] She performed these frantic tasks so discreetly that Walter did not fully appreciate her efforts at the time. More than seventy years later, at a speaking engagement in Rhode Island, he was sharing these experiences when the full import of her action suddenly hit him. Throughout those months of persecution, his father was either imprisoned or exiled. Without his mother's calm determination and quick thinking, they would have been trapped in Germany. In a letter to a cousin, he noted, "It was really my mother who kept us on an even keel."[95]

Toward the end of the month, Annette and the boys packed their bags, said goodbye to relatives and close friends, and prepared to leave a part of the world where their families had been living for more than three centuries and where they had expected to remain for the rest of their lives. On their final Sabbath in Germany, Annette escorted Walter on an hour-long walk through rotten weather to pray at the traditional synagogue in Kriegshaber, which had accidentally been spared during the attacks. They returned home to find another large bouquet of red roses waiting in the empty apartment. This time, they were a parting gift from their congregation.[96]

For the Jacob family, Missouri was
the end of a journey that began with
the destruction of their synagogue in
Augsburg, nearly two years earlier.
Walter recalls a sense of gratitude
permeating his early years in America,
and photographs from the time, such
as this one of him, his brother Herbert
and their mother Annette, taken in
the yard of their home in St. Joseph,
Missouri in 1942, always show the
family in good spirits.

CHAPTER II

An American Point of View

After a queasy trip across the choppy English Channel, Annette and her two sons reunited with Ernst in London in early 1939. They joined another branch of the family that had fled Germany only a few months earlier. These relatives ultimately settled in England, but the Jacobs knew their stay would be temporary. They were waiting until their immigration number was called and they could complete their journey to the United States.[97]

Their nine-month stay in London was the first stage in a period of exile lasting more than three years, until they settled in Springfield, Missouri. By leaving home and starting over, they were taking part in one of the most frequently recurring stories of Jewish history. Walter came to see these periods of displacement as one of the fundamental forces guiding the development of Judaism. Being forced to strip away the physical features of the religion made it easier to recognize the essential qualities hidden within it. "Through a long history we have tried to move from the concrete to the abstract, to think of ideas, not of places, and so we have survived," he said in a sermon. "We have expressed Judaism, not in stones or beautiful buildings. We have erected them, lost them, and have survived. Judaism has been borne in our heads; it is an oral tradition and a wealth of learning."[98] What was true for a people was also true for a family. After the Jacobs were stripped of their ancestral homeland, their citizenship, their apartment and the pleasure they took in leading an enthusiastic religious community, what remained was an enduring commitment to family ties and a deeper sense of security based upon self-reliance and inner strength.

The Jacob family arrived in England with few resources. They knew almost no one, and as refugees they were prohibited from taking regular employment. Eleven relatives shared a tiny house and got by on odd jobs and whatever small amounts of money they were able to smuggle out of Germany. Walter remembers his excitement when a mailman unexpectedly delivered a bicycle, and his subsequent disappointment when his father and uncle quickly stripped the machine to its bearings to retrieve the deutschmarks hidden inside its frame.[99]

Just as he had done in Augsburg, Walter explored his corner of London. In the warmth of spring and summer, he wandered the streets with his brother and their three young cousins to look for the collectible illustration cards tucked inside discarded packs of Players cigarettes.[100] As fall turned to winter, they left the house for other, more practical reasons. The only source of heat in their building was a coin-operated radiator in the front room. "So the result was that you spent lots of time at the library," he recalled. "Or occasionally, if you had enough money, went to the movies. Saw the longest film possible, so that you would get warm."[101]

The adults also kept busy. Annette and Ernst had learned English as schoolchildren, and they kept their skills sharp in Germany by subscribing to the *New York Times*, but now they studied their new language with greater intensity. Within a few months of arriving in London, Ernst already felt comfortable enough writing in English to complete a short manuscript called *The Only Book That Hitler Read*. It traced the roots of Nazi anti-Semitism to the *Protocols of the Elders of Zion*, but was too unpolished to be published.[102] Walter picked up English "by osmosis," as he put it. Being immersed in English in the classroom and on the playground gave his speaking skills a conversational quality that eluded his parents. But entering social settings without knowing how to communicate also carried some risks. Once, a teacher summoned him to the front of the class and swatted him with a switch. "I guess I had done something wrong," he recalled with amusement. "I never knew what it was."[103]

No longer worried about Gestapo spies, the adults now openly discussed politics in front of their children. Ernst vividly described his months of captivity at Dachau. He had spent his nights sleeping on straw mats and spent his days suffering through endless "roll calls." He and his fellow prisoners were forced to stand outside for hours at a time, in the middle of winter, wearing only thin pajamas. Occasionally a weakened prisoner crumpled to the ground and was left for dead.

Everyone in the house in London closely followed the military aggression spreading outward from Germany. They huddled around the radio on September 1, 1939, to listen to King George VI officially declare war against their homeland. With that speech, the Jacobs went from being refugees to being enemy aliens. To avoid internment, the adult men in the household took long walks every morning while British officials went door to door rounding up German immigrants. School had already been sporadic for all children before the declaration and was now cancelled altogether. The Jacobs and their relatives blacked out the windows of their home, carried gas masks at all times, and watched the silver barrage balloons float against the London skyline with distressing gracefulness.

The Jacobs' immigration number came up in December 1939. But leaving England proved to be no easier than getting there. First, the shipping line refused to extract any of the funds the family had arranged for transfer out of Germany. It took a class-action lawsuit and several years to resolve the matter, by which time the family was settled in America. A more urgent problem occurred early in their journey overseas. A few nights after departing Liverpool on the *RMS Samaria*, Walter was awakened by a jolt and squealing alarms. The ship had collided with a troop convoy patrolling the Irish Sea and torn a hole in its hull. The hobbled vessel made it safely back to shore, but the accident upended their departure schedule. The Jacobs spent two weeks living in a cheap Liverpool hotel, playing Monopoly with a hand-drawn board, until they could make a second attempt at departure.[104]

They eventually secured travel on the *MV Georgic*, a larger and better-equipped ship. For safety, and perhaps also in an attempt to calm the fears of its passengers, the ship changed course every half hour and employed a highly visible gun crew on the deck. Walter and Herbert wandered the boat, discovering a herd of racehorses among the cargo. They visited the swanky dining hall. "Good food," he later recalled. "We were seasick the whole time, until the last day, so we couldn't enjoy it."[105]

Even though the remainder of the voyage was uneventful, Walter can still recall the feeling of relief that washed over him as the ship passed through a convoy of American cruisers patrolling the North Atlantic. They briefly docked in Halifax, where Walter traded snowballs with stevedores on the dock, and continued down the New England coast toward New York. The Statue of Liberty welcomed them to America on January 3, 1940.[106]

For his entire adult life, Walter has written a more-or-less weekly letter to members of his family. As he got older, he permitted himself the luxury of reminiscing and began using his first letter of the year to acknowledge the anniversary of his family's arrival in America. "The country has been good to us and remains a land of vast opportunity. Anything which one wants to do can be done by those willing to pursue it," he wrote in a January 2001 letter. "All of us who were fortunate enough to get over here are grateful."[107] He has taken to calling their arrival date his "real New Year."[108]

An uncle met the Jacobs at the pier, loaded them into a large American sedan and took them straight to the Empire State Building. The tallest skyscraper in the world failed to impress Walter. "It really wasn't up to the sky," he noted.[109] What got his attention were all the lights. New York had no blackouts.[110] It had no gas masks or air-raid shelters or barrage balloons, either. War was still far away.

The Jacobs spent their first night in America listening to H.V. Kaltenborn bellow the news on the radio and enjoying a nice family dinner. But soon they were on their own.[111] They rented two rooms in a house in Cedarhurst, Long Island. Their landlords were a family of well-meaning but proselytizing Christian Scientists who were so deeply in debt they occasionally borrowed money from their indigent tenants to pay overdue utility bills.[112] The house was infested with mice, and the boys made a game of sitting on their beds at night, listening to the traps snap shut. As in London, the Jacobs could not justify any unnecessary expenses. Walter still regrets being unable to afford bus fare to Queens to see the marvels on display at the World's Fair.[113]

Even back then, Walter had a positive outlook about his circumstances. Writing to his cousins in London, a month after his arrival, he gamely reported, "I shoveled snow this morning. I was very lucky because some snow was not frozen but it was still very hard." The only sad note he struck in the letter was disappointment over the lack of cigarette illustration cards to be found on the sidewalks of Long Island.[114] Even today, any time Walter recounts those months of limbo in New York, he always gives the grimmer details of poverty and displacement a comic inflection, as though he is telling a madcap story at a cocktail party. When an oral historian once suggested that the experience sounded bleak, Walter quickly changed his tone and insisted, "The stay there was really very content."[115]

Arriving in New York required Walter to adjust to a new culture for the second time in less than a year. He now spoke fluent English, but with a British accent. "Hold onto it, it'll be valuable," his uncle advised, believing that a nice Jewish boy who sounded like a royal subject would have an unbeatable advantage in the marriage market.[116] With typically American confidence, the uncle also told the young immigrant boy that, in the United States, he could become anything he set his mind on — except President, of course. "My ambitions were not so high," Walter joked.[117] But the sentiment certainly left an impression on Walter, and he has repeated it often throughout his life.

Becoming an American boy was easier than becoming an American Jew. As Ernst searched for a permanent job in the New York area, the family visited congregations across the denominational spectrum and discovered the peculiar ways their ancient faith was being practiced on a new frontier.

Ernest I. Jacob   281 Central Avenue
                                   Lawrence L. I.
                                   February 16 th 1940
Dear Father:-
          To-day, 2 full months after leaving England, I am still
without any news from you although I have written you very regularly
every week. It is too strange that we hear every morning over the
radio a man telling us directly from London what was to be read
in your morning papers and that we cannot get any letters from
you over such a large period. Are our letters too long for the censor?
          This evening I have to deliver my first sermon over here in a
special refugee service at Pelham Parkway Jewish center to an auditorium
of American and German Jews. Probably I have to speak in English.
The week was full of the usual hopes and disappointments xxxx. Yet,
we are happy and cheerful and hope for the best. I called on
Dr. Finkelstein, acting dean of the Jewish Theological Seminary,
a very handsome man who was quite amiable. All the conservative
people show much more consideration tham the reform people, at
least to me. He asked what you are doing now and I told him that
exodus is finished too and could be brought to print. He invited me
to a luncheon which was given at the dining room of the Seminary
for the members of the interdenominational studies now held at the
seminary. These are attended mostly by Jewish and Christian clergymen and the lectures are given by the foremost scholars of all
creeds. After the luncheon a protestant professor of theology
gave a lecture on democracy which was really good. But I was most
impressed by the noiseless typrwriter which took every word from
the mouth of the speaker and by a parson opposite to me with a
very spiritual outlook and a very good appetite. Next to me sat an
old gentleman who introduced himself as the great great great great grandson of David Franklin and apparently nothing more than that. He drew from
his pocket Franklin's housekey and his eye-glasses and I gave due admirat-
ionxxxx to these specimens of American history. But to-day this man
sent me photograph of his great ancestor with a very nice dedication,
a piece which I will have framed ; for it looks good in a study and
will give me a real American background. He added a paper of the
refutation of that Nazi forgery of a prophesy of his ancestor against
the Jews and a photostat of the "51 st chapter of Genesis this well
known legend of Abraham and a stranger who did not say grace after
his meal. Franklin used to carry it in his pocket and to put it

The Jacob family settled into their new lives in Missouri as conditions were worsening for their relatives in England. The two halves of the family corresponded frequently during and after World War II and made the most of their limited stationery—all four members of the family added their thoughts on this letter to Benno Jacob.

it into a Bible when in the presence of some clergymen and read it
to themThey always wondered from what book of the Bible it might be
taken.You see I make interesting acquaintances,but you cannot live on
that alone.
We had a terrible blizzard these days,that is a storm of ice;
it was almost impossible to walk on the streets.Winter has returned;
the whole landscape is covered by snow although we had had real
spring weather some days before.
We live here very good as every member of the family
who visits New York feels himself obliged to send us a basket with
food.This week we even received a fine chicken and very fine meat,
liver etc.Milton and May behave very gracious unto us.
And what abou you?How is your life going on?I am so eager to hear
from you and look for every mail whether there is not something
from London,but always in vain.
My cordial greetings for you and much love to every one in
Dunstan Road.
With best wishes and many kisses
most sincerely yours
Ernst Jacob

Dear papa:
I think so often of all of you that I even dreamt post arrived, but
it was a dream only! Many persons have a flue now because
of the change of weather. 2 days it was like spring, now it's
icy cold again. Our boys recovered quickly. Herbert was in
bed on his birthday, but he enjoyed his little presents and
as Milton and May visited us he got a very fine constructive
building box. He is always lucky. Ernst looks and
feels well so does J. He meets many well known persons,
always a new hope turns out but nevertheless we have to
wait for some time longer. The boys like their school very
much and it seems they do well there. They have to help
other boys of their class. I attend English lessons now
but I didn't yet succeed in getting some.
I am mostly alone at home the coloured man who comes every
other day to do housework, of course he drives his own car,
has phone rings for hours then a good breakfast and between
a little bit of work. I try to keep our 2 rooms as an island
without dust. Our landlady is a nice woman who gives me long sermons
of Christian Science she has slave girls and much trouble with her
debtors. How are you? How is it with your landlady? Are you on

The orderly and hierarchical structure of Jewish communities in modern Germany was a byproduct of permanence. It emerged from the long Jewish presence on the continent and from the historically close relationship between church and state in Central Europe. America was a young country with almost total religious freedom, which encouraged decentralized communities. Laymen started the first Jewish congregations in America and often operated without any rabbinic authority. By the time the Jacob family arrived in America in early 1940, a system of national denominations and seminaries had only been in place for about sixty-five years.[118]

American religious communities seemed fragmented and unpredictable to the Jacobs. They were confused when members of a Reform congregation asked them to remove their yarmulkes before entering the sanctuary. In Germany they had covered their heads in this fashion *only* during services.[119] The Orthodox congregations they visited were unacceptably casual. "The difference to more progressed synagogues is the lack of discipline," Ernst explained in a letter to his father. "Walter was quite furious when I attended a Sabbath morning service at the same synagogue some weeks ago. The rabbi, a nice fellow after all and quite European in his education and manners, made a promenade through the synagogue during prayer and stood there, hands in pockets."[120] In any one of these American synagogues, the president of the Augsburg community would have run out of warning cards.

Ernst also marveled at the freedom of American religion and the creativity it fostered. He attended a nominally Orthodox service where men and women sat together, unlike the separate seating at his "liberal" community in Augsburg. "This evening is a ladies service at the same 'orthodox' synagogue! A lady-rabbi will preach, a lady-cantor will sing," Ernst wrote. "Such are things in America!"[121]

Overall, though, Ernst was distraught at what he found in America. "The religious life over here is in a miserable state," he lamented. "All the 5, partly big and marvelous temples in our neighborhood have not so many visitors altogether on Sabbath mornings as my synagogue alone had." Ernst was offended by the way Americans spoke of everything

After a long and fruitless job search,
Rabbi Ernest Jacob took a position in
early 1940 running a religious school
for the small Jewish community in
St. Joseph, Missouri. His sons Walter
and Herbert, seen here in uniform,
were among his students.

in economic terms. Job applicants "sold" themselves to potential employers. Rabbis "sold" religion to their skeptical congregants.[122] As was the case for many of the refugee rabbis who arrived from Central Europe during those years, Ernst struggled to find any work in America beyond a few scattered preaching and tutoring engagements.[123]

Watching his father struggle, Walter quickly realized how things worked in his new country. His mother Annette, in a letter to her family in London, reported on a surprising exchange about the matter with her elder son: "Last week Walter told me, 'I don't know whether I want to be a rabbi or not. Here you get no position for your life only for a short time and I want to earn a lot of money,' 'Wherefore,' I asked. 'Well, mommy, if I save every day 10$, that makes 36500$ in 10 years, then I will build a fine synagogue like ours in A, still finer and then daddy shall be the rabbi there. You see, I have to earn it quickly, that both of you can enjoy it.'"[124]

By late March, Ernst had exhausted all his potential job leads in New York. He embarked on a two-month train trip in search of work. He traveled six thousand miles across ten states to interview for positions in outlying sections of the Midwest and South, including a congregation in one of the small towns near Pittsburgh. (He even spent a night at the Fort Pitt Hotel, or at least took some of its stationery to replenish his letter-writing supplies.)[125]

As he was speeding across the vast American countryside, his homeland was mired in chaos and destruction. Germany invaded Denmark, Norway, France and the Low Countries. Meanwhile, an ocean away, Ernst was marveling at air conditioning units, and electric kitchen appliances, and "clocks which give the time in cipher and not only the time, but the date too."[126] This stark contrast put his frustrating job search in perspective. "What is the personal lot in these revolutionary times?" he asked his father.[127] On his way back to New York in late May, having accepted a modest position as the principal of an Orthodox religious school in St. Joseph, Missouri, he watched the farmlands passing by the window of his train car, and he thought, "Fertile and peaceful as Europe could be too."[128]

The position in St. Joseph was similar in stature to the community religious teachers Ernst had once mentored in Augsburg, and the salary barely covered his living expenses. Even so, he fully embraced the opportunity. He quickly changed the spelling of his name to Ernest, to seem more American. When he found a suitable apartment, he diagrammed its layout in a letter to his father and noted the location of his first study in America.

Soon after, Annette joined her husband in Missouri. She too sent an update to London, and a sense of appreciation spilled from her pen: "It will seem to you to be an idyll, and we ourselves feel like being in a dream in this peaceful little town."[129]

After two years in St. Joseph, Ernest accepted an offer to become rabbi of a Reform congregation in Springfield, ending his three-year absence from the pulpit. By the time he retired from the congregation in 1969, he had become an important figure in the region, serving on many civic and community boards and eventually having a stretch of highway named in his memory. Both he and Annette also became admired teachers at nearby Drury College. For Annette, the college provided the unexpected opportunity to continue the teaching career she had started and enjoyed under her father's tutelage and had set aside for motherhood.

Ernest and Annette never stopped feeling grateful for the pleasant turn their lives took. About a decade into his tenure in Springfield, Ernest participated in a civic event with former President Harry S. Truman, a native Missourian. By chance, the event occurred on November 9, the anniversary of the Kristallnacht attacks. "My father told an individual seated with him that he wished he had been able to peer into the future on that terrible night in 1938 and see himself years later sitting at the same table as the President of the United States; that would have given him hope in the darkest hour of his life," Walter said in a tribute after President Truman's death.[130] Years later, also on November 9, Annette received a bouquet of yellow and red mums "from" her three young grandchildren. "I know, when you sent us those beautiful flowers on the 9th of November, you did not realize, what this day meant to us," she wrote to them, adding, "I thought of many little episodes yesterday and how much better I would have felt, had I been able to see into the future—all of us happily living in the USA."[131]

Walter admired the way his parents approached their journey from Augsburg, to London, to Long Island, to St. Joseph, to Springfield. "It was a principle of their lives not to look back and never to think of what might have been, but to work ahead with what there was, and to enjoy it," he said in a eulogy after his parents died of carbon monoxide poisoning in 1974. "Their settlement in this blessed land was, to them, an opportunity to see life with new perspective. It was a harsh new beginning, but enabled them to understand issues and problems from a European and American point of view."[132]

By "European point of view," Walter meant an understanding of history, a respect for tradition and an appreciation of old manners. By "American point of view," he meant a genius for starting over.[133]

Ernest moved to St. Joseph almost as soon as he got the job, and Annette and the boys joined him a month later. Early in the trip, their westbound train out of New York passed through Pittsburgh, giving Walter his first glimpse of the city where he would spend most of his life. "And I only remember that because we rode on the train for about an hour through what seemed like a fiery furnace," he said, referring to the mills that were starting to become active again as the lull of the Great Depression gave way to the early stages of defense contracting.[134]

Missouri also seemed otherworldly. It was much hotter than temperate Germany, and the Jacobs couldn't even afford a fan that first summer. Ernest soaked in a cold bath for relief, Annette avoided warm dishes at dinnertime, and the boys hawked ice cream on the sidewalk to make a little spending money.[135] A frontier spirit lingered in their rural section of the state. The sanctuary of the St. Joseph synagogue had brass spittoons in the corners. The little Orthodox community regularly attracted *meshulachim*. These were itinerant charity workers— or "Jewish beggars," as Walter described them—who came through

After two years in St. Joseph, Ernest was
offered a position with a small Reform
congregation in Springfield, Missouri in
1942. It was his return to the pulpit after
years of exile. Ernest and Annette lived
at this house at 711 W. State St. until
they retired.

town to raise funds for obscure causes. Walter sat behind a pair of these tattered travelers during services and remembers how the holes in their socks appeared and disappeared beneath their pant legs as they rocked in prayer.[136]

All in all, the Jacobs were content. They had second and third cousins in St. Joseph, which eased the inevitable loneliness of resettlement. Everyone else they met in town treated them pleasantly. "We never felt like outsiders," Walter insists today. "We felt different in a positive way. We were a novelty."[137] Being a novelty defined the two-year stay in St. Joseph. Until the family could afford new clothing, the boys wore remnants of their Bavarian wardrobes to school. Walter recalled his embarrassment when, in the presence of some new friends, his parents finally cracked open their gigantic shipping crates from Augsburg and a pile of toilet paper and soap came tumbling out.[138]

Among the other effects that the family had extracted from Germany was a pair of special bedframes that could be tilted upward to free space during waking hours. These clever beds allowed the boys to share a small room throughout their childhoods, from the early years in Augsburg to their teen years in Springfield. They even worked together at a table nestled between their beds. The close quarters turned the brothers into life-long friends. "If we would have not gotten along, it would have been extremely difficult," Walter said.[139]

The Jacob family followed the war closely. As German forces approached London, Ernest and Annette prepared for the possibility of having to rescue their young nieces and nephew. During those anxious months, Walter paced around the house with a map of Europe in his hands, plotting the locations of cities he heard mentioned on radio broadcasts.[140] He remembers exactly where he was when the Japanese attacked Pearl Harbor—in a movie theater. His job as a school crossing guard entitled him to free tickets. That day, he and his brother attended a double feature. "When we went, we were at peace," he said. "When we returned, we were at war."[141] Even under those heightened circumstances, Walter felt no suspicion or animus from his neighbors. But as America entered World War II, he went from being a novelty to being seen as a potential source of inside information about a part of the world where many of the young local men would soon be sent to fight. Teachers regularly dragged the twelve-year-old boy in front of his class to field questions about European history, geopolitics and current events. "Of course, some teachers would ask things about which I knew absolutely nothing," he said. "You know: *What can you tell us, Walter, about the Junkers?* What could I tell them about the Junkers? I'd never heard of the Junkers!"[142]

By the time the Jacobs moved to Springfield in 1942, they had become accustomed to life in America. But they were still different. They were considered worldly by the standards of southern Missouri. Walter recalled how their American-born neighbors were often astounded by the easy multilingualism of a European family. Using the resources available to them, the Jacobs cobbled together a version of the cultural life they had enjoyed and perhaps even taken for granted in Germany. Springfield was the third largest city in Missouri and the urban center of the rural south of the state. It had an art museum and a chamber orchestra. The nearby Ozarks provided a wealth of natural beauty to enjoy. Drury College and the newly commissioned O'Reilly General Army Hospital circulated outsiders and fresh thinking through the city, and the Jacobs encountered a handful of like-minded souls. They studied Talmud with an Army psychiatrist and his wife. They took an informal music appreciation course at the home of an ophthalmologist who possessed concert-level piano skills and a wonderful record collection. They developed a friendship with a family of American missionaries who had been raised in China and had "a much broader outlook on life" than those families who had lived in Missouri all their lives.[143]

Added to these cultural differences were the religious differences, which existed even within the refuge of their community. Springfield had two synagogues, one Reform and one Orthodox. The Jacobs were nominally Reform, but their European version of liberalism made them much more observant than the rest of the Jewish community of Springfield, including most of its Orthodox contingent. They were one of the few families who kept kosher. Because the congregation was unable to draw enough people on Saturday mornings to justifying opening the synagogue, the Jacobs often held informal services at their home or, on nice days, at some picturesque spot in the mountains.[144]

Beyond those religious differences, the Jacobs were set apart from the congregation by their circumstances. They were a rabbinic family, for starters. And then, as news about the horrors of Europe reached America, they became "a symbol of Jewish history, you might say," as Walter put it.[145]

Added to these were the more profound differences that came from being Jews living in a small town in the Bible Belt. Walter was one of only two Jewish students in his graduating class in high school.[146] His father was leading "a small congregation surrounded by gentiles, mainly enthusiastic Baptists, who tried to convert me, tried to convert my father, tried to convert the whole community," Walter once recalled, decades later, in a speech about the limits of Jewish outreach.[147] The experience of being a religious minority among welcoming people fostered his conviction that, in America, syncretism and assimilation would be far greater threats to Judaism than anti-Semitism.

Walter was a precocious and determined teenager. He exchanged his more frivolous bar mitzvah gifts for books and began taking courses at Drury College while still in high school. As an immigrant teenager still two years from citizenship, he was asked for identification at the American border after hitchhiking through Canada; he used his library card to get back into the country.[148]

He took up photography, which was the perfect creative outlet for a shy, curious child. He enjoyed photographing buildings and landscapes—subjects that held still long enough for the amateur to carefully make all his compositional and technical decisions. When he photographed people, he usually did so surreptitiously. He wanted to capture his subjects in an authentic state of existence.[149]

He enjoyed photographing the railroad yard at the edge of town, or continuing past the city limits to spend afternoons investigating the caves, ponds and forests at the edge of the Ozarks. As night fell, he

Ernest and Annette Jacob worked hard
to translate aspects of the life they
had enjoyed in Germany, especially
their beloved cultural and recreational
activities, to their new surroundings
in Missouri. The expansive Ozarks,
located just beyond their new home in
Springfield, was a suitable replacement
for the foothills of the Alps.

Walter took to photography from
an early age. His photographs of
landscapes and architecture show
a knack for composition and an
attraction to bold perspectives.

would catch a passenger train at some quiet whistle stop and make it home just as dinner was being served.[150] Now, in his mid-eighties, Walter still indulges this inquisitiveness. On his regular trips to Germany, he will occasionally ride a random street car to the end of its line and spend a few hours walking around whatever neighborhood he discovers, just to learn how people live at the margins of a bustling city.[151] He is enthusiastic about high culture, but he is also drawn to alleys, enclaves and other unheralded places. He wants to know how a society dreams but also how it lives.

Walter worked a number of odd jobs as a teenager. He was an apprentice for a heating company, a stock clerk at a department store, a waiter at a Jewish camp in Maine, and a nature counselor at another Jewish camp on the U.S. Gulf Coast. He got the nature counselor job because he had spent three summers in the Kootenai National Forest in northwest Montana, fighting wildfires and controlling an outbreak of blister rust in the white pine trees. The U.S. Forest Service was hiring anyone willing to make the trip and spend a summer in the woods. All that the job required was "a good person to lead you, and a fair amount of *sekhel*," Walter explained, using the Hebrew for common sense. The camp was some thirty miles beyond the nearest road, accessible only by foot or mule. He dug latrines, bathed in streams, climbed the smaller peaks of the Rocky Mountains and panned for gold.[152] The work was hard, but the job included a lot of downtime, which Walter invariably used for reading. Recalling those summers, decades later, a fellow camper wrote, "On nights when lightning flickered across the timbered ridges, he would be immersed in volumes of history while the rest of us concentrated intently on a tutorial in penny ante beneath the wheezing gas lanterns."[153]

When given the opportunity to consider the places across the United States where he spent his adolescent years, Walter often notes the casual generosity he discovered in the hearts of so many of his new countrymen, from the little children at his school on Long Island, to the Baptist preachers who befriended his father, to his bunkmates in the Montana wilderness.[154] He doubts whether most of the other men in the forest camp had ever met a Jew before, let alone one who kept kosher and conducted solitary worship services every Friday night. Yet they all accepted him completely. They called him "Jake." The camp cook knew a few Jewish soldiers from his tour in the Navy during World War II. Without prompting, he always prepared a piece of fish for Walter on nights when the rest of the crew got ham for supper.[155] As Walter got older, and met other Jews, he came to appreciate the value of having grown up in a small corner of the Midwest rather than in one of the big Jewish communities around New York City. "We would not have gotten to really know America," he said.[156]

Added to the general gratitude he felt toward the country that had provided shelter to him and his family at their most vulnerable moment, these warm personal encounters gave Walter a positive outlook about the condition of his new nation. He graduated at the top of his high school class in 1947 and delivered a commencement address on the assigned theme "We Cherish Our American Heritage." While the text has not survived, a brief summary of the speech in the *Springfield News Leader and Press* shows Walter beginning to develop his ideas about the ways a society could pursue progress while still honoring old values. "He saw America as a young nation with energy and vitality and a love of sports, able to act freely because not too tightly shackled by tradition," the article noted. "He called attention to the fact this is an age, not of art and literature, but of science and industry. For the seniors he acknowledged the task of guarding the legacy of past generations to use for greater development for a broader, richer heritage for a new generation."[157]

Walter expressed a similar hopefulness in the commencement address he delivered during his graduation ceremony from Drury College in 1950, but first he reckoned with a growing pessimism he sensed in the culture. "No matter where we turn, we are met by a gloomy outlook on life," he acknowledged. The news made another world war seem both inevitable and imminent. The wonders of science and technology were being used to create tools for global destruction. The best ideas of economics and politics were often dismissed as naïve

Walter spent three summers fighting
wildfires and combating a blister rust
outbreak in the Montana wilderness for
the U.S. Forest Service. Photographs
of him from those summers, such as this
one, are rare. He was usually the one
taking the pictures.

or disingenuous. Religion offered a respite but no real encouragement. Art was completely cheerless. He was particularly dismayed by the evocative yet cruel vision of the coming generation depicted in George Orwell's recently published *1984*. "This is no tale of the far distant future but it is prophesized for the middle of our own life time," he noted. His generation had been raised in poverty and hardened by global war, and now it expected to become "mere grist for the mill of destruction."

Walter countered this fatalism with an idea that would become central to his rabbinate. "The future is ours to shape as we please, for our success, or our needless doom," he said. "Success can only come with hope. We can not look for hope in external sources, we must look toward ourselves as individuals. We must rebuild a faith in the basic goodness of mankind by more fully trusting ourselves as individuals, knowing and believing that each of us can stop the imminent disaster."

Without a higher system of belief, he said, many people felt a "vague pessimism" when they looked at the world. It fostered self-indulgent habits, such as the tendency toward high-minded but ultimately useless philosophizing, or the unwillingness to imagine a better future. The expansion of higher education was teaching an entire generation of Americans how to think. "Yet thought without action avails nothing," he said. "We must regain a faith in ourselves to carry our thoughts into action, to lead us in an optimistic striving toward a goal."[158]

Even though Walter barely referenced religion in the address, his inclination to pin any hopes for the future onto individual actions guided by high ideals was essentially homiletic. With a reference to scripture, it would have made for a nice sermon.

And yet, as Walter moved through high school and college, his father tried to discourage him from entering the rabbinate. Ernest used many of the same arguments Benno had unsuccessfully made to him, such as the potential for great intellectual loneliness and the parade of daily obligations that thwarted private enthusiasms. He told his son to set aside any familial responsibility he might feel and pursue whatever profession interested him most.[159]

Walter briefly took the advice to heart. On his way to Maine one summer, he stopped in New York City to visit his childhood friend George Sturm, whom he had not seen since Augsburg. George remembered Walter from their playground days and was surprised to see a lanky young man with a persistent cowlick, big brown eyes and "a Midwest accent that you could cut with a knife." As they caught up that evening, George remembers Walter telling him, "I don't know what I'm going to do but I know what I'm never going to do: be a rabbi."[160]

Within a few years of that firm pronouncement, Walter was attending a rabbinical school. He has since resisted attempts to pinpoint an epiphany motivating his decision to become a rabbi, the sixteenth generation in his family, although he has acknowledged that maintaining such a long chain involved more than inertia. Before it became a profession, the rabbinate was consciously set apart from the trades. A trade earned money, and the rabbinate was viewed as being above such mundane financial considerations. When it became a paid profession, it also required intensive training, which meant a loss of income for families. Few children justified the financial sacrifice. The Jacob family produced those children in generation after generation. After emancipation, Jewish families in Europe could increasingly send their children to university to pursue almost any vocation they desired. Even with this freedom, the children of the Jacob family still chose to enter the rabbinate.[161]

When pressed to offer a reason for becoming a rabbi, Walter has described the decision as being purely practical. He enjoyed scholarship, and he was drawn to philanthropy. He saw the rabbinate as a way to combine those two interests with far more authority and autonomy than he was likely to be afforded as an academic or as a social worker.[162]

Herbert Jacob went into academia, and his career suggests the type of life Walter might have led in a different profession. Although the two brothers had some key personality differences, they were both interested in the practical side of intellectual pursuits. Herbert was a pioneer in the "law and society" movement, which studied how average people engaged with the legal system. He was an admired teacher and a prolific writer, and he pushed his ideas and beliefs into the public sphere in both conventional and unconventional ways. He regularly wrote letters to the editor on subjects ranging from anti-apartheid to women's rights. He also printed a set of labels with pointed social questions. He stuck these on envelopes, figuring that many sets of eyes would come upon his provocative messages as the letters traveled through postal systems and mailrooms. Walter and Herbert often joked that they divided their father's professional life between the two of them. Walter took the rabbinic half while Herbert took the academic half. "But we also trespassed on each other's territory," Walter acknowledged. Herbert was active at Beth Emet, a Reform congregation in Evanston, Ill. Walter pursued his scholarly interests into areas of the law where his brother was an expert. They both used work as a way to engage with society, rather than as an end in and of itself. [163]

The breadth of Walter's thinking about the rabbinate reflected the influence of his grandfather and his father, as well as his appreciation of the particular opportunities of America. Benno Jacob created a model for maintaining an uncompromising scholarly practice within a congregational routine, and Ernest Jacob created a model for expanding that congregational routine far beyond the synagogue.

Walter was particularly inspired by the way his father conducted "a serious rabbinate in a small community which would have been satisfied with less," he said. [164] In addition to thoughtful sermons and well-prepared classes, Ernest performed his calling far beyond its immediate obligations. As he had done throughout his district rabbinate in Germany, he served both the traditional and liberal wings of the Jewish community in Springfield. He eventually orchestrated a merger between its struggling Reform and Orthodox congregations and oversaw two expansions of the physical facilities of this larger congregation. He also undertook responsibilities outside of synagogue life. He was chaplain of the medical wing of a federal prison and also of the new army hospital. [165] He conducted a Passover seder for thousands of troops and performed weddings for war-bound servicemen. [166]

Ernest became the leading representative of Judaism within a pre-dominately Baptist region. He led synagogue tours for Christians. He conducted interfaith services. He addressed civic groups. He sat on one of the first human rights commissions in Missouri. When important world events occurred, the local news media called him for a Jewish perspective to set alongside Protestant and Catholic perspectives, "as if the Jews constituted a third of Springfield's population," as Herbert once noted.[167]

As a professor at Drury College, Ernest had an opportunity to explain Judaism in great detail to a generation of sympathetic Protestant youth. A pastor named John Loren Sandford has referenced his classes with Ernest in several books. In one, he recalled asking his professor why God had chosen the Jews. The answer changed his perspective about the responsibilities of being a Christian: " 'Gott luffs effryvone,' [Ernest] replied in his heavily accented English. 'He choss de Philistines und de Egyptians, too. De difference iss, ve choss Him back.' "[168]

While the Jacobs were adjusting to their new life in Missouri, they also remained in touch with many of their fellow refugees. The old Augsburg congregation had been dispersed across the world, with members ending up in Italy, France, Great Britain, Denmark, Sweden, the United States, Canada, Mexico, Jamaica, Ecuador, Brazil, Peru, Argentina, Chile, Israel, South Africa, Australia and New Zealand. And, of course, a sizeable group still remained trapped in the prison of Nazi Germany.[169]

Before leaving Germany, Ernest regularly sent news and good wishes from Augsburg to former members who had already fled. He maintained a large number of these correspondences after settling in Missouri. As more and more people fled and the volume of letters started to become overwhelming, he came up with a novel way to stay in touch with his congregation in exile. He published a twice-yearly *Rundbrief*, or circular mailing, between 1941 and 1949. He compiled the small newsletter using whatever information he could learn about the group still in Augsburg, as well as reports collected from the larger group dispersed all over. He structured each issue to highlight accomplishments of the émigré community, believing it would inspire those who were struggling to see that success was possible and that it could shine on them, as well.

Creating these circulars required hours at a typewriter and a mimeograph machine. Walter handled these tasks, and he can still recall his horror as he re-typed a ten-page account of life inside the Auschwitz concentration camp written by a recently rescued former congregant. Ernest worked on this project in free moments, using what little disposable income the family could spare. It was a labor of love for his former community and is thought to be unique within the history of the Holocaust.[170]

Watching his father undertake these wide-ranging responsibilities introduced Walter to the expansive possibilities of being a rabbi in the United States. It was common for American rabbis to serve on citywide communal boards, and it was also perfectly acceptable for them to launch new organizations outside of the synagogue. Walter found a striking example of this freedom in Isaac Mayer Wise, who started two Jewish newspapers and founded the Hebrew Union College and the Central Conference of American Rabbis in the late 19th century, in addition to his congregational work. Walter has called these independent forays "the broader role of the rabbi." He considers them to be an American contribution to the rabbinate.[171] The desire to carry religious energy beyond the traditional duties of the rabbinate was a response to the unstructured and undisciplined state of Judaism in America at the end of the 19th century. It was a way for rabbis to re-assert their authority within religious communities managed by laity. In an essay about this shifting balance of power, Walter wrote, "It is clear that the rabbinate has been resilient and able to incorporate within its framework whole areas which were not originally intended."[172]

Around the time of his retirement, Walter explained that he had chosen the rabbinate because he wanted to make Judaism more attractive to his generation and more understandable to the wider world. By way of an explanation, he noted that all his childhood friends in Germany were Jews, while all his adolescent friends in America were Christians.[173] He seemed to be saying that the sharp contrast between the two halves of his childhood gave him a broad view of the challenges facing his generation. As a child in Augsburg, he was part of a large, unified and active Jewish community surrounded by latent hostility. As a teenager in the United States, he came of age within a small, fragmented and occasionally indifferent Jewish community in the middle of a friendly country.

Becoming a rabbi allowed Walter to address both circumstances. By strengthening Judaism from within, he could help the religion engage with the wider world. "I felt that there was a great deal that could be done in a more modern way," he said.[174]

Walter arrived at the Cincinnati campus of Hebrew Union College in 1950, during a period of transition for world Jewry. It was an era of consolidation. The Holocaust had reduced the Jewish centers of Europe to a series of displaced persons camps, and the State of Israel was a young, war-torn and underdeveloped country. America had unexpectedly become home to the largest, wealthiest and most secure Jewish population in the world. It was also an era of moderation. The traditional wing of Judaism was adopting some of the basic assumptions of liberalism, and the liberal wing was accepting certain cultural traditions from its growing contingent of Eastern European members. A segment of Orthodoxy was beginning to modernize, and the ideological differences that had divided liberal Judaism in America into Reform and Conservative denominations—and had divided those denominations into factions—were easing.

Those changes also touched the school. Walter entered Hebrew Union College in the year it merged with the Jewish Institute of Religion, in New York, to create a unified liberal rabbinic seminary with two campuses. Hebrew Union College had been founded in 1875, when descendants of German-speaking Jews represented the largest segment of the small Jewish population in America. The curriculum of the school had been built on the model of the liberal seminaries of Germany, but designed specifically for American students. The college wanted to translate old-world scholarship to a new setting. The Jewish Institute of Religion was founded in 1922, at the end of the period of great Eastern European immigration. It focused on matters of Jewish identity and promoted Zionism and Modern Hebrew. As Rabbi W. Gunther Plaut wrote in a sourcebook of the Reform movement, the merger combined "the liberal spirit of Judaism" with the "full force of Jewish peoplehood."[175]

The liberal spirit of German scholarship still hung in the air at the Cincinnati campus of Hebrew Union College when Walter arrived. The faculty included American scholars who had trained at the two liberal rabbinic seminaries in Germany before the war and also German scholars who had come to America after surviving the war. Walter ate with Rabbi Leo Baeck in the dining hall and studied with Professor Eugen Täubler. Both men had been faculty members at the Higher Institute for Jewish Studies in Berlin. They and others carried forth a rigorous and orderly style of scholarship. Walter fondly recalls an elective course he took on the 7th century poet Yannai. Each word was so imbued with meaning and subtext that the class reviewed just two and a half poems over an entire semester.

A new American spirit was also blowing through the college. The student body invited the professor of mysticism and philosophy Rabbi Abraham Joshua Heschel to speak, against the wishes of the administration. Walter attended the talk, but he found it too free flowing and unstructured and left early to catch a movie. His disinterest reflected his inherent bias against a certain type of abstract thinking. He is generally averse to philosophy and mysticism unless they are being analyzed historically. In many sermons and lectures he criticized the trend toward "spirituality," which he saw as a way to reap the emotional benefits of a religious life without respecting its practical demands. The closest he has come to experiencing religious transcendence, he said, is the mysterious moment when the mind suddenly grasps a difficult subject after many hours of inquiry.

Walter was an independent student. He was uninspired by the animated and participatory style of Professor Israel Bettan, who was a popular lecturer in the fields of rabbinic literature and homiletics. Recalling his former teacher, Walter wrote, "He may have influenced another generation, but not this one." Even when Walter has mentioned professors he enjoyed, he is quick to assert his independence from them. Although he admired the "approach" of Dr. Samuel Sandmel, Dr. Ellis Rivkin and Dr. Alexander Guttman, he never thought of himself as a disciple of these teachers.[176]

The few surviving essays Walter wrote at Hebrew Union College introduce the themes of his future scholarly efforts. One essay compared the lives, careers and theological approaches of the early American Reform leaders Isaac Mayer Wise and Kaufmann Kohler. The essay was one of his first attempts at writing Jewish history and shows his knack for condensing historical figures and eras into practical and accessible summaries. "It may easily be seen that American Reform Judaism consists of the organizations of Isaac Mayer Wise, while its basic thought and theology stem from Kaufmann Kohler and his disciples," he wrote.[177]

The essay also hinted at the qualities Walter admired in a leader. While he praised Wise for his organizational skills and his efforts to unify the factions within liberal Judaism in America, he thought Kohler had the superior intellect. One practical trick he learned from studying Kohler, he later explained, was to bring a concrete proposal to any committee meeting. "Come with something, and it's likely to go somewhere," he said.[178]

Another essay on "Emergency in Talmudic Law" was among Walter's earliest investigations of Jewish law, which became the centerpiece of his scholarship. Building on the well-known exemption of religious obligations when lives are endangered, Walter concluded that "the teachers of this period did not believe religion to be an absolute force, but they thought of it as benefiting the life of the person and enabling him to develop." A third essay, analyzing the expression "to take the Lord's name in vain," utilized some of the techniques Benno Jacob had developed for determining the intent of the Hebrew Bible. As his grandfather had done, Walter also criticized Jewish scholars for ignoring a subject that Christian scholars ardently pursued.[179]

In his doctoral work, completed over several years after he settled in Pittsburgh in the late 1950s, Walter displayed an ongoing fascination with the world of his ancestors. His first proposal was "A History of the Rabbi and Jewish Teacher Since the Emancipation of the Jews in Germany" and would have allowed him to delve deeply into the lives and careers of his two grandfathers, Jakob Loewenberg and Benno Jacob. Walter ultimately abandoned the project because most of the research materials he needed were only available in British libraries.[180]

Instead, he pursued a comprehensive assessment of Jewish popular literature in Germany between emancipation and World War I. He realized that the scholarly understanding of Jewish identity in Germany during those years came from private sources such as memoirs, diaries and letters. A study of the fiction of the period would show how Jews had presented themselves in public. To research the subject, he had to read more than three hundred novels and short story collections over the course of a year when he was also starting a family and handling new congregational duties. The underlying premise of the project is perhaps more revealing than his other essays from the time. In looking over these books, Walter noticed how a previously isolated community produced "astonishing outbursts of creativity" after it gained admission into the broader society.[181] He was beginning to see similar creative opportunities for Judaism within the welcoming arms of America.

Despite his reputation on campus as a quiet, studious young man, more interested in books than in socializing, Walter pursued the practical rabbinate much earlier than many of his classmates. A few weeks before starting at Hebrew Union College, he led High Holiday services for a small congregation in Okmulgee, Oklahoma. The congregation couldn't afford a student rabbi and hired the twenty-year-old pre-student based upon his affirmative answer to a single interview question: Can you read Hebrew?

After entering Hebrew Union College, Walter worked as a student rabbi at congregations in Ashland, Kentucky and Marion, Indiana, and he made occasional outings to other cities over his years at the school. His description of these peripatetic experiences is a montage of slight embarrassments: fending off too-stiff drinks, being stood up for dinner invitations, quietly suffering while families argued at the dinner table, delivering weak sermons, singing off-key. In Schulenburg, Texas, he sweltered in his only suit, a thick blue garment designed for winter. The congregation put him up in a downtown hotel attached to a movie theater. All day long, he could hear the movie soundtrack on a loop. "And eventually went to see it, to see what the pictures looked like," he said.

Through the student pulpit, Walter learned about the tricks congregants play. The members of the Schulenburg congregation told him about their longstanding tradition of performing all the services of Yom Kippur straight through and finishing the holiday in the mid-afternoon. Eager to respect the local custom, Walter obliged. He only discovered he'd been duped when he overheard a radio broadcast of the World Series and realized everyone had been rushing home to catch the ballgame.[182]

While these forays into small-town America might have been eye opening for student rabbis who had grown up in large congregations along the East Coast, they were familiar to Walter. The towns he visited generally had two hundred Jews or fewer, which was about the size of the Springfield community. He was ready to deal with their limitations, make the most of their opportunities and accommodate their more eccentric personalities.

As a result, he was less interested in using the experience to master the fundamentals of being a rabbi and more interested in testing new ideas. He believed that Reform services should have more music. Being unable to carry a tune, he decided to create a multimedia service using pre-recorded music on a small tape deck. The seamless process he envisioned proved to be highly disruptive in practice. "Here I was trying to lead the service and also push the button at the right time," he said. He also wanted his congregations to engage in regular, serious study. He devised a course and prepared copies of primary texts, only to find that almost no one in the congregation could read Hebrew. "That was a good lesson in asking first what's possible before you prepare yourself for it," he noted.[183]

Perhaps the most instructive example of the gap between rabbinic ambitions and the needs of a congregation occurred in his hometown. After the merger in Springfield, his father's congregation conducted services according to Reform liturgy throughout the year and held a special Orthodox service at the High Holidays. One year, the small Orthodox group asked Walter to lead their special service. Inspired by his recent elective on Yannai, Walter spent the entire summer researching the hidden meanings and subtexts of the liturgical poetry he found in the Orthodox prayer book. The High Holidays finally arrived, and in the middle of the service two congregants nearly came to blows over two of these liturgical poems. Should this poem be read or should that poem be read? As the argument became increasingly heated, Walter had to suppress the urge to laugh. Having spent weeks trying to decipher these cryptic poems, he knew that neither of the congregants understood the intention or deeper meaning of either one. "So what were they arguing about?" he asked. "They were arguing about their family traditions. And they were trying to keep those traditions alive, even if they had no idea what actually led to those traditions."[184]

Even though Walter spent the entirety of his active rabbinate leading one of the largest Jewish congregations in the country, he maintained a continuing interest in the situation of smaller congregations. After his retirement, he coordinated a program to collect historic materials from the dozens of Jewish communities in small towns around Pittsburgh. What attracted him to these congregations were the challenges of perpetuating a tradition in places with little religious education and many conflicting beliefs. He admired how the flexibility of Reform ideology allowed people to come together in the synagogue and still maintain different levels of observance at home. These congregations, he felt, were best served by rabbis who could be flexible about matters of religious custom—rabbis who knew when to read this poem, when to read that one, and when to read both.[185]

He also saw small towns as a place where the cultural pressures facing all of American Judaism would be revealed first. As some of these smaller congregations began to struggle in the second half of the 20th century, Walter took a few surprisingly hardline positions. Early in his tenure as chairman of the Responsa Committee of the Central Conference of American Rabbis, in the 1970s, he received a question from the president of a congregation in South Dakota asking whether it was appropriate for a layman to conduct a wedding in a city without any rabbi for miles. Walter insisted that the congregation find a rabbi to conduct the ceremony. He believed that a wedding should only be conducted by someone with "the ability to deal with all the ramifications of the marriage, which include pre-nuptial counseling, as well as the ability to counsel afterwards."[186] In a speech in the early 1990s, Walter said it would be wiser for small congregations to close than to accept non-Jewish members in an effort to revitalize their ranks.[187]

These conservative positions came later in his career, though, as he sought to bolster the authority of the rabbinate at a time of tremendous cultural change. Early on, his primary interest was to promote creativity and engagement within the American Jewish community, which, despite its growth and strength, could seem spiritually adrift.

Walter was ordained in a class of nineteen in a morning service at the Rockdale Avenue Temple in Cincinnati in June 1955. It was a tradition for rabbinic fathers to participate in the service, and Rabbi Ernest Jacob delivered the invocation.[188]

In those days, Hebrew Union College required its graduates to serve a two-year stint as military chaplains. Soon after his ordination, Walter reported for basic training at Lackland Air Force Base in San Antonio, Texas. The coursework was designed for chaplains pursuing military careers. "I decided very early that this was a path of education where I did not need to excel," Walter said. "I sat in the back behind a very big chaplain … and spent most of my time reading. And passed the course, but also got a fair amount of reading done."[189] His industriousness was commensurate with the value he assigned to the endeavor. A similar pragmatism is one reason why his personal letters are often filled with typographical errors. When a cousin once asked him about these simple mistakes, Walter wrote back, "I am usually two lezie too ron de spell-sheker."[190]

At the end of basic training, each recruit was asked where he would prefer to be stationed. Walter requested Europe and was instead sent to the Philippines. "Of which I knew nothing," he said. He tried to research the country using whatever books he could find around the house in Springfield, including an outdated German encyclopedia called the *Judisches Lexikon*. It anachronistically told the reader to check for the Philippines under the entry for Spain, which had ceded control of the island nation in 1898, after the Spanish-American War.[191]

Walter arrived in Manila in the fall of 1955, during the fragile calm between the end of the Korean War and the escalation of American involvement in what would become the Vietnam War. As a chaplain, he was made a first lieutenant "from the first day, didn't even know how to salute," he said.[192] His duties were prosaic. He led services, taught classes, delivered lectures and counseled the few dozen Jews among the thousands of servicemen at Clark Air Force Base, Subic Bay Naval Base and Naval Station Sangley Point.[193] To get around these large bases, he bought a spiffy scooter that he emblazoned with a Star of David.

Walter soon realized that the remote posting was another invitation to experiment. "It gave me an enormous opportunity to speak with absolutely no consequences," he said. He enjoyed the challenges of ministering in peacetime, such as the long "character guidance" lectures he had to deliver to hundreds of troops of all faiths. A chaplain could speak from one of several prepared texts, but Walter always wrote new material. He wanted to learn how to make a nearly hour-long lecture interesting to people his age. He often had to compete with small annoyances, such as pilots who revved their engines on the nearby flight line, or times when his audience suddenly stood to salute a senior officer who had happened to wander through the lecture hall.

HEBREW UNION COLLEGE-JEWISH INSTITUTE OF RELIGION

Upon your arrival to attend the

ORDINATION SERVICE

*please present this card to the usher who will
direct you to a section of the Temple reserved for
friends and relatives of the candidates for degrees.*

Walter received his ordination from
the Hebrew Union College-Jewish
Institute of Religion in June 1955.
According to a seminary tradition,
the rabbinic parents of graduates
participate in the ceremony, and his
father delivered an invocation.

Walter bought a scooter to zip around
the vast Clark Air Base in Manila,
where he spent two years as a military
chaplain. He affixed a Star of David
to the back.

After so many years of book learning, Walter enjoyed dealing with the "very human problems" on the bases. He learned how to be sympathetic and savvy at the same time. He was moved by a sad story from a military prisoner, only to discover that the man had carefully omitted the more heinous details of his rap sheet. He figured out ways to convince soldiers with pregnant girlfriends on the island to meet their paternal responsibilities. He learned about the value of gracefully navigating territorial boundaries when a Greek Orthodox soldier came to him for a "second opinion" after consulting a military priest about a personal matter.

Even at its busiest, the job was easy. Walter had a lot of downtime and soon grew restless. A few months into his tour, he started visiting a small community of civilian Jews living in Taiwan. A few months after that, he began arranging trips to the new Military Assistance Advisory Groups that were being established as training centers throughout Southeast Asia. By the end of his first year, he was making a monthly flying tour throughout the region, from Manila to Taipei to Bangkok. During the High Holidays, he completed portions of this wide circuit over the course of a single day, conducting a service in Manila in the morning and repeating the service in Taipei in the afternoon. He also visited civilian communities in the countries surrounding the South China Sea. In Saigon, he wore street clothes to bypass quotas on military personnel in Vietnam. In Manila, he discovered a small and scrappy congregation of "the odds and ends of Jews who fate had parked there," as he described the German refugees and Soviet exiles he quickly befriended.

Walter playfully called these communities his "area rabbinate." The term recalled his father's "district rabbinate," albeit on a notably different scale. "It was probably the largest rabbinate in the world with the smallest number of Jews," he said.[194]

Between his official duties, Walter frequently traveled for pleasure. He went to Japan, Hong Kong, India, Guam and Singapore, visiting cultural sites and also witnessing daily life. With his camera around his neck, he toured a rubber plantation and a tobacco farm. He attended a cockfight and a religious flagellation ceremony. Between the responsibilities of his area rabbinate and his vacations, he logged more than fifty thousand miles during his two-year tour of duty. It was his first experience traveling around the world for business and leisure, rather than for safety. He was hooked.

Walter produced a weekly bulletin for his dispersed congregation. He mimeographed a sheet of paper and folded it once to make a modest four-page pamphlet. He called it *M'mizrach*, meaning "From the East." It was a *Rundbrief*, of sorts.

The primary purpose of the bulletin was to disseminate the times and dates of upcoming events, but Walter used the remaining space as a forum for ideas and inspiration. He published sermons. He offered capsule reviews during Jewish Book Month, classifying his reading recommendations into two categories: "for pleasure" and "for information." He wrote essays on Jewish symbols, Jewish holidays, Jewish thinkers and Jewish denominations. After visiting a new country, he created travel guides focusing on Jewish history and culture. He even decorated his bulletin with drawings, including one of Rodef Shalom, where he had filled a temporary post for several months before his ordination.[195]

M'mizrach was his first foray into self-publishing, which became an important tool of his rabbinate. He has used the printed word far beyond the bibliographic pursuits that are typical of his profession. Adapting an existing tradition at Rodef Shalom, he published an annual booklet of sermons in each of his thirty years as senior rabbi of the congregation. Any time he organized a symposium, he later published a simple volume containing all the lectures. He often created simple, informative newsletters to accompany new projects. His preferred method of honoring a friend or family member was with a personalized book dedication.

One reason for congregational rabbis to maintain a rigorous scholarly practice, according to Walter, is that congregants are more likely to glance through a book if they know the author, even if they are just trying to be polite. When counseling a congregant, he will often recommend books on relevant subjects and occasionally mail unsolicited copies.[196] "We cannot expect people to flock to courses; they never will. We must bring material to them in the simplest and easiest, but also most stimulating way as possible," he once said in a sermon with the ambitious title "Where Are We Going As American Jews." In it, he called for more high-quality publications written for a general Jewish audience. The more reading material that was scattered around a house, he argued, the more likely a person would be to pick up a book or a magazine now and then and learn something new.[197]

This emphasis on the written word goes beyond the enthusiasms of a bookworm. It reflects one of his central ideas about the role of a rabbi. A rabbi can guide, teach, counsel and instruct, but a rabbi cannot be religious on behalf of congregants. The daily task of adhering to a faith will always be an individual responsibility. In his final issue of *M'mizrach*, as he prepared to return to civilian life, Walter gently chastised his fellow servicemen for spending so much of their downtime on Clark Air Base when the friendly Jewish community of Manila was just a short drive to the south and the Air Force offered religious retreats to Japan. "The opportunity exists, but you must avail yourself of it; no invitations will be extended on a silver platter," he wrote.[198] A rabbi can recommend the right book, but the congregant must decide whether to read it.

Walter accepted a position as an associate rabbi at Rodef Shalom Congregation in Pittsburgh after he returned to the United States in late 1957. He stayed with the congregation until he retired forty years later. In the decades since his retirement, he has remained a "senior scholar" of the congregation.

He has attributed this long association entirely to the graciousness of providence. A mismanaged attempt to graduate from Hebrew Union College as quickly as possible left him taking only one class during his final semester, in early 1955. When Dr. Solomon B. Freehof, who was senior rabbi of Rodef Shalom, asked the college to send someone to Pittsburgh to be a temporary assistant, Walter was the only student rabbi available at the time.[199]

Walter tells a story about his first meeting with Dr. Freehof. It goes like this: "He talked to me for an hour, and I listened. At the end of that time, he said, 'I think you'll do.'"[200] The line usually gets a laugh from those who knew firsthand how Dr. Freehof could hold court. Pressed to provide details, Walter will admit that Dr. Freehof conducted the interview rather skillfully. He started by casually discussing a book on his shelf and wove a "quiet interrogation" through the resulting chat.[201] In this way, the interview process lost its usual formality and became a way to judge the personality and intellect of the applicant. Several younger rabbis who have worked with Walter say that his first question to them was: "What are you reading?"[202]

Dr. Freehof was said to have divided the rabbinic profession into two categories: those who lead with their heads and those who lead with their feet. He was undeniably the former, a brilliant scholar and a gifted orator who happily delegated pastoral responsibilities to subordinates. Walter was technically still a student, but Dr. Freehof immediately gave him many of the day-to-day responsibilities of an established pulpit rabbi. That summer, Dr. Freehof took his annual vacation to Maine and left more than two thousand members in the care of the twenty-five-year-old rabbinical student. Walter was so baby-faced and inexperienced that when he got up to address a confirmation class, he was mistaken for one of the high school students.

Walter welcomed these responsibilities. "If it was all right with him, it was all right with me," he said. Thinking back, he also seemed to recognize an underlying respect in this hands-off management style, which he described this way: "If you've got an area, you take care of it. And if you want to talk about something, talk about it, but as far as the normal details are concerned, it's yours." He later copied this approach when he became senior rabbi and gave his associates and assistants a long leash.

Walter only stayed with Rodef Shalom for about six months during that first stretch before leaving for the Philippines. Returning to the congregation in 1957, as a full-time associate rabbi, he was again made immediately responsible for practical aspects of the pulpit. He

In his weekly bulletin at Clark Air
Base, Walter published sermons,
book reviews, travel guides and
other news for Jewish servicemen
across the South China Sea region.
He illustrated the bulletin and
occasionally added drawings of
Rodef Shalom.

performed weddings and funerals, and he visited the ill and the elderly. "My father, when he heard the number of funerals I was involved with, was kind of astonished. Because funerals were so few and far between in Springfield you had to look at the rabbi's manual to see what were the prayers." Walter was also made the rabbinic liaison for the religious school and for the Junior Congregation, which put him in contact with young couples who later became his advocates.[203]

Rodef Shalom Congregation was the oldest and largest Jewish congregation in Pittsburgh, with a history of strong rabbinic leadership. It began as a burial society founded by German immigrants in 1848 and was chartered in 1856, after a series of breakaways and mergers within the small Jewish population in the city. Rodef Shalom was originally a traditional congregation and adopted Reform liturgy after Rabbi Isaac Meyer Wise visited the congregation in 1863. The change led a faction to break away and form a more traditional congregation. Both congregations did better after the split than before, as each became free to pursue an uncompromising agenda. When the leaders of the Reform movement decided to hold a conference in 1885 to set forth a bold, new vision, they asked Rodef Shalom to play host. The result was the Pittsburgh Platform, which described Judaism as a religion of ethical monotheism, rather than of ritual.

The spirit of Rodef Shalom gradually shifted over the following decades from small and German to expansive and American. It became especially known for its rabbinic leadership under Rabbi Lippman Mayer, Rabbi J. Leonard Levy, Rabbi Samuel Goldenson and eventually Dr. Freehof. By the time Walter arrived in the mid-1950s, Rodef Shalom was at the pinnacle of its size and its influence. Even with another Reform congregation just a mile away and two more emerging in the suburbs, its senior congregation had approximately two thousand members, and its Junior Congregation had another two hundred and fifty. High Holiday services filled the main sanctuary and overflowed to a second service at a rented hall nearby. The religious school spread its classes across both days of the weekend to accommodate the large student body. The need for space and classrooms led the congregation to construct a large, modern social hall onto the side of its grand and historic sanctuary.[204]

Congregational life was busy enough to justify hiring a second associate. Walter recommended Rabbi Frederick Schwartz, a former rabbinical school classmate. They shared a youthful vision for the rabbinate, but Rabbi Schwartz brought a more outgoing sensibility to that vision. "We'd always been friends at school, both of us very different personalities, as different as you can get, but we got along extremely well and made it work out," Walter explained. Working closely with a peer for the first time, Walter established a collective approach. "We decided right from the beginning that we would essentially do everything together. And so neither one of us was assigned to something. We did religious school and the auxiliaries and pastoral visits and preaching together," he said. [205]

Walter replicated this model in all his major leadership positions over the years, from his tenure as senior rabbi of Rodef Shalom, to his years with the Central Conference of American Rabbis, to his ongoing efforts to establish the Abraham Geiger College. In all three cases, he found partners who shared his approach and beliefs, but had a style or a sensibility that he was unable to provide himself.

Dr. Freehof rarely mentored his two younger associates. "He was a very good teacher by example," Walter said. "You could see what he did, and see how he did it." Walter watched carefully, especially when it came to the nuances of speaking publicly, a skill he was working to develop. Dr. Freehof was a master. His book reviews drew as many as a thousand people, Jews and gentiles alike, to the synagogue on Wednesday mornings. His sermons and lectures were published and widely read. He spoke eloquently and articulately without notes. He would introduce a theme and develop it extemporaneously, gauging the mood of his audience and revising accordingly. Walter has often recalled a time he watched Bishop John Wright of the Catholic Diocese of Pittsburgh dictate a statement to his secretary and work through several revisions before he was satisfied. Seeing this, it occurred to Walter that Dr. Freehof rarely changed more than a word or two when he gave dictation.[206]

JUNIOR CONGREGATION   RODEF SHALOM TEMPLE

NEWSLETTER

VOLUME 5—No. 1   SEPTEMBER, 1957

TEMPLE WELCOMES RABBI AFTER TWO YEAR ABSENCE

RABBI JACOB

Rodef Shalom's new assistant rabbi isn't really new at all. Rabbi Walter Jacob has returned to Temple with a permanent status, to resume the duties he performed as a temporary assistant two years ago. We welcome him back, with the hope that we will enjoy the association with his "first" Temple as much the second time.

Born in Augsberg, Germany, Rabbi Jacob came to the United States with his parents in 1940. He attended Drury College in Springfield, Missouri and later, Hebrew Union College in Cincinnati. Rabbi Jacob came directly to Rodef Shalom from HUC, and was here for five months until he left to serve two years in the U. S. Air Force. As an Air Force chaplain, Rabbi Jacob was stationed in the Phillippines, and was responsible for duties throughout the Southern Pacific area.

Now back with us, Rabbi Jacob will be concentrating mainly on the younger element at Rodef Shalom. His unofficial title might be "Rabbi of the Religious School." Questioned about this he said: "as Rabbi of the Religious School, I am working closely with Mr. Levin in a continued effort to improve the school. For example, this year the Rabbis will have closer contact with the confirmation class than heretofore. Sections of the class will be taught by the Rabbis throughout the whole year."

Although our children may see

COMMITTEE WORKERS WANTED

It is an unqualified truth that the way to enjoy fully and receive benefit from any organization is to give of one's self. As Junior Congregation begins another active season, it is the hope of all officers, board members and committee chairmen that this year will see many new recruits for the various committees. Give a bit of your time, your interest, and find the rewards of self-satisfaction and many new friends.

If you think you would be interested in one or more of the following committees, please contact either the chairman, or assistant chairman for further information.

RELIGIOUS ACTIVITIES COMMITTEE

This committee is interested in the development of the spiritual life of the members of Jr. Congregation. To this end, it conducts the annual Jr. Congregation Service. In addition, it sponsors a Sunday Nursery so that members may attend services. It reminds members of Holidays and of several home services and distributes menorahs to all new members.

Chairman: Bill Behrend
Asst. Chairman: John A. Stein

MEMBERSHIP COMMITTEE

The Membership Committee contacts prospective members of Jr. Congregation and, with their consent, recommends them for approval to the Board of Trustees. The committee also makes personal visits to new members whenever possible and provides for the integration of such members into Jr. Congregation activities.

Chairman: Stanley Barbrow
Asst. Chairman: Leslie Dukehart

PUBLICITY COMMITTEE

The Publicity Committee publicizes the activities of the various committees. This is done through the frequent notices sent to the members and through articles published in local periodicals. The committee also pub-

lishes the Newsletter and the Jr. Congregation Directory.

Chairman: Janet Nieman
Asst. Chairman: Johanna Barbrow

FORUM - ADULT EDUCATION COMMITTEE

This committee is responsible for the planning and presentation of a series of forums dealing with timely and controversial subjects. It also offers the Congregation, as well as the community at large, a series of adult seminars covering significant areas of our intellectual and religious life.

Chairman: Don Schneider
Asst. Chrmn: Robert Frumerman

HOSPITALITY - TELEPHONE COMMITTEE

The Hospitality Committee plans and serves at the Social Hour following all forums and religious meetings, assists with the breakfast preceding the Annual Service, and sponsors a party for all women members.

Chairman: Bea Jacobson
Asst. Chairmen: Natalie Smith, Rita Rosenson

COMMUNITY SERVICE COMMITTEE

This group plans and carries out programs for the good of the Congregation and for the community at large, such as the sponsoring of parties for children in the Juvenile Detention Home and the Industrial Home for Crippled Children. It is also responsible for planning seminars with Rabbi Gershon and Rabbi Jacob.

Chairman: Joan Sherman
Asst. Chairman: Norma Steiner

SOCIAL COMMITTEE

The Social Committee plans and executes arrangements for all social functions sponsored by Jr. Congregation, including dances, the annual Election Dinner, and other novelty social affairs.

Chairman: Jacques Blum
Asst. Chairman: Charles Solof

more of him, we of Jr. Congregation will certainly come to know Rabbi Jacob as he conducts services, and also become acquainted through the Adult Education series which we sponsor. Says Rabbi Jacob, "I will be working with Rabbi Gershon on the Adult Education Series and I hope that many of you will participate in the programs and classes which will be held during the coming year." During these High Holy Days, Rabbi Jacob will preach at the morning service for Yom Kippur at the Temple, and the morning service for Rosh Hashonah at Syria Mosque.

Through a quirk in his academic calendar, Walter started working for Rodef Shalom Congregation in Pittsburgh six months before he was ordained. The experience was mutually beneficial, and he had a job waiting when he returned from the service.

Developing a logical structure in a spontaneous way made Dr. Freehof an exceptionally effective speaker. Walter admired how people could recreate the basic argument and sequence of these talks after hearing them once.[207] Walter also possessed a clear, logical mind, but he had to learn how to engage a large crowd of people. After his mother visited Pittsburgh during his second summer on the job, she wrote, "I can't tell you how I enjoyed that service—the way you conducted it—good thoughts in your sermon—but don't be too shy, give it a little more warmth, personal feeling."[208] Even as Walter gained proficiency in the art of preaching, he had to learn to carry this energy into other aspects of public presentation. After he led a High Holiday service in 1966, one congregant wrote to critique his performance on the pulpit. He praised the "vim and vigor" of the sermon but complained about an overall lack of engagement. "There must be things you can do to help us become participants instead of just ticket-holders," the congregant wrote.[209]

Walter developed several subtle techniques for creating intimacy within a roomful of people. He learned how to speak without notes, started sprinkling personal recollections throughout his talks and added modest hints of theatricality by using dramatic pauses or strong endings to particularly long sentences. Most important, he incorporated his dry and subtle sense of humor, which has the rare quality of being sharp without being cutting. His jokes are incisive and consequential without coming at the expense of anyone (except, with some frequency, himself).

Even as Walter grew more comfortable on stage, it never became his favorite place. He had a habit of holding onto the sides of the podium when he led services. Rowna Sutin, a cantorial soloist who regularly shared the stage with Walter, described this instinctive action as a way for an inherently private person to rise to the demands of being a public figure. "It was defining his space: Now, I'm not Walter. I'm the Rabbi," she said.[210]

Effective preaching was only one of the many skills Walter learned during his years under Dr. Freehof. He has had numerous opportunities over the years to pay tribute to his predecessor, and the attributes he chose to praise reveal the virtues he values in a rabbi. He admired how Dr. Freehof delivered his annual "bar mitzvah sermon" year after year, always on the same section of the Torah, without rehashing old ideas. He appreciated how Dr. Freehof mediated conflicts with an authoritative presence and a carefully worded suggestion. He noticed how Dr. Freehof always returned compliments to those who offered them.[211] Walter became a master of this rhetorical maneuver and the related art of deflecting praise: "It was, of course, an honor to receive the American Jewish Committee's Human Relations Award, although I find these occasions somewhat embarrassing. It is, after all, this community which has enabled some progress to be made in various areas of human relations, not any individual." "I see these honors as basically a challenge to do more and to work a bit harder." "The praise was certainly excessive and I will have to atone on next Yom Kippur." "Dr. Freehof and Mark Staitman said a lot of nice things and I restrained myself from providing a rebuttal."[212]

As Dr. Freehof passed eighty and then ninety and approached the century mark, Walter praised his eagerness to keep pursuing his interests as his body and mind allowed. Walter often said he would be happy if his retirement proved to be as active as that of his predecessor, and it has turned out to be even more so. In an essay about the Jewish view of aging, Walter noted, "Our tradition may help us to a different understanding of the aged. It feels no need for exact definitions and does not segregate the elderly into a separate class that has lost its usefulness to society. The Talmudic tradition sees involvement and learning as continuous throughout life."[213]

Rodef Shalom had just celebrated its centennial when Walter started as an assistant rabbi. Like many of the older Reform congregations across the country, it still maintained an air of seriousness inherited from the Germanic sensibilities of its founding families. Services were mostly in English, with little Hebrew. Music came from a grand pipe organ and a choir, not from a cantor or from much congregational singing. Rabbis wore traditional morning dress on the pulpit, and a degree of formality was also expected outside the sanctuary. "If Dr. Freehof would see me now, sitting in his former study, in short sleeves, without a jacket, he would have been shocked," Walter recalled, four decades later. "This was not done."[214]

The dress code reinforced an idealized view of the clergy that was common throughout Judaism at the time, and not only within Reform. A rabbi was supposed to personify religious perfection on behalf of the congregation. Walter respected the office of the rabbinate, and he appreciated decorum, but certain pretensions annoyed him. In a letter congratulating a former Hebrew Union College classmate who had accepted a position with a suburban congregation on Long Island, he warned, "I hope your new position won't make you too Rabbinical. That's the worst of all curses. Every month we have a meeting here of local Rabbis. Some of them sound as if they are preaching when they say hello and any normal person's reaction would be to tell them to go to hell."[215]

Walter was too polite to make such statements publicly, but he began to develop and articulate a vision of the rabbinate based on his personality and his interests. His writing career expanded beyond the sermon outlines he contributed to the weekly temple bulletin and the book reviews he occasionally submitted to the local newspaper. His bibliography developed in a highly idiosyncratic fashion. His first four book projects promoted the works of other people. In 1964, Walter and his brother Herbert co-edited a collection of their father's sermons from Springfield. That same year, Walter co-edited a collection of essays in honor of Dr. Freehof. The following year, Walter wrote an adult study course based on a popular work of biblical commentary that Dr. Freehof had published fifteen years earlier. Throughout those early years, Walter also helped his father translate Benno Jacob's massive Genesis commentary into English.

Walter also used his growing confidence as a public speaker to promote a message of action and engagement to accompany the intellect and erudition expected of his position. The traditional worship schedule at Rodef Shalom offered plenty of opportunities to speak, including a sermonette on Friday evening, a full sermon on Saturday morning, and a long lecture during a Sunday morning service that the congregation had started at the turn of the century to accommodate businessmen who worked on the Sabbath. Such a rigorous homiletic program reflected the values of an earlier era and was already becoming passé by the time Walter arrived in Pittsburgh. In an essay on the subject from 1964, he blamed this "decline of the sermon" on the persistent pessimism throughout the culture, from the alienation behind much art and literature to the tendency of the social sciences to focus on broad trends instead of the actions of individuals.

The purpose of a sermon, he wrote, was to encourage people in the pews to change. But a preacher could only speak from "the mood of our age." In an age of hopelessness about the power of individuals, Walter saw many preachers using their sermons to consider strictly Jewish questions or matters of personal growth. These were areas where it was still possible to imagine how words could inspire change among a large group of people.

Walter agreed that these subjects were important, but he believed they fell short of the prophetic ideal of liberal Judaism—its desire to use the particular values of the religion for universal benefit. "What is likely to happen to this vehicle of public rabbinic expression in the years to come?" he asked. "Those of us who believe that an individual can bring about changes in the world and who feel that we will be understood, will continue to preach; the rest will have to sit quietly and wait until the times and academic fashions have changed sufficiently to give new meaning to the sermon."[216]

Walter always used the pulpit to discuss current events, but history was a more pervasive theme. He wanted the congregation to see the inherent dynamism in Judaism. He described the forefathers as radicals, not elders. He showed how earlier generations borrowed from their surrounding culture, rather than isolating themselves from it.[217]

In those early sermons, Walter was developing his thoughts about the state of American Judaism, about the opportunities and challenges it faced. He expressed these most forcefully in a provocative Sunday

Rodef Shalom was at the peak of its
influence when Walter became its
associate rabbi in 1957. It was the oldest
and largest Jewish congregation in the
city and had recently expanded its
historic synagogue to accommodate
its growing membership.

lecture from February 1965 titled "The United Jewish Federation: An Appraisal and A Critique." He described the Jewish community in America as being on the verge of an important historical moment, a "third stage of Jewish philanthropy," as he described it. The first stage was the effort to help an immigrant population become economically and culturally established in America around the turn of the 20th century. The second stage was the effort before World War I to make Jewish philanthropy both efficient and effective by establishing a system of Jewish social services.

But now, with the Jewish population of America fully acculturated, and the federal government increasingly providing social services that had once been the sole responsibility of religious communities, a third stage was possible. If approached properly, he believed, it could "lead us to a creative Jewish life." In a rare example of Walter preferring the abstract language of poetry to the concrete examples of prose, he called for the next determinant of philanthropic endeavors to be a strong commitment to Jewish ideals. He proposed adult education as the only way to instill those ideals across the entire Jewish community. "In our land we now have an opportunity to become as glorious as the Jewish community of Spain," he said. "The leaders of that golden age combined success, wealth and status with a fine knowledge of Judaism. The great men of that community were able men of the world, but they also knew Jewish ideals. They were not rabbis, but well-educated laymen…We need a thousand such men like that who will inspire not only our desire to give but also our sense of idealism. We must have leadership with learning—not just giving and spending."

The younger generation might currently be estranged from Judaism, he said, but they would eventually return. When they did, they would demand high ideals, intellectual depth and spiritual stimulation. If they failed to find these in Jewish institutions, they would take their idealism elsewhere. In other words, to use Dr. Freehof's two categories for leadership, the Jewish community needed to lead with its head and also with its feet.

In the harshest moments of the lecture, Walter explicitly criticized the professionals who oversaw Jewish organizations and the lay leaders who ran Jewish congregations. These men and women were "dedicated," "highly-motivated," "good" and "hard-working" people, he acknowledged, but they were often unlearned. "Their Jewish knowledge is limited, despite the other degrees they might hold. No one can be blamed for ignorance but it is reprehensible to be unwilling to learn," he said.[218]

The intention of the lecture was much broader than any immediate discussion of communal fundraising practices. Walter was calling for the Jewish community to take greater responsibility for its religious destiny. He wanted people to give for the sake of giving, to learn for the sake of learning and to use those virtues as the basis for change.

Even though Dr. Freehof was the second-oldest active Reform rabbi in the world, he took many people at Rodef Shalom by surprise in January 1966 when he announced his plans to retire after the upcoming High Holidays, in the fall. He was the longest-serving rabbi in the history of Rodef Shalom, having led the congregation for a third of its existence. For the last thirteen of those thirty-three years, Dr. Freehof had worked with the same president, Marcus Lester Aaron, and the same executive director, Vigdor Kavaler, creating a degree of stability that many took for granted.[219]

Walter felt he was ready for leadership, as did his fellow associate, Rabbi Schwartz. After the news broke, they proposed the idea of forming a co-rabbinate to succeed Dr. Freehof. Even years later, Walter believed it would have worked. But the board of trustees could find few examples of a successful co-rabbinate and decided against it. A few weeks later, when Rabbi Schwartz accepted a position in another city, the matter of succession seemed to be resolved. But a segment of the congregation doubted whether Walter was the right person for the job. At issue was whether a reserved and modest young man like Walter would be a good choice for a congregation accustomed to a grand figure like Dr. Freehof. "In retrospect, becoming senior rabbi of this large congregation and succeeding one of the most prominent people in the Reform movement at age thirty-six was perhaps a little bit of chutzpah, you might say," he generously acknowledged decades later, after he had retired.[220]

Those who supported Walter saw his temperament as an asset. The most common words used by his supporters were "warmth," "kindness," "intelligence" and "integrity." In his presidential address at an annual meeting in late February, Lester Aaron thanked Walter for his "selfless devotion" to Rodef Shalom during his nine-year apprenticeship and added, "He has given us new insight and new hope—insight and hope which we shall need in the days to come." Most of Walter's support came from emerging leaders within the congregation, specifically from members of its Junior Congregation. These were the men and women who would run the Brotherhood and Sisterhood and serve on the Board of Trustees in years to come. They saw Walter as a leader who could create a personal rabbinate, one focused on spirituality and justice as well as on learnedness.[221]

The clearest expression of this desire came from Louise Marcovsky, Walter's first secretary. As someone who had worked closely with Walter on a daily basis, her letter of support during the weeks of deliberation offered a unique perspective on the type of rabbi he had become by 1966. "In my lifetime I have met few people like Walter Jacob, a true man of the cloth. He is kind and understanding and most tolerant," she wrote. "I have seen the little Nursery School children look at him with adoring eyes as he tells them about our holidays. I have seen the teen-ager girls also look at him adoringly and see in their eyes a wish that he weren't married, that he were younger and they were older." She noted the patient way he interacted with the elderly, his graceful approach to resolving marital disputes, his habit of quietly donating honoraria to the congregational library, his ability to set aside his personal problems to help others with theirs and his willingness to be a public representative for the congregation. "As long as I have to work to feed, clothe, house, and educate my children, I hope it will be with this fine man, Rabbi Walter Jacob."[222]

Although Marcovsky's comments touched on Walter's rabbinic achievements, she was trying to describe a deeper quality. It was the aura many people notice after spending a significant amount of time around Walter. It is a spirit of calmness and kindness radiating from his actions, even when he takes a firm position, and it is just as important to his rabbinate as the scholarship contained in his bibliography and his practical obligations at Rodef Shalom. Walter has cited his grandfather as a model for his scholarly life and his father as a model for congregational activities.[223] Perhaps his mother was a model for his temperament, which elevated the other aspects of his rabbinate into righteousness.[224]

Through the early months of 1966, a pulpit committee interviewed six candidates to replace Dr. Freehof, including Walter. In early April, the committee endorsed a rabbi from Milwaukee. He was fifteen years older than Walter and had already served as the senior rabbi of two congregations.

What happened next was "an introduction to politics, which I had largely avoided beforehand and also subsequently," Walter later said. He was referring to the way segments of the congregation privately lobbied for him and against him during those months. "During all of this, one had to keep doing everything else, more or less as if nothing was happening, and make sure that everybody was treated fairly, including people who you knew were opposed to you," he said.[225] His introduction to politics also demanded a new assertiveness. When the other candidate asked Walter to consider staying on at Rodef Shalom as an associate rabbi, Walter politely declined. As a result, Aaron withdrew his support for the other candidate. His endorsement, he explained, had been predicated on Walter remaining with the congregation. At a board meeting, Aaron explained that he now felt Walter was "ready for leadership—also that the Congregation wishes to retain him because of the expressions from all arms of the Congregation," as the minutes described it.[226]

The board invited both candidates to present their ideas. Before introducing his program, Walter mentioned both his lineage and his youth. He reminded the board of his tenure at the congregation and his long rabbinic heritage and also pointed out that he was energetic and in the prime of his life.[227]

His program sought a balance between the desires of an older, established generation and the needs of younger members. "Our congregation is highly diversified; we should offer a program which will meet the religious needs of all members," he wrote. His proposal was exceedingly conservative on its face and slightly radical in its undertones. It promised to retain many of the best-known features of the congregation and add only those ideas that congregants either requested or would accept. But the details of his proposal followed the path he set in his critical lecture about fundraising priorities. He proposed new services with more involvement from the congregation, longer religious school hours and increased pastoral work.[228] These changes would require more interaction between clergy and laity, and greater participation from a congregation that had become accustomed to quiet observation.

A few weeks later, in late April, the board of trustees approved a resolution recommending that the congregation elect Walter to a three-year term as senior rabbi. It scheduled a congregational meeting for early May to vote on the recommendation. But opposition remained. The vote to recommend Walter was close, and a subsequent motion to make the recommendation unanimous was defeated.[229] A board member privately offered to withdraw his opposition if Walter agreed to accept a one-year contract on a trial basis. Walter politely declined.[230]

Until that point, Dr. Freehof had stayed out of the debate, as was his way. A few days after the board recommended Walter, he sent a letter to the congregation. "The Congregation has had almost a decade in which to learn the fine qualities of Rabbi Jacob, but I am glad of the privilege of being able to add certain characteristics of his which the Congregation cannot easily know," Dr. Freehof wrote. "Besides his sterling character, he has a fine, clear mind and excellent judgment. He is a man devoted to his duty, and the complex task of leading Rodef Shalom Temple will be in good hands."[231]

Walter was already receiving congratulatory letters and had tentatively begun looking for an associate when six of the seven members of the pulpit committee, everyone except Aaron, sent an open letter to the congregation. "We want you to know that this meeting is not to be a perfunctory one — a cut and dried affair at which the above recommendations will be blindly followed and accepted," the committee wrote. Noting the close tally of the board vote to recommend Walter, they concluded that more work was needed to make sure the congregation was choosing the best candidate.[232]

The congregational meeting on May 1 has assumed a legendary quality in the minds of many longtime members. The sanctuary and its balcony were completely packed. Some children even crept into the room to witness a moment they sensed would be historic. The minutes from the meeting are discreet. They record procedural measures and list the trustees who spoke that evening but provide no details about exactly what anyone said. Several people in attendance recalled one moment in particular, when a trustee and third-generation congregant named Silas Adelsheim paused at the pulpit when he rose to address the crowd. He explained that it was the first time he had stood on the stage since his confirmation ceremony, decades earlier. He was overcome by his reverence for that spot and believed Walter would serve it well.[233]

After several hours of discussion, the matter was finally put to a vote, and the congregation elected Walter by a margin of four to one. He celebrated with a glass of champagne and spent the following weeks responding to the hundreds of congratulatory letters he received. He felt that the election had given him a "very clear mandate for the years to come," and that there was much work to do.

When members of the pulpit committee offered their congratulations and apologized for the unruly nature of the debate, Walter dismissed the whole ordeal as part of the "Democratic process." A few of his responses to these committee members were tardy, which, he noted, "only indicates that I am paying more attention to the future than the past."[234]

Walter and Irene encouraged
congregants to turn their personal
interests into communal endeavors, an
idea exemplified by the Biblical Botanical
Gardens at Rodef Shalom Congregation.
They conceived and designed the garden
almost entirely on their own, and they
undertook much of its daily maintenance
responsibilities for decades.

CHAPTER III

Initiative and *Sekhel*

The debate about whether Walter was the appropriate person to succeed Dr. Freehof emerged from a change in the mood of the Reform movement in America. Walter acknowledged this change a few days after his election, when he told *The Jewish Chronicle* of Pittsburgh, "A good many things here at Temple may change, but we expect evolutionary smooth changes. We want the old and the new to be maintained in proper balance…We hope to continue the Rodef Shalom tradition which we know is strong. At the same time, there is a great need to innovate and change and try all sorts of new things. Each generation must go its own way."[235] In one of the hundreds of thank-you notes he wrote to his supporters after the election, Walter privately acknowledged the skepticism he would have to overcome as he pursued a new path at Rodef Shalom. "I realize that for some even the slowest evolution looks like a revolution," he wrote.[236]

Walter worked quickly. Between his election in May 1966 and his installation that November, he implemented several significant aspects of the six-point program he had outlined while campaigning for the position. The congregation began offering bar and bat mitzvah ceremonies, a late Friday evening service for families, a weekly Hebrew class and a more varied and robust program of adult education. The pace of these changes might have struck some as revolutionary, but the multifaceted nature of a large congregation meant that congregants could easily ignore almost any new offering they disliked. In the case of bar and bat mitzvahs, Walter limited the involvement of the student to reading the Torah, instead of leading the service, to make sure the addition would enhance rather than overwhelm the Sabbath service. [237]

Walter described his overarching goal at Rodef Shalom as "moving the congregation more toward the center," which suggested a deeper cultural shift, beyond the details of programming. [238] The nature of this shift was apparent in the address he delivered at his installation ceremony and in the way it differed from the addresses delivered by his rabbinic elders.

A recurring theme of the day was the tension between continuity and change. Following brief greetings from Episcopalian and Catholic priests and an Orthodox rabbi, Dr. Freehof took the stage to offer some thoughts about his protégé. He started by presenting a view of Jewish history where the office of the rabbi was given greater and greater responsibility with each passing generation. A rabbi was once a "first among equals" within highly learned Jewish communities, he said, but over time, as laymen devoted more attention to their professional lives, rabbis became the "sole repository of a great literature." Rabbis had become the last representatives of sacredness in an otherwise irreverent world. "Now I have known Walter Jacob, as you know, for a decade, a changing decade," he said. "I am sure of this—he is a scholar; better still, he is a potential scholar. He has a taste for learning and a love of learning and the ancillary love of the possession of books. You will not have a shallow rabbi. You will have someone whose mind deepens every year and his dignity you know, his natural sense of respect. He will not be an echo. Only a parrot repeats exactly the words as talked and can do no more. The human mind hears, receives, changes and embodies the personality. Walter Jacob will be himself, in his temperament, but of this I am sure there will be intellectual depth and spiritual dignity."

After Dr. Freehof spoke, Rabbi Ernest Jacob delivered the keynote address. He described the occasion as "a symbol characterizing Judaism." He said that the Jewish religion was a heritage to be preserved

Walter was installed as the senior
rabbi of Rodef Shalom Congregation
in Pittsburgh on November 6, 1966,
almost 28 years to the day after the
Gestapo had arrested his father, Rabbi
Ernest Jacob, during a raid of their
synagogue in Augsburg.

by each generation, rather than a faith to be individually confessed. By installing his son, just as *his* father had installed him forty-two years earlier, Ernest felt he was maintaining that chain of tradition in a very literal way. The job of the rabbi, he explained, was to find ways to both preserve and to adapt that heritage. "It must never fall victim to stagnation. Each generation has needs, requires a different emphasis, even speaks a new language, and it is the task of the rabbi to translate the old insight, the old wisdom, the moral and spiritual values of our tradition into the language and into the life of our times," he said, before laying his hands on his son and reciting the priestly blessing.

Walter also spoke about the importance of preserving and adapting the tradition. But where his predecessor and his father had assigned the responsibility for these tasks solely to the rabbi, Walter expanded the responsibility to include all those seated before him. "And now for us here, this congregation, today we begin," he said. "We begin to build towards the future and, please God, we will build for many years together. There is much to be done and if we seek to express the essence of what ought to be accomplished, we can say it very simply—to take the traditional past and make it meaningful for our life, for each of our lives—to interpret, to change, to bring through [that] which has been brought through dozens of generations. It is easy to speak of our goals. It will not be easy to carry it into practice. It is my task...but beyond that it is our task. Each of us must work together.

"In this grand congregation we can do this, not only for ourselves but for all of American Jewry. We are accustomed to be leaders. We shall lead. Rodef Shalom shall lead as it has in the past. What needs to be done can be expressed by a simple picture. All of us are working together in the garden of God which is our religion. There are times of harvest—and we have had a grand time of harvest through the life of Dr. Freehof—and there are times to begin again. A garden cannot be neglected. We must plant again, work again, so that we will have another harvest, many other harvests in the future. In a garden there is work for everyone. If we wish to have it beautiful and grand there is a task for each to plan, to work, to look towards the future, to mend the fences which keep us from the outside world; there are tasks for all of us in this garden of God and if we work together and work diligently and well, we will make this our Garden of Eden."[239]

By announcing his intention to make "evolutionary smooth changes" and to maintain a "proper balance" between the old and the new, Walter was promising to consider the needs of the entire congregation, even as he pursued a new path. If he had ended up leading a smaller congregation, he said, he would have worked with its lay leaders to rapidly implement broad changes and would have met directly with individual members who felt overlooked. In a large congregation like Rodef Shalom, with such a strong identity and such a large membership with so many different needs and desires within it, he felt it wiser to be patient.[240]

Walter was willing to take the heat for some of his changes, particularly those he had outlined while campaigning for the position. For others, he found clever ways to allow his ideas to gradually infuse the institution. He relied heavily on the tradition of a completely free pulpit at Rodef Shalom, which gave the rabbi permission to speak and to preach without restraint. He also partnered with other people. If there was a provocative idea he wanted the congregation to hear, he might invite a national figure to come speak about it. If he wanted to implement some new program, he found congregants who also desired it, preferably people who were "less radical in their thinking" and could accommodate opposing viewpoints, and he would make sure those people ended up on the right committees. He sought to reduce conflict by gauging the mood of the congregation to determine what it would accept and what it was not yet ready to accept. For this way of enacting change to be effective, he explained, "there's two things you need: one is initiative and the other is *sekhel*."[241]

By restraining his initiative with *sekhel*, or common sense, Walter often had to wait years or even decades to implement seemingly minor changes. In one of his favorite examples, he recalled how an Israeli flag became a permanent feature on the pulpit of a congregation that had been openly skeptical of Zionism in the decades before the founding of the State of Israel. The flag was placed on the pulpit temporarily to decorate the sanctuary for a community-wide event for Israel. "After that happened, I simply instructed the custodian not to remove it," Walter said. When a congregant complained that the Israeli flag was taller than the American flag on the other side of the pulpit, Walter had someone slice a few inches off its flagpole.

Similarly, toward the end of his tenure, Walter and his rabbinic staff wore prayer shawls during a special service to honor Sephardic traditions, as part of a commemoration of the five hundredth anniversary of Columbus's voyage to North America. When the congregation resumed its usual services, the rabbis continued to wear the shawls, which, in an earlier era, many in the congregation would have considered to be an outdated relic of Orthodoxy. For both the flag and the prayer shawls, Walter figured out a way to implement changes proposed by other people with minimal furor.

Walter described the case of the flag and the prayer shawl as changes "of a more emotional character," as opposed to more substantive matters of liturgy or congregational policy.[242] Like the two congregants in Springfield who had fought about which poem to read during High Holiday services, the people who felt most strongly about these emotional matters were responding to symbolism and tradition. For that reason, these cases were likely to spark fierce debates if they were first brought up for public consideration. By instead choosing the right moment or the right person to make a change, the same skeptics could be made to accept the change and possibly even to embrace it.

Walter was also patient and creative when it came to implementing major changes. Rodef Shalom was among the last Reform congregations in the country to start using *Gates of Prayer*, a new Reform prayer book published in 1975. The congregation resisted the prayer book because Dr. Freehof was an editor of its predecessor, a newly revised version of the *Union Prayer Book* from 1940. "If you're adopting a new prayer book, you can't half adopt it," Walter said.[243] And yet, long before Rodef Shalom formally adopted the new prayer book, Walter found ways to expose the congregation to new forms of liturgy. One of the more radical experiments was a jazz-rock service called "Sim Shalom." It was created by his Associate Rabbi Frederick Pomerantz and later toured the country. In the 1990s, his Assistant Rabbi Debra Pine started a Rosh Chodesh service and a Passover Seder for women and a "Tot Shabbat" for families with toddlers. "As various groups sought more individualized services, we established family services, youth services, singles services, tot services for the very young, an intimate library service, and daily services," Walter recounted in a sermon shortly before he retired.[244] By encouraging these experiments while also keeping the *Union Prayer Book* for regular services, Walter allowed the congregation to both change and stay the same. As a new generation came of age, copies of *Gates of Prayer* began to appear in a small chapel of the synagogue and finally in the main sanctuary, too.[245]

Walter promoted gender equality at Rodef Shalom in a similarly incremental fashion. He officiated at the first bat mitzvah ceremony in 1967, invited some of the first generation of female rabbis to address the congregation as pulpit guests starting in the late 1970s and early 1980s, and supported a series of female cantorial soloists throughout his time as senior rabbi. Starting in the 1990s, he worked alongside the first female executive director and the first elected female trustees. Over the years he also took advantage of unexpected opportunities to acclimate the congregation to the idea that women within the Reform movement could hold any leadership position. When a young woman from a prominent family within the congregation entered Hebrew Union College, he engaged her as a student rabbi over the summers. By the time Rodef Shalom hired a full-time female assistant rabbi in 1992, any lingering dissent was faint and easy to dismiss.[246]

The changing mood of the Reform movement in the decades after World War II also gave Walter an opportunity to approach activities outside of the congregation in a new way. A move to right within Reform and a move to the left within Orthodoxy created opportunities for promoting Jewish unity. In his first year as senior rabbi, he helped establish the Greater Pittsburgh Rabbinic Fellowship, which brought together more than one hundred Reform, Conservative, and Orthodox rabbis from across the tri-state area of western Pennsylvania, eastern Ohio and northern West Virginia. The group held regular meetings and organized a sermon column in the *Jewish Chronicle*. But unlike the similar rabbinic fellowships that his father and grandfather oversaw in Germany, this group did not limit its activities to private discussions about the problems facing religious professionals. It also advocated for shared standards across the entire Jewish community of the region, and it issued public statements about world events on behalf of a unified Jewish community.[247]

The Fellowship was able to speak forcefully because the Jewish community in America had become strong enough and stable enough to direct its attention outward. Walter also took advantage of that momentum in his interfaith activities. He realized he was living in an era when Judaism could address Christianity on an equal footing, without the defensiveness demanded of those conversations at earlier points in history. "Christianity is weaker than ever before, while Judaism and the Jewish people feel a new confidence," he wrote in the preface to his 1974 book *Christianity Through Jewish Eyes: The Quest for Common Ground*, which traced how relations between the two faiths moved from debate to dialogue. "As a result, it may now be possible to find a new ground for a common understanding."[248]

Walter continued the Rodef Shalom tradition of establishing strong relationships with Christian clergy and using pulpit visits to bring congregants into those relationships. He also sought out opportunities to address Christian students, scholars and lay leaders. He taught courses for six years at the Pittsburgh Theological Seminary, a Presbyterian academy, through a lectureship created in 1968 by the Rodef Shalom Brotherhood and the Jewish Chautauqua Society. After the lectureship ended, he partnered with an executive from a local multidenominational Christian organization to create the Milton Harris Interfaith Institute, named for a Rodef Shalom trustee. Each year, the institute brings an important Jewish thinker to Pittsburgh to address an interfaith audience. Along similar lines, Walter spent many years as a director of the Religious Education Association of America and also served a term as its president. He used his involvement to bring more Jewish religious educators into an organization with a far greater representation among Christian scholars. Through these classes, meetings, books, articles and friendships, he slowly and steadily improved the understanding of Judaism among Christians.[249]

This was particularly true for Catholicism. In the program Walter outlined for the trustees of Rodef Shalom, he announced only vague intentions to work with other Jewish congregations throughout the city and to maintain the strong tradition of interfaith activities established by his predecessors, but he was explicit in his desire to actively pursue relationships with Catholic groups. His affinity for Catholicism emerged during his childhood in Missouri, where Catholics were the only other religious minority aside from Jews in the overwhelmingly Protestant environment of the Bible Belt.[250] In Pittsburgh, the enduring heritage of European immigration made Catholicism more prevalent, but historic prejudices had sometimes strained the relationship between Catholics and Jews. The relationship was starting to improve as Walter stepped into the role of senior rabbi, in large part because the Second Vatican Council, which closed in 1965, made significant changes to Catholic doctrine, including a more sympathetic and welcoming attitude toward Jews and Judaism.

During this wave of Catholic goodwill toward Jews, Rodef Shalom welcomed pulpit visits from local Catholic clergy and joined newly formed interfaith dialogue groups. And when Bishop John Wright of the Roman Catholic Diocese of Pittsburgh was elevated to Cardinal in 1969, he invited Walter to join the large American delegation traveling to the ceremony at the Vatican. In a lecture at Rodef Shalom upon his return, Walter described the invitation as a "grand and dramatic gesture" but also encouraged a deeper and more nuanced look at the relationship. Amid the festivities and official ceremonies, Walter used his time in Rome to explore the attitudes of Catholic laity from all over the world. He wanted to see whether the welcoming statements of the

Vatican had entered the hearts of the faithful, especially in regions where Jews had never lived in great numbers, such as sub-Saharan Africa and South Korea, or parts of Eastern Europe where prominent Jewish communities were now a thing of the past.

These personal conversations left him feeling slightly concerned about the future of the Catholic-Jewish relationship. The historic nature of the Second Vatican Council had inspired widespread excitement within Catholicism. But as the Council moved further into the past, he said, the excitement would fade and a new set of prejudices would emerge, perhaps from feelings about the Holocaust, or from a Jewish government controlling important Christian sites in Israel, or simply from the different political inclinations between different faiths and denominations. The Second Vatican Council had addressed prejudices embedded within doctrine, particularly those arising from the blame directed at Jews for the death of Jesus. The only way to address the deeper emotional prejudices, he said, was by continuing the slow and steady process of dialogue through personal relationships. "The drama is gone and the day-to-day work remains," he said.[251]

Nearly a decade after Walter retired from Rodef Shalom, he wrote a long essay comparing the pulpit work of his rabbinic predecessors at the congregation. He titled it "Showing the Way," and the phrase concisely expressed his views about the ideal relationship between a rabbi and a congregation. He relied on personal example more than any other tool of leadership. His warmth, gentleness and compassion showed his congregants the value of small voices, incremental progress, personal commitment, communal obligation and maintaining peace while also pursuing progress. In most matters, Walter favored small concrete actions over large symbolic gestures and preferred maneuvering around obstacles to confronting them directly. In conversations about the progressive causes of his day, he usually responded to idealistic fervor with a sense of practical obligation. When draft-age men came to him during the Vietnam War seeking the required clerical endorsement for conscientious objector status, he always asked them to consider taking active steps toward peace in addition to taking a strong stand against the war.[252]

Walter took a similar approach toward the civil rights movement. He encouraged Associate Rabbi Pomerantz' eagerness to stand alongside protesting farm workers and Associate Rabbi Mark Staitman's advocacy on behalf of Soviet Jewry, and he defended both of those efforts to his congregation, when opposition arose. But he never marched in those or any other protests.[253] He instead favored an interfaith initiative called Project Equality. It sought to marshal the economic power of religious institutions to the cause of civil rights. If churches and synagogues patronized only those businesses that employed minority workers and treated them fairly, the group argued, it would go a long way toward improving lives and changing attitudes. The effort stalled, which Walter blamed on the mundane nature of its mission. Contract negotiations simply did not ignite the imagination of the general public.

The results forced him to again consider the importance of drama in awakening the American conscience. "We are different from Elijah ... For him, it was not the earthquake nor the storm, but the still, small voice at Mt. Sinai which mattered," he said in a sermon about the fate of the project. "For most of us mortals, it is not the small voice, but the drama of the earthquake which moves us."[254] Instead of trying to inspire people through drama, Walter promoted the idea of infusing daily tasks with a sense of prophetic idealism. In his first year as senior rabbi, especially on holidays when the pews were full, he often preached about the "path of Reform Judaism."[255] He asked congregants to view the Reform movement as an ongoing process, rather than a one-time revolution—as "Reform" Judaism rather than "Reformed" Judaism, as he once put it, cleverly distinguishing between the two ways Jews have colloquially referred to the movement.[256] He described this path as a willingness to continually adapt the outward expressions of religious observance to fit the contours of a time and a place, while also preserving the inner ideals of the faith, even if they were at odds with the wider culture. "A reform movement or a revolution can succeed only by building on the fundamental existing structure of a people," he said in one of those early sermons.[257]

Amalgamation is an important theme of his preaching and writings. He is inspired by moments in history when Judaism built upon the social structures of its surroundings. The Jews of ancient Greece borrowed emerging literary techniques to produce great works of history and philosophy. The Jews of Spain during the Middle Ages felt more comfortable among Muslims than Christians and, as a result, wrote in Arabic rather than Spanish. The symbiosis of religious and national identity in Germany fostered the scientific approach to Judaism, where Jewish scholars used the tools of the German academy to reveal insights about Jewish history, culture and religious observance.

All of those examples involved environments where Judaism had been in close contact with the surrounding culture. Walter believed that a similar process was well underway in America. Prolonged exposure to American society had infused Judaism with pragmatism, optimism and openness. He saw those traits recurring throughout the early history of the Reform movement in America, as its first generation of leaders arrived from Central Europe and took advantage of the freedoms they found in their new country. A perfect example was the Pittsburgh Platform of 1885, which defined Judaism as a system of moral laws supported by only those rituals and ceremonies that "elevate and sanctify our lives." The platform had been built upon the ideas of radical German and Hungarian reformers. "What was added?" Walter said. "A spirit of hopefulness, of optimism which proclaimed that we would stay here and build grandly. That is American!"[258]

As the Jewish community in America absorbed these traits, it assumed a set of priorities, he said. It became committed to social justice, charity and addressing threats to Jewish welfare around the world.[259] Walter wanted to expand this list to include a sense of "personal piety," where prophetic ideals were married with the concrete demands for daily living, including prayer, study and new religious practices. He wanted his congregants to act out of a sense of *mitzvot*, or divine obligation.[260]

This was the deeper shift Walter was trying to encourage at Rodef Shalom. It was what he meant when he talked about moving the congregation "more toward the center." Asked how he measured his effectiveness at the task, he acknowledged, "You really can't."[261] To look at hard statistics like membership or attendance missed a deeper matter of whether anyone was internalizing the message.

Others have found it easier to articulate the nature of his accomplishments. During an annual congregational meeting in February 1986, Dr. Freehof made a special trip from his winter home in Florida to offer a tribute to his successor, who was celebrating his twentieth year as the senior rabbi of Rodef Shalom. Looking over the changes of those two decades, Dr. Freehof saw reflections of a broader societal change. "Reform Judaism began in the age of philosophy in which the most important test of any action was sheer logic. What isn't logical, what isn't rational is to be rejected as error," he said. "This is no longer the mood of our age. We've moved from the age of rational logic to the mood of emotion. We judge things differently now; it's part of the world atmosphere. We used to say testing an observance, does it make sense, now we say does it make sense for me. What does it mean, we used to say? Now we say what does it mean to me. We [as] a whole world [have] moved from the age of philosophy to the age of psychology and every movement that's aware of the state of mind of its people must make necessary changes. And these are the changes Rabbi Jacob made. He moved Reform Judaism, as represented here, from the age of philosophy to the age of psychology, from mere rational thinking to emotional; a change that was necessary to fit the mood of the people everywhere and this he has accomplished."

Dr. Freehof also pointed out an important similarity between him and his successor. Through his scholarship, specifically his study of Jewish law, Walter had preserved the strong intellectual tradition of Reform Judaism. "The emotional field he changed and what needed to be maintained on the intellectual field, he maintained," he said.[262]

A little more than a decade later, at a June 1997 symposium marking Walter's recent retirement as senior rabbi, his successor, Rabbi Mark Staitman, elaborated on the nature of this balancing act. He said that Walter had led Rodef Shalom through an era when the role of the rabbi changed for Jewish communities all over the world. It was a period of time when the rabbi "went from being the one whom the congregation perceived as acting for them to being the exemplar of what they ought to do and be."[263] Walter had managed to bridge those two archetypes, acting both as a proxy and as a model.

Looking over the major projects Walter had undertaken in his years at Rodef Shalom, Rabbi Staitman discovered a theme. "It is the ability to bring one's outside interests into the congregation for the benefit of the congregation as a whole...To take one's interests and find a way of making those a part of congregational life and, through them, to enhance the life of the congregation means there is a principle here that says a successful rabbinate recognizes the unique qualities of the individual rabbi and allows the interest of the rabbi to be manifest in the life of the congregation," he said.[264]

A preference for day-to-day work over drama is why Walter usually made changes gradually, as conditions allowed. This method was inclusive and lasting. But it could also be slow. When something mattered deeply to him, he responded much more forcefully. Or, to use his word, he had "initiative."

This was the case with three of his best-known undertakings in Pittsburgh: Horizon Homes Inc., the Biblical Botanical Garden and the Associated American Jewish Museums. All of these projects can be categorized as part of the "broader role of the rabbi," as he once described it. They were communal institutions that emerged from personal interests. Each provides an example of how one can turn individual expression into a common good by infusing mundane tasks with prophetic idealism.

Walter was a bachelor when he returned to Pittsburgh in 1957, after completing his military service. He rented a one-bedroom apartment a few blocks from Rodef Shalom and filled it with books, art and classical music recordings. In one of his early letters home to his parents, he drew a small map of the apartment, just as Ernest had done for Benno after arriving in St. Joseph.[265] Walter left his scooter in the Philippines and bought a brand-new Chevy sedan, which he drove to the state parks of Pennsylvania, across the plains of Ohio, and into the mountains of West Virginia. On evenings when he wasn't busy with a function at the synagogue or reading novels for his doctoral work, he attended plays and concerts. And, of course, he was invited to many dinners, where, as he later noted, "there was always a young woman at the dinner, too. I know from that, by looking back, in a humbler sort of way, how King Ahaseurus must have felt. Well if King Ahaseurus had taken a trip to Italy, the problem would have been solved for him, too."[266]

At the end of his first year on the job, Walter planned a summer vacation to Italy, Switzerland, France and England. It was his first trip to Europe since fleeing in early 1939. His cousin Irene Loewenberg also happened to be passing through Italy at the same time. It had been nineteen years since they had last seen one another as refugee children in the cramped house in London, and they decided to meet in Rome and get reacquainted.

Knowing they might have trouble recognizing each other as adults, they arranged to meet at the steps of the Basilica di Santa Maria Maggiore in Rome. But the grand church had steps at multiple entrances. "We kept walking back and forth, looking to see if there was someone looking for someone," Walter remembered. After they finally spotted each other, they set out on an ambitious sightseeing tour. But Rome was on holiday, and every landmark they visited was closed. They spent all that day and most of the next strolling through the quiet city, slowly getting to know one another.[267]

Irene was coming from Israel. The Loewenberg side of the family had stayed in England after the Jacob side left for America. After the war ended, Irene worked for several Zionist organizations in London. She closely followed the creation of the Jewish State and moved to the new country in 1948, shortly after it declared independence. She briefly tried living on a kibbutz, but frequent rat sightings convinced her to pursue a conventional life in the city instead. She was a secretary for a social work agency and later worked as an X-ray technician.[268]

After her excursion through Rome with Walter, Irene visited her parents in London. Walter joined her a few weeks later, after finishing his tour of Europe. He stayed in London for a week. By the time he returned home, he and Irene were engaged.

Asked once in an interview whether their whirlwind courtship was love at first sight, Walter guardedly said, "Well, we both felt that this was right." But in a videotaped oral history for the Survivors of the Shoah Visual History Foundation, his strong inner feelings briefly overtook his controlled demeanor and generally private nature.

"How did you propose to her?" an off-screen interviewer asked Walter. "How did you do that?"

A knowing smile crossed his face as he listened to the question. But he became shy as he answered, and looked off to the side. "Well, we were walking home from an outing on the, I guess on the river. We were on the Thames. So I—" he started to say, before stopping himself. He chuckled, and through a wide smile, he added, as an aside, "I said this, in a rather roundabout way…" He wanted to finish the story but, again, laughter got in the way. He finally managed to say, "We talked about visiting America." At this point he paused for five seconds, to regain his composure. "And I said to her, 'Would you like to come?' And she said, 'Well. Maybe.' "

Now he raised his eyebrows and, turning toward the interviewer with a big grin, recalled what he asked Irene next: "Would you like to come *permanently*?" After he delivered this punch line, his shoulders shook with laughter and delight.

"And what did she say?" the interviewer asked.

"And she said, 'Yes!' "[269]

After proposing to Irene, Walter immediately returned to Pittsburgh to assist with the upcoming High Holiday services at Rodef Shalom. But he quickly booked a return flight to London. He was so private about his personal affairs that even his secretary didn't understand why he was crossing the Atlantic Ocean again so soon after returning from his European vacation. "What," she teased him, "are you getting married or something?"[270]

Walter and Irene had a simple, traditional ceremony in London. The only flourish was the top hat Walter wore, according to British custom.

His parents had been to Europe the year before and were unable to afford another trip. But Herbert and his wife Lynn happened to be in Europe and attended. "We looked enough alike that he received half the congratulations," Walter recalled. "And I guess I should have given him half the presents, but I never did that."²⁷¹ Walter and Irene honeymooned in Torquay, a seaside resort billed as the "English Riviera." (The comparison fell short in blustery November.) After some immigration trouble—"It took about five weeks and a fair amount of congressional pressure to get her over here," he recalled—they started their life in Pittsburgh.²⁷²

The transition to American life was more challenging for Irene than it had been for Walter, eighteen years earlier. He had been a child; she was an adult. She was a European coming to America, an Israeli re-entering the Diaspora, a traditional Jew taking a highly public position within an iconic classical Reform congregation. The malleability of childhood had allowed Walter to easily switch languages and slough off accents he encountered during his journey from Germany to Missouri, and by the time he arrived in Pittsburgh he spoke like any other Midwesterner. Irene piled casual American English onto guttural Israeli Hebrew onto formal British English onto her precise native German to create a highly idiosyncratic way of speaking. Her voice sounded clipped and mellifluous at the same time. Even her name, which was spelled "Irene" but pronounced "Eye-ree-nee," with the vowel sounds elongated, made her exotic.

Before she arrived in Pittsburgh, all Irene knew of the city came from the descriptions of the steel mills and ethnic neighborhoods in the bestselling family melodrama *Valley of Decision*. What she found as she settled into her new community was more prosaic than the novel and also more inscrutable. During her first week in Pittsburgh, she attended a crowded Sisterhood luncheon at Rodef Shalom where all the women seemed to her to have the same hairstyle, the same wardrobe and the same way of speaking. She was surprised by American formalities. People always called before making a social visit, rather than simply showing up at the door, as they did in Israel. As she gained

Walter and Irene grew up together in
Germany, but the chaotic early months
of World War II split and separated their
families for decades. They reconnected,
got engaged and were married within
a few weeks during the late summer and
fall of 1958.

a better understanding of the culture of Judaism in her new country, she was dismayed by the status of the rabbi. The demands made on the profession seemed to her to be closer to the job of a social worker than the traditional duties of a clergyman as she had known them from her childhood in Europe. "But Walter happened to be that way and also a scholar," she later explained. "He was able to combine it."[273]

Walter, in turn, admired her pluck. "That these decades went so well is almost miraculous, as we did not know each other at all when we married and only really became acquainted on our honeymoon," he wrote to a relative after her death. "Irene's ability to resettle in a strange city, another country in which she knew no one except relatives she had met only the previous summer, is a tribute to her adaptability and her sense of adventure, which never left her."[274]

Walter and Irene shared many interests and had similar tastes, and the differences in their personalities were complementary. Walter was diplomatic, and Irene was direct. Walter was reserved, and Irene was ardent. Walter often had to force his way through his inherent shyness to perform his duties, and Irene occasionally retreated into her shyness when circumstances demanded humility. If she happened to speak with a little too much candor at a social gathering, Walter would lovingly sigh, "Now *Irene…*" If he said something impressive at the dinner table, she would turn to those around her and ask, "Ain't he sumpthin?"[275]

Walter has a reputation for being a quiet, cool person who spends more time in his head than his heart, but his passions guide just as many of his rabbinic decisions as his intellect. In a Yom Kippur sermon delivered in his fifth year as senior rabbi of Rodef Shalom, he described romantic love as a sudden, inexplicable realization. "Has anyone among us chosen our wife or husband rationally?" he asked. "When we find a girl we like, we do not list her qualifications—she is intellectual, cooks well, sews nicely, is able to put us through medical school or law school. All that is secondary. We love her and we will sing her praises when we describe her." He used this ode to love to introduce a larger point about devotion. "Love can lead to belief in an individual and in God," he continued. "We are not as far removed from it as we think. Whatever is meaningful to us in Judaism is expressed through the heart." The societal value of religious ideals can be explained rationally. But the desire to pursue those ideals, for generation after generation, despite the impossibility of the task, can only be explained emotionally. "We can name hundreds of obstacles instantly. Yet, we willingly forget them," he said. "Our heart proclaims that we may succeed."[276]

Walter always admired the way his parents undertook activities together, from studying languages, to taking hikes, to traveling the world, to telling each other about the highlights of their private intellectual pursuits. The element of friendship within their marriage "helped overcome some of the natural isolation which is part of the rabbinate," he said in his eulogy for them.[277] Walter and Irene followed this example. Their best-known and most lasting contributions in Pittsburgh emerged from a quiet partnership. In some cases they worked as equals. In other cases, one led while the other followed. In all cases, they were a team.

A year after they married, Walter and Irene had their first child, a daughter they named Claire Helen Jacob and affectionately called "Poopsie." By the following spring, it was clear that Poopsie was developing differently than most infants. She had trouble feeding, and doctors soon discovered cataracts, cerebral palsy, and a range of intellectual disabilities known then as "mental retardation."

Poopsie was sweet and cuddly and loved to be held, especially by her parents. Going on walks pleased her, and returning to the comfort of her home at the end of those walks pleased her even more. She had a joyful disposition and an innocent appreciation of the world. Walter fondly recalled a morning when he came downstairs to find her standing on a kitchen stool, removing glassware from a cupboard and delighting in the noise and sparkle as she dropped each piece to the floor.[278]

At that time, people with physical or mental disabilities were still strongly stigmatized. "The first advice of some colleagues was, 'Find yourself a good institution,'" Walter said.[279] The Jacobs instead kept their daughter at home and made her a part of their lives. Walter put a playpen in his office at Rodef Shalom for Poopsie to use when she

The liberal Judaism that Walter and
Irene knew from their childhoods in
Germany was grounded in more ritual
than the version they discovered in
the United States. Some of the rituals
that they performed in their home,
such as closing out the Sabbath with
the havdalah service, were not initially
performed at Rodef Shalom.

spent days at the synagogue, and he found a helmet to protect her head from hard corners when she explored.[280] He regularly took her around to the religious school. "I felt that was useful—not only for her but also to show kids you can have handicaps and still be okay," he said. He would even take her along on house calls and let her crawl around on the floor. Afterwards, he could tell how well his hosts had been cleaning their homes by examining the state of her once-white stockings.[281]

After Poopsie was born, Walter and Irene worried about risking their genetic compatibility again. They adopted their sons Kenney in 1962 and Danny in 1966. Walter revealed something of his strong feelings toward his sons when a rabbi asked him whether the Reform movement should create a welcoming ceremony for adopted children. Walter adamantly opposed the idea. "When an adoptive child enters the family, the parents will probably feel quite at ease with that child and will, from the beginning, be able to treat it as if it were a natural child. Such an attitude will develop only slowly among grandparents and other relatives who must be shown that this child is to be considered the *complete equal* of a natural child," he wrote in response. "For this reason, all procedures should follow the pattern taken with natural children. This will help the acceptance of such adopted children. For this reason, we would *not* favor adding any new ritual for adopted children. They should be treated like any other child in every way, be brought into the covenant and raised as Jewish children."[282]

Walter and Irene wanted their children to have normal lives. They purchased a house just beyond the neighborhood where many of their congregants lived, hoping to shield their children from some of the scrutiny of the congregation.[283] "The children grew up—as all rabbi's children, I guess—full of mischief," Walter said, with pleasure.[284] The children saw a side of their father that others rarely saw. He attended their sporting events. He took them camping and taught them how to pitch a tent and build a fire. After they had prepared the camp, he took them wandering through the woods to make sketches of the trees. Any species he couldn't identify he named a "Kentucky Coffee Tree."[285]

Walter encouraged his sons
Kenney and Daniel, seen here,
and his daughter Claire to visit
his study at Rodef Shalom, even
though they sometimes made
a mess of his things.

Claire "Poopsie" Jacob was born
with an array of physical and mental
disabilities that required intensive
treatment as she aged. She lived for
years at the D. T. Watson Home
outside the city but always returned
to Pittsburgh on the weekends.

His calm demeanor at the synagogue carried over into his home. The two boys reveled in the single time they drove their father to anger through excessive rowdiness on a road trip. Exasperated, he finally yelled, "Shut the hell up!" The uncharacteristic expletive sent the boys and their father into a fit of laughter, and they teased him about it for years.[286]

As the boys got older, Walter contrasted the stability of their childhoods with the uncertainty of his and Irene's. Instead of fleeing from country to country, his sons grew up in one city and even in one house. While many people reflexively saw Jewish history as exclusively a story of constant migration, Walter disagreed. "By stressing this, we are emphasizing the wrong aspect of our past. Ours has been a surprisingly stable history, and we have remained in many lands for centuries," he said, pointing to Egypt before slavery, ancient Israel before exile, and Babylon, Spain, Italy, Germany, Poland and other countries before expulsion.[287]

These periods of stability had always been the most productive and creative eras throughout Jewish history, he noted. His children and their contemporaries would likely come of age during another one of those periods of stability, and he expected them to take full advantage of it. If Walter ever encouraged either of his sons to consider the rabbinate, he never did so publicly. In the sermons he delivered at their bar mitzvahs, he told each of them to follow their interests. He reminded them that their family line, in addition to its many generations of rabbis, also included poets, teachers and businessmen. "Each has taken a different path; you and your contemporaries will take other paths," he said. "Yet, all of us continue to seek similar goals of outer and inner religious experiences."[288]

Walter, Irene and their three children lived together for several years. But while the Jacobs fully embraced Poopsie emotionally, their ability to help her develop physically and intellectually was limited. Eventually they enrolled her in a special program at the D. T. Watson Home for Crippled Children, where Jonas Salk had recently performed the first successful tests of his polio vaccine.

They escorted Poopsie to the suburban facility each Sunday evening and returned on Friday afternoons to bring her home for the weekend. At least once a week, Irene drove the hour each way to meet with therapists and learn about the puzzles, games and other activities designed to help Poopsie learn and grow. The Rodef Shalom cemetery happened to be halfway between the city and the D. T. Watson Home. If Walter had a Friday funeral he would tell the hearse driver to continue deeper into the suburbs after they had finished at the cemetery, and would collect his daughter in a grand fashion.[289]

As it became clear Poopsie needed care beyond what the D. T. Watson Home could provide, Walter and Irene searched for a permanent home. They toured one of the large institutions where children with disabilities were kept at the time and were appalled by what they found. "Have you ever been to one of our schools for the retarded?" he asked his congregation in a Rosh Hashanah sermon soon after. "You will see beds by the hundreds in rooms designed for fifty or sixty; there may be a foot between each bed. Dozens of children are locked in a room with a single attendant. Individuals are forgotten and may be left in a section alone all day. The State violates all of its own laws in its own buildings. The vast majority of these individuals could live in the general society with limited supervision, but someone must first train them."[290]

The Jacobs envisioned a home where Poopsie could get the intensive daily care she needed while also remaining close enough to feel the warmth of her family. Walter elaborated on his feelings about the matter many years later in a *responsum*, a formal response to a religious query. A rabbi wanted to know what obligations Jewish tradition placed upon the parents of a child with severe intellectual disabilities. Was arranging for permanent care sufficient or were the parents also required to assume the emotional responsibility of regularly visiting their child? In a rare instance where one of his *responsa* contained an explicit reference to his life, Walter noted that Jewish tradition required a father to provide for his children. "Nothing in the traditional literature limits such care to normal children," he continued. "In other words, the obligation is universal and applies to every child regardless of her mental and

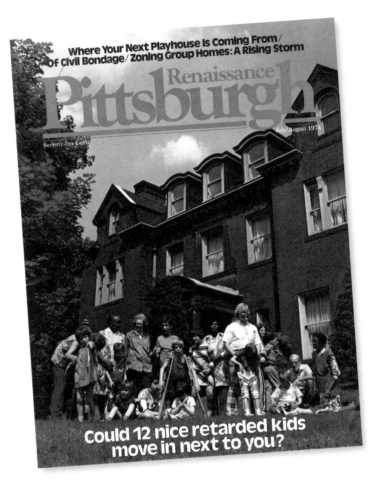

Where Your Next Playhouse Is Coming From /
Of Civil Bondage / Zoning Group Homes: A Rising Storm

Pittsburgh
Renaissance

July/August 1974

Seventy-five Cents

Could 12 nice retarded kids move in next to you?

Dissatisfied with the state of state-
run institutions, Walter and Irene and
a group of like-minded colleagues
set about bringing the "group home"
model to Pittsburgh. Their idea met
strong opposition from neighborhood
groups around their proposed site.

physical abilities. Tradition, therefore, indicates that this child, despite its very limited abilities, deserves both the maintenance and affection which the parents can provide. As I view this problem through my personal experience with a severely handicapped daughter and that of others who have dealt with parents of handicapped children, it is clear that unless ongoing relationships of some kind are established with such a handicapped child, the parents and other children will always feel guilty. Obviously this child can not be made part of the normal family life, but ongoing visits and continued concern with his welfare rests as any obligation upon all the members of the family. Practically speaking, such visits also assure a higher standard of care for such an individual, as those institutionalized children who receive no visits are frequently neglected."[291]

As they looked for options other than the state-run institutions, Walter, Irene and sympathetic congregants from Rodef Shalom learned about an alternative being tried at a few places around the country. A small number of people with disabilities were brought together to live in a single home, situated within a residential neighborhood, close to their families, with trained caregivers who lived on site around the clock. A delegation from the congregation toured one of these "group homes" in Connecticut in late 1968.[292] They were impressed, and so, a few months later, they decided to replicate the model in the Pittsburgh area. They chartered a nonprofit organization called Horizon Homes Inc.[293]

E ven though Horizon Homes emerged from their personal needs, Walter and Irene saw the undertaking as part of the civil rights movement. "It is our premise that these children are human beings who deserve the same treatment and opportunities as the rest of society; the birth of a retarded child may occur in any family; it is our premise that the parents of these children deserve a life as nearly normal as can be provided by helping them take care of their children," they declared early on.[294]

They envisioned a building with four wings extending from a central commons. It would comfortably house twenty-seven children and would have classrooms, play areas, kitchens, dining halls and infirmaries. It would even have short-term apartments for visitors.[295] Reality quickly thwarted this vision. Their construction plans were not only prohibitively expensive but also impractical among the narrow streets and crowded neighborhoods of the East End of Pittsburgh. They decided instead to renovate an existing building. They visited more than forty potential sites. Some were too large. Some were too small. Some were appropriate but unavailable. Some were available but in poor condition, or abutting railroad tracks, or hard to reach. They finally found a workable option when a Gilded Age mansion went on the market just a few miles from their house. The building had been well maintained by a local architect, but it was too large to be practical for any modern family. The main house covered more than nineteen thousand square feet, with another seven thousand in a carriage house behind it. It sat on a spacious corner lot near the entrance to a large city park and the local zoo.[296]

Even as the best of all available options, the mansion posed several significant problems. The asking price was high, and the house needed extensive and expensive renovations to make it appropriate for the children and the caregivers who would be living there. Additionally, the house was zoned as a single-family residence, and two previous attempts to convert the building for other uses had failed in the face of neighborhood opposition.[297]

These challenges fell into an entirely different category than those Walter had encountered as he oversaw religious school curricula, or delivered sermons, or attended committee meetings, or visited congregants in the hospital. But while raising funds, hiring contractors, applying for zoning variances and lobbying neighborhood groups would have fallen beyond the purview of a rabbi cast in the traditional European mold, they were well within the "broader role of the rabbi" as it had developed in America.

Horizon Homes had just $202 in its bank account when it launched a $300,000 fundraising campaign in June 1969. By October, it had raised approximately $15,000 in pledged donations and was waiting to hear back from public agencies about several grant applications. Even if all those grants came through, the organization would still need to raise some $130,000 from private sources. When the large philanthropic foundations of Pittsburgh expressed skepticism about backing an unproven venture such as group homes, Walter and his team undertook an ambitious person-to-person drive.[298]

They launched this drive just as the first recession in nearly a decade was spreading its full weight onto the national economy, yet they managed to raise $36,000 by July 1970 and $75,000 by February 1971. Their grassroots success won over some previously reluctant private foundations. By June 1971, they had raised more than $200,000.[299]

It was the first time Walter had raised any significant funds for a project, a skill he practiced often and improved over the decades. He once described his fundraising philosophy in a sermon about Joshua and Caleb, the two spies of the Hebrew Bible who brought back optimistic reports about the land of Israel while their cohorts all warned of impending doom. Walter sensed a similarly dour attitude among the emissaries of his day. "If the economy is good, the doubters will say that this is not the time as too many other organizations are attempting the same goal. If times are bad, and there is a recession, the same bearers of gloom will say, 'It can not be done now; we can not approach anyone during this bad period,'" he said. "Both of those points of view are totally wrong. If those involved in the cause possess enthusiasm and dedication, they will always succeed. Never mind the times!"[300]

The experience of creating Horizon Homes also taught Walter how to navigate government bureaucracies. He was forced to abandon a large grant because minor contradictions on matters as trivial as the width of doorways made it impossible to satisfy both state and federal guidelines. In pursuing state funds, he often found himself in the Pennsylvania Capitol, making the case for group homes to public officials who had already endorsed the idea. In response to a request for data from one governmental funding agency, he spent an entire summer compiling a comprehensive report about the need Horizon Homes would fill. The final document was three inches thick. When he carried the ten required copies to the government office, they nearly obscured his vision. Through these incidents, Walter learned when to play along and when to stand his ground, when to patiently persevere and when to strategize. "There was some data that simply wasn't available, census data," he recalled about the government proposal. "And I looked high and low for it, and after a while I decided if I couldn't find it, they couldn't find it either, and I made it up."[301]

When citizen groups from the neighborhood challenged the proposed zoning change, Walter learned the intricacies of community organizing. He and his team scheduled public meetings, secured endorsements, prepared traffic studies and appealed to members of the city Planning Commission. They launched a petition drive. Groups of idealistic teenagers went door to door through the blocks around the mansion to collect signatures of support from nearby residents. When a few holdouts in the neighborhood still remained opposed, and the Planning Commission rejected the request to change the zoning, Walter appealed his case to the City Council, thereby making the matter far more visible than it had been as a technical dispute within one neighborhood. In late October 1971, the City Council unanimously approved the zoning change, allowing renovations to begin on the building.[302]

H orizon Homes, though nonsectarian, became an informal congregational project. Rodef Shalom members filled its initial board of directors. An early Horizon Homes administrator was given a desk and a telephone in the religious school office while the operation was coming together. Through congregants, Walter learned about a restaurant getting rid of some useful kitchen equipment and a vacant storefront where the equipment could be stored until the renovations were finished. Irene led a team of volunteer decorators drawn from the congregation. They sewed curtains, selected wallpaper and planted gardens.[303] Over the years, Rodef Shalom congregants made Horizon Homes a regular part of their charitable giving, donating money and supplies and volunteering their time.

By the time the first Horizon Home began accepting residents in 1972,[304] Poopsie was able to spend only a few years living there. She died in February 1975, at the age of fifteen. Walter dedicated his annual sermon booklet that year to his daughter, "whose brief, limited life brought our family much happiness. She widened our horizon and taught us understanding, patience and the enjoyment of simple pleasures," as he wrote in his dedication. Below this tribute, he included a verse from Psalms: "The stone the builders rejected became a cornerstone." He printed the epitaph in Hebrew, which meant that anyone who was curious about its meaning had to seek out a translation.[305]

Poopsie's death came just ten months after another, unexpected family tragedy. In the middle of Passover, in April 1974, Ernest and Annette Jacob died from a carbon monoxide leak at their home in Pittsburgh, where they had come to live in their retirement. When Irene entered their house, she found them sitting in the living room with a Beethoven recording spinning on the phonograph.[306]

Walter acknowledged the sorrows in his personal life when the Jacobs celebrated Kenney's bar mitzvah, in March 1975, just two weeks after Poopsie's death. "We have been together several times on family occasions lately; unfortunately, all of them have been sad," he said in a sermon. "It is good that this fine and happy family event brings us together now. A change of mood is needed in our family."[307] A few years later, at Danny's bar mitzvah, Walter again reminded his congregation of the varied circumstances under which both he and they had come together over his quarter century with the congregation. "We have been together on occasions both sad and happy in your life, in mine, and so we have become friends," he said.[308] By formulating the sentence as a cause and its effect, Walter revealed his view of friendship. It was not the result of having mutual interests but of having shared experiences. Ernest had made a similar point during his installation ceremony in Springfield, when Walter was young. Seeing his Augsburg congregants at the lowest moments of their lives made them more precious to him, he said. Their distress brought out their best characteristics. "So you will understand that I shall approach you differently after having lived through these experiences," he said. "I want to come to you not as the newly appointed rabbi, but as a friend."[309]

Walter experienced something similar, albeit in reverse. He became more precious to his congregation in the wake of his personal tragedies, as those around him saw his faith, his stoicism and his fortitude, and were inspired by his example.

As the children and grandchildren of public figures, Walter and Irene understood the importance of drawing a boundary around a portion of their lives and keeping the contents private. They rarely discussed their losses unless asked. But from the outside, their bond appeared to be strengthened by experiencing tragedies together. They always stopped to remember the anniversaries of these deaths, but they both preferred to look ahead rather than behind. When a congregant who had recently lost a child asked Irene how she had coped with her losses, Irene replied, "You just keep very, very, very busy," which is exactly what the Jacobs did.[310]

By the time Walter started his fourth three-year term with Rodef Shalom, in October 1975, the demands being made on his time were commensurate with being the spiritual leader of the largest Jewish congregation in a major city. In addition to fulfilling his daily responsibilities at Rodef Shalom, he had served on nearly forty local and national boards. Among these groups were a great many local and national Jewish organizations, of course, including his recent appointment to the board of governors of the Hebrew Union College-Jewish Institute of Religion and his anticipated advancement to the chairmanship of the Responsa Committee of the Central Conference of American Rabbis. The full list illustrates the scope of his diverse interests. It includes health care and disabilities groups, a field he had come to know through the effort to establish Horizon Homes. It also includes arts and cultural organizations, such as the local public television station WQED, the Pittsburgh Chamber Music Society and the International Poetry Forum, among others.[311]

Irene was similarly busy in her role as the *rebbetzin*, an honorific title given to the wife of a rabbi. When she arrived in Pittsburgh in the late 1950s, Dr. and Mrs. Freehof were still the senior rabbinic couple at Rodef Shalom, and there was no immediate expectation for Irene to act as the *rebbetzin* for the entire congregation. Her involvement more closely resembled that of a committed member. She attended religious services every week and Sisterhood meetings every month, but otherwise she took advantage of her freedom from congregational responsibilities. Like her husband, she also turned her personal interests into communal ventures. She played the recorder and helped start the Pittsburgh Recorder Society. She liked art and was among the first class of docents trained at the Carnegie Museum of Art. She was a mother of three and established a Mothers' Day Out program at Rodef Shalom, providing babysitting so mothers could enjoy art, music and other cultural excursions, take classes and socialize with adults.[312]

Gardening was her greatest passion, and horticulture became her biggest contribution. Her interest in the natural world started in child-hood, when her grandfather taught her the names of wild mushrooms they spotted on long walks through the forest. Her father had maintained a rose garden at the cramped house in London. He rushed outside whenever carriages passed, to collect the horse droppings for fertilizer. In the years when Walter was filling his first apartment with books, art and classical music recordings, Irene was tending to her first garden on the rooftop of her Tel Aviv apartment building. She lugged pots, plants and soil up several flights of stairs, and she worked night shifts to free her daylight hours for gardening.[313]

On her first day in Pittsburgh, in the middle of winter, Irene visited the nearest nursery and filled her new American apartment with plants. She traded pots and window planters for a proper garden when she and Walter bought their house in the Point Breeze neighborhood of Pittsburgh in 1966. Irene had a positive and accommodating outlook toward gardening. "If a plant is grown nicely, any plant is fine," she once said. Their home garden became a lifelong enterprise, always expanding to accommodate new ideas. They replaced a dying elm tree with a compact red maple to allow more sunlight into the backyard, and they eventually purchased a neighboring lot to create a spacious garden that unfolded through a series of thematic "rooms" arranged along a dramatic right angle.

Irene and Walter undertook the work of the garden in their typically pragmatic fashion. They divided chores between them, both the daily tasks of weeding and the larger renovations. On their own, they buried pipes for irrigation, installed wires for lighting and hauled all their supplies—all the dirt, all the plants, all the heavy paving stones—into the yard by hand because most of their garden was inaccessible from the street out front and from the alley out back. Employing a gardener would have lessened their budget for plants, and they enjoyed the daily devotion of caring for a plot of land.[314]

They had a small greenhouse built off of a second-floor room that Irene used as her study. A year after Poopsie died, Irene turned the green-house into the headquarters of a new landscaping business she called The Plant Hunter. She searched for striking and exotic plants to liven up homes and offices and occasionally created outdoor settings, including small gardens for the entrance to Rodef Shalom and the grounds of a senior living facility operated by a Jewish communal agency. One of her greatest congregational pleasures was using her expertise to help the Sisterhood decorate the large indoor sukkah erected on the pulpit of Rodef Shalom, a beloved tradition of the congregation.[315]

She also spent much time visiting the nearby Phipps Conservatory and Botanical Garden. The garden is one of the cultural gems of the city, set inside a magnificent Victorian greenhouse bequeathed to the city of Pittsburgh at the end of the 19th century by an early investor in the Pittsburgh steel industry. Inspired by her experience at the Carnegie Museum of Art, Irene decided to create a docent program at Phipps. "I thought, 'If you could do it for pictures, you could do it for plants,' " she said. She asked the city for permission to start a docent program at the garden and was told she could do anything she wanted, so long as it didn't make any demands on their budget. Over the years, she created a comprehensive education program, entirely as a volunteer.

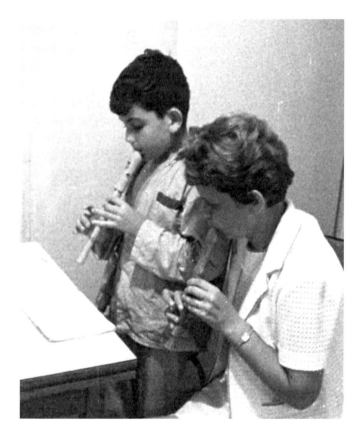

Irene was passionate about the
recorder and co-founded the
Pittsburgh Recorder Society.
In this photograph, she practices
with her son Kenney.

She labeled every plant in the garden, trained more than one hundred docents, and taught classes for the public. She gave her docents and regular visitors a broader perspective about plants by organizing visits to nearby gardens and even a few longer excursions, including a trip to Florida, where many of the northerners in her delegation got their first look at tropical plants.[316]

Irene's career in horticulture mirrored Walter's rabbinate. It was both practical and scholarly, both emotional and intellectual. She enjoyed the work of tending to the garden as well as the pleasures of learning about the ways people had used plants throughout history. She studied how different cultures had grown the food they ate and the beverages they drank and had turned plants into textiles, dyes, cosmetics and medicines. During the winter months, she spent several hours each week in the old Science and Technology Department of the Carnegie Library of Pittsburgh, reading through horticulture books. "Bring me a stack of what I need and I have a grand old time," she said.[317] Her personal horticultural library contained hundreds of volumes, including some odd, rare or hard-to-find editions procured during her travels around the world with Walter. She found one of her favorite volumes tucked behind some knick-knacks in the gift shop of the Cairo Hilton. It listed the scientific names of common plants in numerous languages, serving as a Rosetta Stone for plant research.[318]

W alter and Irene took an extended vacation every year, leaving all their work behind. They went on family road trips throughout North America, and, after their boys left the house, they traveled the world together, visiting Asia, Africa, the Middle East, Australia and South America. They often returned to Europe, especially Italy, where they had fallen in love. Between visits to the country, they occasionally enjoyed it vicariously by watching Audrey Hepburn charm Gregory Peck in *Roman Holiday*. They also visited their mutual family in England and made increasingly regular visits to Germany, their homeland. Aside from personal connections, they chose their travel destinations based on cultural offerings—museums, gardens, architecture, orchestras, operas and theaters.[319]

They planned extensive itineraries well in advance, but they also always included time for unstructured exploration. Some of their most memorable travel experiences came from wandering through cities with no destination in mind. They followed the sound of hammering in Myanmar to discover a village of goldsmiths and silversmiths. While wandering through a neighborhood in Central America, they attracted two benevolent rifle-wielding guards who were concerned for their safety and followed at a few paces, warning away troublemakers. Dismounting an ostrich in South Africa, Walter broke his leg.[320]

Even when work was the reason for their travels, they always tried to add a day onto their itineraries to accommodate personal activities. If a day could not be spared, they took a few hours wherever they could get them. Walter traveled to Poland in the 1970s with a delegation of rabbis to visit Nazi concentration camps. "But you know, there's a lot more to Poland than that," he said. At each stop along the way, he slipped away to wander the city streets and "left the group to do whatever the sponsoring agency thought was appropriate."[321]

As part of their travels, Walter and Irene visited gardens all over the world, including hundreds across North America. "If I have a meeting some place, I'll find time to go to some gardens. There's always a boring segment of a meeting where you can go see a garden," Walter explained when a television reporter asked the Jacobs how they fit so many gardens into their busy schedules.[322] From time to time, Walter and Irene overlooked an interesting garden, simply because they hadn't known it existed. So they decided to create a comprehensive guidebook. *Gardens of North America and Hawaii: A Traveler's Guide*, published in 1985, listed the location, operating hours, contact information, admission fee and basic offerings of more than fourteen hundred gardens across the United States and Canada. They ranked each garden using a four-star system. "We have tried to be conservative," they wrote in their introduction, "some sites probably deserve an additional star, but we feel it is better to be surprised than to be disappointed."[323]

As they were compiling the guide, they were surprised by the lack of biblical gardens. Irene had created several wintertime displays of biblical plants at Phipps, and the encouraging response led her to believe that the public would support an entire garden devoted to the theme. The Jacobs decided to create one at Rodef Shalom. They claimed an unused patch of lawn along the side of the synagogue and sketched a design on a sheet of used wrapping paper. Irene envisioned a diamond-shaped garden approximating the shape of Israel, with a stream for the Jordan River and a pond at the center for the Dead Sea. A path would wind diagonally through the rectangular plot, making the garden feel much larger than its third of an acre.[324]

Based on the infrastructure projects they had undertaken at their home garden, Irene and Walter figured that their design could be built for about $10,000. They took their rough sketch to a local architect to be turned into a working plan. By the time the architect was finished, their initial cost estimate had grown tenfold. And so, while Irene decided what plants to include and where to procure them, Walter tackled the organizational technicalities. In the fifteen years since his first fundraising campaign for Horizon Homes, he had become so skilled in the art that he was able to raise approximately $100,000, by himself, in about six months. He accomplished this feat by carefully pre-selecting potential donors and restricting donations to $10,000 or more. He even turned away a few sizeable donations that fell below his threshold.

I rene wanted the Biblical Botanical Garden to enliven scripture. "To the monochromatic black and white print of the Bible, which for too many may remain a drab and closed book, the Biblical Botanical Garden continues to add color and life," she wrote. Her original plan was to fill the garden with plants mentioned in the Hebrew Bible, but soon it occurred to her that a garden composed exclusively of species native to a moderate Mediterranean climate would bloom in the spring and become barren by summer. She decided to expand her concept to include plants with names inspired by Scripture. The wider focus allowed her to showcase not only the flora and fauna of the ancient

Middle East but also the ways in which the Bible had inspired people throughout history.[325]

A desire to combine beauty and education drove much of the early planning for the garden. Irene included a shaded pavilion to host summer lectures and a docent program to help visitors understand the full significance of the plants. She chose docents who were flexible and personable. "Once a docent, always a docent," she liked to say, meaning that true talent of being a docent was the ability to size up a group of strangers and cater to its needs.[326] A headful of knowledge was also necessary but not enough. Her docents were dedicated to the garden and loyal to her. After a decade, the entire original class—except the few who were ill or deceased—was still volunteering. Her approach to the docent program reflected her view about education. After dropping out of school at sixteen, she became an autodidact. She appreciated knowledge, regardless of any degrees or titles associated with those who offered it. She taught horticulture classes at local colleges and universities and was tickled when a student once referred to her as "Professor Jacob."[327]

After the Biblical Botanical Garden at Rodef Shalom opened to acclaim in the summer of 1987, the Jacobs divided the responsibility of maintaining it. They handled smaller tasks each day and arrived early on Sunday mornings throughout the summer months to trim and weed for several hours before the garden was opened to visitors. "Sunday school in the winter was relaxation, after working the garden in the summer," Walter said. As the weather turned cold around the High Holidays each year, they hauled all the plants inside, either to empty rooms in the basement of Rodef Shalom or to the greenhouse at their home. Even now, in his mid-eighties, Walter can often be found in the garden on summer mornings, carrying a bucket and a spade.[328]

Irene was diligent about keeping the garden intellectually interesting. She planned a new exhibit each summer. Her first exhibit highlighted plants brought to Israel after the biblical era. Another used the five-hundredth anniversary of the Columbus expedition to consider how the explorer influenced horticulture in the New World. Over the years, she created exhibits on medicine, on perfumes and cosmetics, on bread and beer, on papyrus, paper and textiles. Her research for these exhibits often became the basis for short books. She organized symposia, inviting scholars to Pittsburgh to speak and collecting their papers in scholarly books. Each year, she published a monthly summer research journal called *PapyruS*. She co-wrote the entry on "Flora" for the Anchor Bible Dictionary. Her enthusiasm for horticulture of the biblical era made her a recognized expert on the subject worldwide.[329]

As the Biblical Botanical Garden appeared in major travel guides, it began to attract visitors from all over the world. It became especially popular among Christian travelers, making it one of the most effective interfaith initiatives at a congregation with a history of reaching out to other faiths. The garden differed from earlier interfaith efforts at the congregation in one crucial regard. The Sunday morning lectures started by Dr. J. Leonard Levy and the Wednesday book reviews made famous by Dr. Freehof both drew their value from the voice and the presence of a single, charismatic leader. The garden was the work of many volunteers, who worked either in private or with small groups of visitors.

Walter appreciated the contrast of the small, unassuming garden beside the beautiful and historic synagogue. "The garden is a very humble spot. The synagogue is a grand spot. We have turned to God in both ways," he said in a speech during a twenty-fifth anniversary celebration of the garden. "We built, long ago … a magnificent Temple in Jerusalem, which had all the grandeur that those ancient Jews could manage. And we have built magnificent synagogues throughout the world. But they don't always do it for us. That may not be the way to some spiritual renewal. That may not be the way to God."

The garden, he continued, provided another option, "a quiet place, a place of retreat through which you wander, and … think of how your life can become somewhat better. As I watch people going through it, I see some reading every sign and every educational board, trying to learn. That's wonderful, and we intend that. But others look at nothing. They look at the plants. They wander through it, they sit down and they think. Perhaps for five minutes, perhaps for a half hour. I've seen it go both ways. And that's a major part of the intent of this garden: to provide a spiritual haven for whoever enters, Jew or non-Jew, it doesn't make any difference."[330]

The relationship between beauty, intellect and spiritual development guided another major effort Walter oversaw during his rabbinate. After Horizon Homes became self-sufficient in the early 1970s, his next big undertaking was an effort to widely promote Jewish art and culture. Synagogues and Jewish community centers around the country were beginning to create small museums to display their collections of Jewish art and ritual objects. None of these collections was particularly impressive on its own, but he realized that if they could be combined, the whole would be greater than the sum of its parts.

His idea was to organize a series of traveling exhibitions. Participating small museums would lend materials to these exhibitions and would be added to the touring schedule in return. The arrangement would allow people living outside of major cultural centers to see objects they might never otherwise have the opportunity to encounter.

He started a non-profit organization called the Associated American Jewish Museums. He quickly attracted members and even commissioned what he called an "idiot-proof" display case that could be easily and affordably mailed from one museum to the next as exhibitions toured. Unfortunately, insurance made the idea impractical. Over the next twenty years, until Walter once again had time to revive and revamp his idea, the organization served in an advisory role, helping the administrators of Jewish museums learn how to host exhibitions.

In the early 1990s, just as Walter was completing his tenure as an officer with the Central Conference of American Rabbis, Rodef Shalom hired two part-time assistant rabbis. With a larger rabbinic staff and fewer national responsibilities, Walter decided to use some of his newfound spare time to start a new undertaking. He wanted to create a gallery at Rodef Shalom where he could display art and historical exhibitions. He had been hosting exhibits within the synagogue for decades, such as a popular traveling exhibit on Jewish life in the Lower

East Side. He usually displayed these exhibits in Freehof Hall, but as demands on the social hall increased through the 1980s, he decided it would be useful to start an independent gallery. The only available space he could find was a long and unpromising hallway outside Levy Hall, a small sanctuary and auditorium at the side of the synagogue. He had to share the hallway with the religious school, whose classrooms were along the same hall. As he had with the Biblical Botanical Garden, Walter proceeded with his idea with only the most minimal review from his board of trustees and no financial help from the congregation. He raised approximately $50,000 — this time restricting donations to $5,000 increments — to build and install a series of lighted panels along the hall. [331]

The hall led out to the garden, and during the summer months Walter created indoor exhibits that both introduced and complemented the plants. He created exhibits on "The Ancient Near East Farmer" and "Papyrus to Paper — Jewish Books through the Centuries" to accompany similar exhibits Irene was creating in the garden. During the rest of the year, he created exhibits around themes he found interesting, from beautifully illuminated haggadot to exotic Jewish costumes. His loving and ambitious exhibition "Our Crowd" displayed more than fifteen hundred photographs of Rodef Shalom congregants past and present. The exhibit subtly showed how the congregation had grown, generation by generation, from the initial vision of a few founding families.

To make installation easier, Walter developed a series of Velcro boards for mounting these exhibitions. The simplicity of the system gave him an idea for the Associated American Jewish Museums. Rather than shipping actual artifacts, he would ship photographs and reproductions, which required no insurance or security. Throughout the 1990s and early 2000s, he created five traveling exhibits — on synagogue architecture, synagogue interiors, modern takes on traditional Jewish marriage certificates, specialized museums throughout Israel and remnants of the Eastern European synagogues that had survived World War II. An accompanying display system gave each participating museum all the equipment it needed to mount the exhibit, pack up the materials at the end of the run and mail them to the next museum. Aside from a small membership fee, each museum paid only for postage to send the exhibit to its next stop.

The Associated American Jewish Museums also provided a local forum for Walter to host annual symposia. During the years immediately after he retired as senior rabbi, he invited local and national scholars to present papers on "Small Town Synagogues of Western Pennsylvania," "Museums and Ideas" and "Art and the Ancient and Medieval Rabbis." The Associated American Jewish Museums also partnered with other organizations to present scholarship on topics of mutual interest, such as a popular symposium on the painter Samuel Rosenberg, who got his start in Pittsburgh by teaching art classes at a Jewish settlement house.

In an accompanying newsletter called *Gallery*, Walter offered advice on everything from how to properly display materials, to the best way to pitch exhibits to local media, to tips for training Jewish docents to lead tours for non-Jewish visitors. The newsletter also provided reviews of interesting Jewish exhibits in other cities, as well as original research on Jewish art and artists. These simple exhibits toured nationally, attracting more than fifty thousand visitors on an extremely small budget.[332]

Freedom underpinned the idea of the "broader role of the rabbi." The combination of religious liberty and individual expression in North America allowed the rabbinate to expand in ways that previous generations would have thought to be outside of the purview of the profession. Walter used this freedom to turn his personal interests in disability rights, gardening and Jewish culture and history into communal projects: Horizon Homes, the Biblical Botanical Garden and the Associated American Jewish Museums. He encouraged his colleagues to do the same, which is how Rabbi Pomerantz came to manage a Greenwich Village-style coffee house at Rodef Shalom in the 1960s.

Walter also recognized a downside to individual freedom and cautioned about its excesses.[333] One particularly far-sighted warning came during a book review he delivered as part of the popular Wednesday morning series that the Rodef Shalom Sisterhood sponsored each fall. Walter had canceled the series after becoming senior rabbi. He was less interested in popular literature than Dr. Freehof, and he suspected that he would be unable to meet the high oratorical standards set by his predecessor. The decision to cancel the book review series was a rare example of Walter choosing the wrong time to make a change. Demand from congregants forced him to revive the series just two years later. As was the case with many of the changes Walter made to institutions he inherited, his contribution to the book review series was to expand its format. Instead of relying on one reviewer, he had a rotating group.[334]

Walter usually reviewed works of history when his turn came around in the rotation, but in October 1983 he reviewed Orwell's *1984*. He made no mention of the earlier review of the novel he had included in his commencement address at Drury College, in 1950. At that time, he had dismissed the oppressive vision Orwell prophesied for the coming generation. He saw the story as an expression of doom and pessimism, disconnected from the real way that his generation could improve the world.

Now, at the dawn of the era imagined in the book, he still believed that an extreme authoritarian government was unlikely, at least in the West, and he still had faith in the power of individual efforts. But he took a starker view of the general state of affairs. "For us the danger is completely different," he said. "No one will impose such a pattern on our society. No government, no matter how power hungry, could succeed. Where then is the danger? It lies in imposing it upon ourselves; we may take this path carelessly and with little realization of potential changes. Yet the results may be the same."

He wondered whether the theme of constant surveillance was really so far-fetched, even in America. He found it easy to imagine a television set capable of two-way communication, or corporations advertising their products through subliminal methods, or savvy computer operators stealing personal information by hijacking the account numbers attached to every aspect of modern life, or governments monitoring every communication made by citizens. In many cases, the technologies needed to turn those hypotheticals into reality already existed. In fact, people had willingly accepted them into their lives. "What can we do about the problem?" he asked. "No technical solution will help us; only a high level of morality and a renewed feeling of trust can aid us."[335]

Even though the review was more prescient and dystopian than most of his talks, Walter had been making a similar case for decades. "All morality must begin with restraint; if it cannot be exercised in simple matters, then we are unlikely to carry it into other aspects of our lives," he said in a sermon.

By the time he became senior rabbi of Rodef Shalom, Walter believed that the biggest problems facing the Jewish community in America were no longer discrimination or integration but figuring out what to do with unprecedented wealth and nearly unlimited freedom. The same opportunities that allowed Jewish communities to experiment with observance also allowed individuals to withdraw from communal life without any consequences.[336] In an era when religious observance was voluntary, he sought to temper this freedom with a sense of religious obligation. "In this permissive age we expect Judaism to go along. When we come to the rabbi with a request, any request, we expect him to say 'Yes,' " he said in a Yom Kippur sermon. "But it is the rabbi's duty to say 'No' far more frequently than to say 'Yes.' Look at the Ten Commandments; they are primarily negative and prohibitive. Society may say, 'Okay,' but Judaism says 'No.' "[337]

Walter made this idea a recurring theme of his preaching as Rodef Shalom was restoring its historic synagogue in 1989 and 1990. The project was complex and arduous, involving a large fundraising drive, considerable historic research and setbacks including an electrical fire and the death of a construction worker. "When we think about this building and its restoration we soon realize that our concern extends beyond walls and roof," Walter said in a sermon at the start of the project. "We are interested in our spiritual restoration and it is more important than the structure. What is this building unless it is filled with individuals who feel their Judaism? If we look at the Temple of our soul we may find it as chipped and faded as the building. Just like the terra cotta on the side of this building, it needs restoration. Shall we restore the religion of 1907?" he asked, referring to efforts by Dr. Levy, around the time of the construction of the building, to help a population of immigrant Jews become more accepted in their new country. "That was his path. Our path is different. We do not need to be Americanized, but we need to be Judaized."[338]

To Walter, becoming "Judaized" meant giving more attention to the daily demands of being Jewish. It was one of the central messages of his rabbinate at Rodef Shalom and also of his years as a national figure within the Reform movement. He promoted the idea locally through preaching and through communal projects, and he developed it nationally through scholarship, specifically through an age-old process of answering religious queries.

Walter succeeded Dr. Solomon B. Freehof
as chair of the Responsa Committee of
the Central Conference of American
Rabbis in 1976 and made Jewish law the
primary research interest of his career.
He wrote three volumes of *responsa*,
answering pressing questions about
Jewish law from dozens of rabbis and
congregants.

CHAPTER IV

Standards Now

Walter once speculated that his interest in Jewish law could be traced to the day his grandfather Benno Jacob improvised a highchair by setting the small boy atop a tall stack of legal volumes.[339] The playful claim to scholarly osmosis contained a hint of truth, because Walter certainly absorbed his sense of religious discipline from the context of his childhood. The liberal Jewish community in Germany before World War II was closer to the center of the spectrum of religious observance than most Reform congregations in North America. When Benno had described himself as "a liberal rabbi but not a rabbi of the Liberals," he was distinguishing between the practical reforms occurring within congregations and the radical ideas being proposed in journals and debated at conferences. He showed little interest in those ideas. He cared about modernity only "in a practical sense," as Walter put it.[340] He endorsed changes that allowed his congregants to participate fully in both religious life and national life but vigorously opposed any change that he felt was predicated on insufficient religious knowledge or on mere ideology. "When a rabbi is nothing but popular," he said, "that raises my suspicion."[341]

When Ernest Jacob, in his introductory textbook to Judaism, outlined the basic necessities of any Jewish community, his prerequisites also would have sounded foreign to most Reform congregations throughout North America at the time. He declared that every Jew should feel obligated to join his or her local congregation; that every community should have a cantor, a cemetery, a kosher butcher and a ritual bath; and that a strong rabbinic figure should oversee education and set religious standards. He closed his description with a verse from Deuteronomy that highlighted the communal nature of Jewish religious obligation: "Moses charged us with the law, as a possession for the assembly of Jacob."[342]

According to Walter, if a liberal rabbi in Germany could address a religious matter using traditional sources of Jewish law, he generally did, and "if changes seemed in order like those in liturgy, personal practices, etc., they were made and then defended as necessary in the various journals available to the exponents of Liberal Judaism."[343] The result was a Jewish community with traditional observances built upon a liberal ideology. Rituals were often practiced for untraditional reasons. Europeans interpreted this state of affairs as a reformation, but by American standards it might have resembled orthodoxy.

The liberalization of Judaism in the 19th century is usually defined by its disruption of the legal tradition within the religion. When the early reformers challenged the inherently conservative nature of religious law, questioned the divinity of the oral law and began to view the law historically, they "created a real break with the Jewish legal tradition," as historian Michael A. Meyer wrote in his history of the Reform movement in Judaism.[344]

Walter views that history differently. In his many writings on the subject, he has argued that liberal Judaism is simply the latest manifestation of a pattern of preservation and adaptation going back to the creation of rabbinic Judaism in the aftermath of the destruction of the Second Holy Temple in the 1st century. Asked once to distinguish between the source of authority within Judaism generally and the source of authority within Reform Judaism, Walter began his answer, "The source of Judaism's authority lies in the word of God." The only difference for Reform, he continued, was its willingness to explicitly allow present generations to interpret and change religious practices as they saw fit. "The source of authority for Reform rabbis, therefore, lies in divine revelation, the tradition both written and oral, as interpreted by scholars of the past and our own time for our day," he concluded.[345]

Interpreting that tradition became Walter's primary scholarly endeavor. He pursued it through lectures, essays and most significantly through the time-honored process of answering religious questions. For as long as the rabbinate has existed, Jewish laypeople have turned to rabbis for guidance about practical observance. Questions cover a wide range of everyday concerns, from what conditions make a piece of food stop being kosher, to whether a community should pay a ransom to save a kidnapped member, to who can read from the Torah during worship. Questions can also cover irregular cases. For example, when does the Sabbath begin above the Arctic Circle, where the common understanding of "sundown" doesn't apply for much of the year? And questions can present purely theoretical situations, such as the religious implications of human cloning. This process of seeking and receiving religious guidance is known in Hebrew as *she'elot ve-teshuvot*, meaning "questions and answers." It is also known by the Latin legal term *responsa*, which covers similar activities in other religions.

In the scattered and decentralized landscape of Jewish history, *responsa* have been the leading edge of *halakhah, or* Jewish law. *Halakhah* literally means "the way to walk" and is a comprehensive system of conduct, established before the modern divisions between religious and civil law. The precepts of *halakhah* are drawn from the basic texts of Jewish literature, starting with the Torah and the Talmud and continuing through many centuries of rabbinic writings to the present day. Attempts have been made throughout history to codify these laws, most notably with the publication of the *Shulchan Arukh* in the 16th century. But these attempts have always been complicated by the unpredictability of real life, which is continually creating new scenarios and circumstances outside of the scope of the existing laws. *Responsa* can either expand or narrow that scope. It is a process for turning life into law.

By the time Walter was born, *responsa* had fallen out of favor within liberal Judaism. The first generation of reformers in the early 19th century had unsuccessfully used the *responsa* process to defend their reforms against the criticisms of traditional authorities. When those defensive efforts failed, a new generation of liberal Jewish scholars in the mid-19th century used the *responsa* process to refine ideas among themselves. As liberal Judaism became the dominant form of the religion in Central Europe, toward the end of the 19th century, its leaders had less of a need to justify their positions to traditional authorities or to define their philosophy for adherents. They largely stopped developing Jewish law and focused on reforming other aspects of the religion, such as the details of worship. They installed organs in their synagogues. They allowed women to sit with men during services. They revised prayer books. They introduced a sermon in the vernacular. They started reading the Torah instead of chanting it.[346]

At the beginning of the 20th century, the emergent Reform movement in America saw the *responsa* process as a useful way to temper its early radicalism. Enthusiasm for *responsa* waxed and waned over the next four decades, depending on the mood of each generation of leaders and the needs of their congregations, but the process gained popularity in the decade after World War II, as Walter was beginning his rabbinic training.

Walter discovered *responsa* as a rabbinical student, but not in the classroom. In his first year at Hebrew Union College, he took a part-time job as a clerk at the campus library, pre-cataloguing and shelving books. The work proved to be much more interesting than he could have expected it to be.

In the aftermath of World War II, Allied soldiers discovered hundreds of thousands of stolen Jewish books in Nazi archives. A reparation campaign attempted to return as many of these books as possible to their original owners. In many cases, though, the owners were no longer living, or in the case of institutions, no longer existed. The unclaimed books were instead distributed to Jewish institutions throughout the United States.[347]

2,000 Volumes Tell of Middle Ages Ghetto Life *6 / 26 / 1965*

Antique Jewish Books Saved

Dr. Freehof Aids In Recovery Of Scorched Pages

By JAY GOGGIN
Post-Gazette Staff Writer

Charred and water-curled pages recording life in the Jewish ghettoes of Europe during the Middle Ages were saved from a modern pulp mill by an Oakland rabbi and a generous congregation.

Dr. Solomon B. Freehof, rabbi of Rodef Shalom Temple, was asked last year by an insurance company to estimate the value of an Hebraic library, that had been extensively damaged during a fire in the East End residence of the late Rabbi Abraham Zilberberg.

Close To Destruction

In May of this year the insurance company was going to destroy the cartons containing the books. The Philanthropic Committee of Rodef Shalom intervened and purchased the books.

For four weeks Dr. Freehof and his associate, Rabbi Walter Jacob, unpacked cartons and sorted books and manuscripts in the basement of the temple. The room where they worked still has the acrid smell of a fire-gutted building.

After the initial sorting, which uncovered nearly 2,000 volumes, the rabbis crated the bulk of library and last week shipped it to the Hebrew Union College in Cincinnati.

—Post-Gazette Photo
Rabbi Walter Jacob pages through charred volumes of Responsa.

everyday problems of family life, such as the one cited, a picture, not only, of the Jewish community emerges, but the country where the

Walter developed his love of Jewish law through a series of remarkable occurrences, such as when Rodef Shalom Congregation purchased two thousand damaged volumes of Jewish scholarship from an insurance company in 1965.

The Hebrew Union College campus in Cincinnati received nearly ten thousand of these books between July 1949 and the end of 1952, when Walter was working as a clerk.[348] "The library was short of help, so I was given tasks with much more responsibility than usually assigned to a beginner," he wrote. The shipments included a wide array of Jewish books. The work was fairly straightforward for most of the books, but the cataloguing system at the library was too rigid to accommodate the nuances of the *responsa* collections. A single volume might have multiple editions, or different volumes might have identical titles, making them difficult to catalogue.[349] To better understand the context of these books, Walter approached experts at the college. He was able to persuade Professor Alexander Guttman to teach an elective in the Talmud, even though most rabbinical students showed no interest in the legal text. Professors Moses Marx and Isaiah Sonne gave Walter an introductory overview of the field of *responsa*. Hebrew Union College library director Herbert Zafren allowed Walter to buy duplicates from the collection. These were the first volumes of *responsa* in Walter's rabbinic library.[350]

By a stroke of good fortune, Walter landed the perfect job for a young Reform rabbi with an interest in Jewish law. Rodef Shalom's Dr. Solomon B. Freehof was the undisputed authority on the subject within the movement. After several decades as a noted expert in the field, he had recently become the chair of the committee responsible for answering religious questions within the Reform movement — the Responsa Committee of the Central Conference of American Rabbis. Being an associate rabbi to Dr. Freehof, and later his successor, gave Walter the unique opportunity of observing a present-day manifestation of the ancient *responsa* process he had discovered in those books at the library. Dr. Freehof showed Walter the questions coming from colleagues around the country, and he often asked Walter to read early drafts of his responses.[351] The experience exposed Walter to the religious concerns of people in the Reform movement and introduced him to the ways of addressing them.

Intrigued by the possibilities of *responsa*, Walter shifted his personal studies toward Jewish law. It was impractical to take even his small *responsa* library to the Philippines, but he convinced the Jewish Welfare Board to send him a complete set of the *Mishnah Torah*, a code of Jewish law compiled by Maimonides in the 12th century. After returning to Pittsburgh from his tour of duty, Walter began a private course of Talmudic study, which he felt had been underrepresented in the seminary curriculum. He often studied long-distance with his father. They read independently and shared thoughts in letters. Ernest once pointed to a Talmudic passage where the sages allowed active manipulation in the reporting of the new moon, and therefore the workings of the ancient calendar. "There is always a way even in the strictest orthodoxy to get what you want," he told Walter.[352]

An unexpected opportunity drew Walter even deeper into the literature of Jewish law. In early 1965, an insurance company asked Dr. Freehof to appraise a library of religious books that had been damaged in a house fire in Pittsburgh. To ensure that any salvageable books from the collection would be preserved, and that any ruined books would be disposed of respectfully, Rodef Shalom acquired the entire collection, more than two thousand volumes. Dr. Freehof had the books delivered to a basement room at Rodef Shalom and asked Walter to help him sort through them. "We soon proceeded with the dirty work of going through this mountain of ash-covered books and sometimes were ankle deep in half-burned pages," Walter recalled. "After an hour we looked and smelled more like fire-fighters than rabbis. It was a dirty labor of love for two bibliophiles."

They shipped most of the books, as well as several cartons of assorted pages, to the Hebrew Union College library, and they also made copies of hundreds of title pages to distribute to other academic and governmental institutions. But before they did, Dr. Freehof selected a few volumes for his library and gave several hundred duplicate volumes of *responsa* to Walter. Added to his earlier treasures from the Nazi archive, these books became the foundation of Walter's extensive *responsa* library.

The books were badly damaged. Bits of charred binding flaked off any time Walter handled them, and he had to wrap each volume before he could add it to the shelves in his study. Over the following decade, Dr. Freehof rebound all of these books for Walter.[353] Dr. Freehof bound books the way Walter gardened, as a productive hobby to divert his mind from other responsibilities. He was prolific. He rebound most of the volumes in his professional and personal libraries. He regularly borrowed books from congregants to rebind. He even offered his services to libraries. He took a utilitarian approach to the craft, covering the book boards in wallpaper swatches or used giftwrap and binding the spines with bright scraps of materials salvaged from the bindery at the Carnegie Library of Pittsburgh. This gave his work an instantly recognizable aesthetic: modest covers with mismatched spines and vibrant book boards.[354]

After the two of them finished processing the collection, Walter spent the next few months reviewing his new books. They came from Poland, Germany, Austria and Italy, and some dated back several hundreds of years. The books had emerged from Jewish communities where there was little or no distinction between religious law and civil law, and the questions Walter encountered as he read the books offered glimpses into the social and cultural concerns of each community, as well as their religious lives. "It is fascinating work," he told a newspaper reporter who came by to see some of the books. "Like being transposed to another place."[355]

A round that time, the Central Conference of American Rabbis asked Walter to become an associate member of the Responsa Committee. It was a committee in name only, with no meetings and few discussions other than a perfunctory review of the more controversial subjects. But the appointment encouraged Walter to devote more of his private studies to the nuances of Jewish law.[356]

Between the books on his shelves and the much larger collection of books in Dr. Freehof's study, Walter had access to one of the finest rabbinic libraries in the world.[357] These books allowed him to become more familiar with the idiosyncrasies of a vast and decentralized literary genre. Most of the *responsa* volumes were written in an older style of Hebrew and had archaic systems of shorthand and citation. They often lacked the conveniences of modern scholarship, such as subject headings or indices or even a consistent approach to the endeavor. One rabbi might answer a question directly while another might expound on the given subject for several pages, turning a practical matter into an excuse for intellectual acrobatics. It was not uncommon for two scholars to offer different answers to a similar question, nor was it uncommon for one scholar to rule one way and future generations to take the law in a different direction. Through these private studies, Walter absorbed the spirit of the enterprise. He learned how to apply the examples of tradition to the circumstances and the needs of modern society.

Under the chairmanship of Dr. Freehof, the Responsa Committee was gaining new prominence within the Reform movement. The Central Conference of American Rabbis had formed the committee in 1906 to resolve a debate among its members. Some rabbis wanted to create a handbook of guidelines to assist younger colleagues, while others worried that such a book would be a step toward replicating the rigidity of orthodoxy. Both sides saw the age-old *responsa* process as an acceptable alternative. The informal nature of asking questions and receiving answers from wise elders would allow all rabbis to absorb examples from tradition without demanding adherence.[358]

Through its first forty years, the committee was used sparingly and mostly to provide the Central Conference of American Rabbis with scholarly research to guide its decisions. Dr. Freehof turned the committee into an active channel for influencing practical observance. He wanted the Reform movement to become more familiar with Jewish law, as he had known it as a child in an Orthodox setting in England. He was also skeptical about establishing a code of practice too soon, before religious practices had a chance to emerge organically from within congregations. Again, the Responsa Committee provided a way to address the demand for a code of practice without actually implementing one. He treated the examples of tradition as *minhagim*, or customs. Customs have always held great importance within Jewish communities, but, because they typically involve matters at the edges of Jewish law, they often vary drastically from place to place. Dr. Freehof believed that providing information about the varieties of Jewish observances in the past would encourage new patterns of observance in the present. The example of tradition, he famously said, would provide "guidance, not governance."[359]

Dr. Freehof freed the work of the Responsa Committee from the insular world of the Central Conference of American Rabbis. He encouraged his rabbinic colleagues to send questions, and he made his answers more public than previous chairs had done. By the time of his death in 1990, he had published nearly six hundred *responsa* across eight books and had written perhaps an equal number of unpublished *responsa* through direct correspondence with the people who sought his expertise. In the introduction to each of his books, he took a step back to offer his current thoughts about developing *halakhah* from a liberal perspective. Through these efforts, Dr. Freehof essentially inverted the way liberal Judaism thought about religious practices. Instead of using rituals and ceremonies to bolster a commitment to ethical ideals, he wanted those ideals to emerge from the routines of observance. "We do not begin with theology, we arrive at theology," he wrote.[360]

Dr. Freehof retired from the Responsa Committee in 1976, and Walter was the obvious choice to be his successor. In addition to his long apprenticeship and his access to Dr. Freehof's library, he shared his predecessor's vision. He saw the value of building philosophy from practice.

Rodef Shalom contributed to this vision. The first four chairmen of the Responsa Committee were academics during their tenures. Dr. Freehof and Walter were the first congregational rabbis to chair the committee. Combining their back-to-back terms as associates and chairs, they sat on the Responsa Committee for forty-two years, from 1947 until 1989. By extension, Rodef Shalom and the broader Jewish community throughout the greater Pittsburgh area became a testing ground for the work of the committee. More questions came to the committee from western Pennsylvania than from any other part of the country. Perhaps more importantly, the many Jewish communities in western Pennsylvania provided a living example of the ways religious practices were being observed or ignored. The idea of using the *responsa* process to encourage greater practical observance required a connection to the daily life of a congregation and its wider community. Being among "real Jews," to borrow an admiring term Walter often uses for laypeople, influenced how Dr. Freehof approached his *responsa*. As senior rabbi of Rodef Shalom, Walter consciously took a more pastoral approach than Dr. Freehof, and so his considerations of daily congregational life were even more nuanced.

Dr. Freehof's enthusiasm for Jewish law did not prompt him to discuss the subject from the pulpit with much frequency, and although his congregation was proud of his accomplishments in the field, it rarely called upon him to expound on his work. By the time Walter became the senior rabbi, the interests of the laity had started to change. "This generation of congregants wished to know how Judaism responded to contemporary issues and what the tradition had to say about them," he wrote. "These were often issues of national policy as well as personal interest. The death penalty, abortion, drugs, pollution, medical problems among other issues became themes." In addition to growing curiosity about the Jewish view of contemporary American problems, many congregants wanted to know more about the Reform movement in particular. They wanted to understand the Reform perspective on Jewish rites of passage and wanted to understand the thinking behind changes to Reform liturgy. Congregants also had concerns about broader trends of assimilation and secularization. Others throughout the Reform movement had similar questions, and these matters eventually reached the committee.[361]

Walter treated his *responsa* as literal responses to actual questions, rather than as opportunities to write about a particular subject. "I have always considered writing *responsa* a religious task. The guidance provided must have a spiritual basis that needs to be clear in each answer," he wrote.[362] Being a congregational rabbi helped Walter appreciate the personal consequences of his legal decisions. Back when he denied the request from the president of the remote South Dakota congregation who had sought permission to conduct a wedding as a layman, Walter attached a personal letter to his *responsum*. "This answer in no way reflects on your abilities and commitment to the Jewish community," he wrote. "Certainly, you show that you are one of the leaders in your State and I hope that that may continue for many years to come."[363]

Walter also had a first-hand understanding of intricate communal dynamics. For example, when the Responsa Committee was asked in 1983 whether a rabbi could start a new congregation in a city that already had many existing congregations, the question was almost certainly referring to a young Reform rabbi who had started a congregation in Pittsburgh using once-controversial ideas from the Reconstructionist movement. In his answer, Walter acknowledged that there were overarching historical concerns about the potential institutional damage that could result if people left an existing congregation to join a new one. But he also pointed to the many instances throughout history where a single city maintained multiple synagogues. "In a large community such as Pittsburgh nothing should stand in the way of attempting to establish a new congregation, if that seems desirable to some members of the Jewish community," he concluded. "Tradition favors the establishment of synagogues which will satisfy the needs of the worshipers."[364]

In the *responsum*, Walter made no mention of his personal experiences, but it is easy to see how they might have influenced his thinking. The liberal congregation in Augsburg preserved a stable and friendly peace with the traditional congregation in nearby Kriegshaber. The merged congregation in Springfield required a delicate touch to maintain the fragile equilibrium between its two factions. Rodef Shalom started as a breakaway congregation and became ideologically stronger after another congregation broke away from it. All three cases illustrated how forming a new congregation could limit conflict within a wider Jewish community, which may or may not have been obvious simply by looking at the legal rulings of earlier generations.

W alter quickly reorganized the membership and operations of the Responsa Committee after he formally assumed the chair in early 1977. He saw the work of the committee as "a way of connecting the Reform movement more closely to the *halakhah*, which has always been the central expression of Judaism," he once wrote.[365] To that end, he favored congregational rabbis over the academics who had typically populated the committee. Outlining his thoughts about associates in a letter to the incoming president of the Central Conference of American Rabbis, Walter suggested limiting academic representation on the committee to one professor each from the four campuses of Hebrew Union College. Doing so would "still leave us with a strong practical rabbinic representation," he wrote. "This remains essential for the committee; otherwise the *responsa* becomes too theoretical."[366]

Despite his desire to more closely address the needs of congregations, Walter balked at the idea of appointing laymen to the committee. "It was decided that this would not serve our purposes as a thorough knowledge of the traditional literature is necessary for our procedures and we do not want our results to be akin to the resolutions of other committees," the minutes of an early meeting bluntly noted. Instead, he wanted members of the committee to encourage younger colleagues to take an interest in *halakhah*, in the hopes of developing future scholars and gaining a wider range of learned viewpoints.[367] By limiting the committee to rabbis, he was reasserting the authority of rabbinic scholarship in an age of individual autonomy.

Walter wanted associate members to become more involved in the process of crafting *responsa* than they had been under previous chairs. He soon discovered a reason for the imbalance: the chair usually possessed a better library than any of his associates and often possessed greater enthusiasm for the task. Walter decided he would answer each question on his own and then circulate his *responsum* by mail to the rest of the committee for comments. To ensure that this process remained speedy enough to be useful to petitioners, he asked that each *responsum* make the rounds within a month of the committee receiving the question. The timeline proved to be impractical in the days of postal mail, especially given the increasing volume of questions coming to the committee with each year. Within a few years, the associate members of the committee had asked Walter to pass along only those *responsa* on truly consequential subjects.[368]

Even though circumstances thwarted Walter's collective approach at the time, his desire for collaboration infused the committee and was fully realized in the 1990s, when the widespread use of email made his vision practical. As a result of his proposed changes to membership and operation, the Responsa Committee eventually became a fully deliberative body, rather than a sounding board for its chair. Today, any member the Central Conference of American Rabbis is allowed to contribute to the *responsa* process in an ex-officio fashion, which means that the work of the committee reflects a much broader array of views from within the movement.[369] In that sense, the Responsa Committee followed the pattern Walter had set with other institutions he inherited. By eliminating the dependence on a single leader, he elevated the importance of the entire institution.

Walter took a similarly expansive approach to distributing the work of the Responsa Committee during his tenure. The committee was only required to pass along its most important decisions to the wider Central Conference of American Rabbis. These were considered at conventions and published in yearbooks, which made them difficult for the wider public to access. Dr. Freehof disseminated his work more widely by collecting his *responsa* in a series of books for a general audience. Walter continued both measures. He sent consequential *responsa* to the wider conference and published two collections of his *responsa*. He also undertook two new publishing ventures that were designed to further his broader goal of connecting the Reform movement to *halakhah*.

One venture was a *responsa* column in *Reform Judaism* magazine. The former quarterly magazine of the Union for Reform Judaism was touted in its day as being the most widely circulated Jewish magazine in the world, which gave the *responsa* column a potentially wide readership. In a sense, the column fulfilled the proposition Walter had made years earlier of incorporating accessible scholarship into general-interest publications to create more opportunities for Jewish learning.

The other venture was an anthology of Reform *responsa*. The volume, titled simply *American Reform Responsa*, included all the *responsa* issued by the Central Conference of American Rabbis between 1889 and 1982. Walter organized the anthology according to the categories used in the *Shulchan Arukh*, the best-known code of Jewish law. He even included the Hebrew titles for each category.[370] An earlier anthology of *responsa* was organized chronologically, rather than by subject matter. Dr. Freehof implicitly organized his *responsa* collections according to the traditional categories of Jewish law, but only those who knew the categories would recognize the structure he was using. By explicitly associating the anthology with traditional codes, Walter took one step further toward developing liberal *halakhah*—a working system of Jewish law from a liberal perspective.

The structure of the anthology allowed readers to see how the Reform movement had evolved on many issues, such as the question of whether or not to establish a bat mitzvah ceremony for girls. In a series of *responsa* written in 1913, 1954 and 1979, the committee twice rejected the bat mitzvah ceremony in favor of a confirmation for both girls and boys and later endorsed both a bar mitzvah and bat mitzvah ceremony without reservations. The three *responsa* show the committee trying to treat men and women equally while resisting the desire of many congregants to bring traditional religious ceremonies into liberal Judaism. Over time, as more and more congregations ignored the nuances of those earlier *responsa* and began offering both bar mitzvah and bat mitzvah ceremonies, the committee fully endorsed the custom.[371] "When we recognize that we are children of our age and are deeply influenced by it," Walter wrote in his introduction to the anthology, "we do not differ from those who lived in the creative periods of the past as we seek to understand the underlying principles and develop specifics, i.e. *Halacha*."[372]

By taking such a practical approach to the process of writing *responsa*, Walter encouraged demand for his services. It was not uncommon for him to receive urgent telephone calls from people with pressing questions, such as a dispute about burial customs among the mourners standing at a gravesite. He was forced to answer on the fly, and then revise, or at least expand, his initial decision when he followed up with a written response. "How fortunate were the *gaonim* in Baghdad who received an inquiry from hundreds or thousands of miles away and had months, till the departure of the next caravan, to prepare a reply," he once wrote.[373]

Walter started fielding questions from his first day as chair and typically received more than one question each week throughout his tenure. The volume, frequency and urgency of these questions could cause intellectual vertigo, as he researched one subject for only as long as it took to answer the question and immediately started researching a completely different subject. Handling the great flow of questions while also meeting his congregational duties was often a challenge. "Only long evenings and early mornings of study along with tight personal organization has made it possible," he wrote.[374] He developed tricks for getting the most out of his days. One of his tricks was arriving at large social gatherings on time but spending most of the event working on a manuscript in a nearby room and joining the festivities a few minutes before they ended, when everyone had tired of chatting with each other and appreciated a fresh face. Another trick involved visiting his congregants. One of his assistants, Rabbi Debra Pine, asked once how he was able to make a dozen or more hospital visits in a day. "He said, 'Here's the answer: You never sit down,'" she recalled.[375]

Supplying answers quickly enough to be helpful to those who had asked the questions also meant sacrificing some conceptual thoroughness. Walter admits that there were inconsistencies in his work before he gained experience and confidence in the endeavor. More to the point, he was perfectly willing to set aside the larger philosophical issues that emerged during the process of responding to religious queries. He prioritized answering questions over creating a system of thought.[376] Like Dr. Freehof, he made decisions on a case-by-case basis and looked back later to find emerging trends.

Walter called this "implicit theology." In an essay explaining the phrase, written shortly after he assumed the chair of the Responsa Committee, he argued that anyone who insisted on crafting a comprehensive theological system before making a practical religious decision was "doomed to fail." The desire to provide a comprehensive philosophy or theology for Judaism, Walter believed, was a common response at moments of spiritual crisis in Jewish history. Every encounter with outside influences—from the Hellenism of ancient Greece, to the Arab culture of medieval Spain, to the rationalism of modern Germany, to the secularism of America—had prompted soul-searching among the Jewish people. "Philosophy in each case has tried to strike a balance or bring a synthesis between Judaism and the tempting outside culture," he wrote, concluding, "We will probably continue to use this approach among others when other cultures threaten to engulf us, although history should teach us that this path has not succeeded. The philosophers and the systems espoused in each of these periods have remained peripheral to Judaism."

By contrast, "implicit theology" started with the daily responsibilities of being Jewish. "We build our foundations slowly through our actions, our sermons, our lectures in a fashion akin to *midrash*," he continued, using the Hebrew term for rabbinic commentary. "This has been our path from the beginning, so the Book of Genesis did not start with theology, but with creation. We learn to understand God and the Covenant through the Exodus and Sinai; sometimes our ancestors wished to express their concepts more explicitly and did so through poetic theology as in the *Shir Ha-Yam* (Song of the Sea). Such statements and those by prophets, Ecclesiastes, Job, as well as the later *midrashic*, poetic and mystical literature, provided a better basis for Judaism than any philosophical system."[377]

"Implicit theology" was a more systematic way of describing a general preference for action over discussion. His combination of "initiative" and "*sekhel*" was an attempt to respect the will of his congregation without explicitly seeking consensus from it. He believed that seeking consensus too explicitly could create "other bureaucracies," beyond the unavoidable ones. When he and Irene were developing the Biblical Botanical Garden in 1985 and 1986, another group in Pittsburgh was pursuing a similar venture, albeit on a much larger and more ambitious scale. This group started by establishing a horticultural society, forming a new non-profit, inviting a wide array of area gardeners to provide suggestions, creating a master plan, holding meetings and hosting workshops. It took more than twenty-five years for the first section of their garden to open to the public. "Meanwhile, we've had twenty-seven lectures," Walter said.[378]

The challenge of "implicit theology," of course, is sincerity. It can only work if the people making decisions consistently have higher values in mind, rather than self-interest. By relying so heavily on this approach, Walter was displaying his fundamental faith and optimism in humanity, as well as confidence in his vision and abilities.

A preference for action is also why Walter is skeptical of philosophy generally. While many people rely on a philosophical framework to make sense of the world, Walter prefers the objective examples of history. As both a scholar and a teacher, he likes to follow a subject over a long period of time to understand how it was handled in different eras or different places. One of his favorite museum exhibits in recent years considered the government propaganda of several countries involved in World War II, turning an emotionally charged subject into an objective comparison. His greatest skills as a scholar are summary (the ability to convey the essence of a subject in a few words) and synthesis (the ability to describe the relationship between disparate ideas). His essays use both skills in combination to articulate the implicit theology demonstrated by human behavior.

Walter viewed the task of writing *responsa* from both a legal perspective and a historical perspective. As a scholar of Jewish law, he wanted to know what earlier rabbinic authorities had decided when they faced questions similar to the ones he was currently facing. As a historian, though, he also wanted to know how Jewish communities had actually behaved. A lawyer will consider what people were told to do, while a historian will consider what people were actually doing.[379] By combining these two approaches, Walter followed in the spirit of those Talmudic sages who resolved theoretical debates by advising, "Go see what the people are doing."[380]

Following the will of the people was easier to do when it came to questions about ritual. Walter considered most rituals and ceremonies to be customs that had developed during specific eras or within specific communities throughout Jewish history. "They remind us of our ethical duties; they are important as they are an emotional and nonrational connection to Judaism," he wrote.[381] In his attempt to make *halakhah* more central to the Reform movement, he liked to illustrate how these customs fit into the larger system of Jewish tradition.[382] When people asked him about the appropriateness of placing an Israeli flag on the pulpit, or using non-traditional fabrics in a Torah mantle, or dipping challah into salt at the start of a Sabbath meal, he approved of the customs, even when they had no legal basis. Instead of answering these questions briefly, he used the opportunity to provide a few pages of historical analysis.[383]

Along these lines, one of the first *responsa* he wrote as the incoming chair considered the question of dress codes. Did a congregation have the right to impose standards of dress for worship services and religious school classes? The question came from his son Kenney, who was about fourteen at the time and inconvenienced by such dress codes on a regular basis. A matter that could have been handled over the dinner table instead became a history lesson. Walter started his answer by referring to the rabbinic prohibition against "crowns of the bridegroom" during the 1st century War of Vespasian, and his *responsum* continued through the many centuries of similar sartorial prohibitions to make the case for dress codes.[384]

Walter assigned more importance to the ethical and moral aspects of *halakhah* than to its ritual and ceremonial sides, and he quickly faced some truly consequential questions in those areas. The increased prominence of the Responsa Committee under the chairmanship of

Dr. Freehof made the Reform movement—rabbis and congregants across the country, as well as Reform institutions—increasingly willing to seek its guidance. Almost immediately upon taking over the committee, Walter began fielding questions from agencies, commissions and committees of major Reform organizations. The Family Life Committee of the Central Conference of American Rabbis sent him a long list of generic questions about changing sexual mores and family structures. At the same time, individual rabbis were also sending questions about unexpected religious dilemmas emerging from the increasing rate of intermarriage.[385] Areas of Jewish law that had been mostly theoretical in previous generations were now becoming practical.

Walter once outlined five ways of approaching the difficulties of interpreting Jewish law. The first treated *halakhah* as a "unified whole" and worked hard to resolve any apparent contradictions within it. The second tried to ascertain the original intention of the earliest generations of scholars and then charted a path from that starting point through the work of subsequent generations. The third reinterpreted *halakhah* according to the spirit of the present, with due consideration for the past. The fourth attempted to codify *halakhah* according to a particular understanding of its intentions. The fifth used a legislative system to create new standards.

Walter followed the third and fifth paths. He cared more about addressing the immediate moral and ethical considerations behind a particular question than about the broader issue of preserving a conceptual whole. If the modern understanding of a subject contradicted the traditional view, as was the case with many issues involving women and religious practice, he allowed for a break with the past. He also assumed that previous generations had been making similar calculations, and therefore he was willing to follow an older path that later generations of scholars had abandoned. Along similar lines, he also accepted the possibility that later generations might take an entirely different approach than the one he took. In either case, he felt it was important to reach a clear decision, whenever possible. "Any decision, especially if made in writing places the author on the firing line…I would rather make a decision and have another generation of writers of *responsa* take a different path, than make no decision," he wrote.[386]

This approach allowed the *responsa* writer to drink from the "vast reservoir" of tradition, as Walter put it, but properly balancing the needs of the present and the past required a discriminating mind. Walter explicitly noted this challenge when a rabbi asked the committee whether a committed, unmarried couple could join a congregation as a family. In a *responsum* from 1980, Walter replied, "We now have a problem between the rather strict tradition and its ideals and modern circumstances. We must also ask about the difference between quietly condoning a certain style of life and publicly accepting it, as would be the case through congregational membership. On the other hand, we do not want to discourage young people from joining congregations." He suggested accepting the couple through two individual memberships.[387]

Maintaining that balance proved to be most difficult when societal norms directly conflicted with traditional Jewish values. Walter assumed the chair of the Responsa Committee as mixed marriage became a central concern of the movement.[388] His approach to the subject illustrated the way he relied on tradition and also the way he departed from it.

In 1979, a rabbi asked the Responsa Committee whether he should recite a traditional pre-wedding prayer for a Jew who was planning to marry a Christian. Walter decided it would be inappropriate "because such action would lend public approval to such a marriage." After the couple married, though, Walter felt that the congregation should recognize the marriage and "do everything possible to make the non-Jewish partner feel at ease and at home in our midst."[389] The following year, a different rabbi asked explicitly whether it was appropriate or inappropriate to officiate at a wedding between a Jew and a non-Jew. In the longest *responsum* of his career, Walter surveyed the history of Jewish views about intermarriage from the Hebrew Bible through modern times, including both the Reform and Conservative perspectives as well as the statutes contained in modern Israeli law. And while he ruled definitively against officiating at the wedding, he again referenced the "provisions" that the movement had made to accommodate the growing number of families with one Jewish spouse. "They are welcome in our congregations, and we continue to urge them to convert to Judaism," he wrote.[390]

A third question, from 1982, asked the committee to make the case for and against a rabbi officiating at a wedding between a Jew and a non-Jew. Walter provided fifteen reasons against the practice and none for it. He ended his *responsum* by issuing a broad statement about the matter. "It is clear that mixed marriages will continue and that the percentage will rise and fall depending upon circumstances beyond our control. That is a risk of living in an open society. Some non-Jewish partners will convert, others will not. Some children will be raised as Jews, others will not," he wrote. "But we have never depended upon numbers alone. It is far more important to have a strong commitment from a smaller group than a vague commitment from a large number who are at the very periphery."[391]

In all three cases, Walter was unable to lend rabbinic support for mixed marriage, even within the "broad avenue" of Jewish law, as he once described the varied examples of tradition. The prohibitions against the practice were too consistent to be reinterpreted in good faith. When it came to the children of those marriages, though, Walter participated in one of the sharpest breaks with tradition in the history of the Reform movement. In a lecture from 1979 surveying the history of *halakhah* in the Reform movement, Walter offered patrilineal descent as a case where *halakhah* could be used to expand the boundaries of observance, rather than exclusively narrow them. The parliamentary procedure within liberal Judaism, he noted, allowed the movement to create new laws when its needs could not be accomplished by reinterpreting old laws. The movement had used that system, he noted, to give women the ability to perform religious observances once reserved for men. These changes were based on the belief that men and women should be treated equally, and if gender equality was to be a core principle, he continued, then the movement should also consider those situations where women had more rights than men. "There is no reason, for example, why we should define our answer to the question 'Who is a Jew' by only following the female line," he said.[392]

The Central Conference of American Rabbis took precisely that step in 1983 when it passed a resolution endorsing patrilineal descent in cases where a family raised its children as Jews. By creating a way for the child of one Jewish parent—mother or father—to be considered Jewish, the resolution directly opposed the traditional insistence on matrilineal descent. To ground its decision in Jewish law, the conference asked the Responsa Committee to explain the origins of matrilineal descent and to determine whether or not *halakhah* could be used to justify patrilineal descent. With the second-longest *responsum* of his career, Walter used the examples of the biblical patriarchy and the Temple priesthood, both passed through the father, to challenge the standard of matrilineal descent. He concluded that education and upbringing should be equally important for establishing Jewish identity.[393]

The three *responsa* that Walter wrote about mixed marriages were more or less in line with mainstream Jewish opinion on the subject. His *responsum* on patrilineal descent, though, was a sharp break with other denominations, and even put the Reform movement in America at odds with its counterparts in Europe and Israel. The discrepancy came from his view of Jewish history. He refused to lend rabbinic support for mixed marriage because he was unwilling to upend a central norm of Judaism. But after the Central Conference of American Rabbis endorsed patrilineal descent, he treated the resolution with the same authority as any other precedent he might find within Jewish tradition. Over the years, he invariably cited the resolution anytime the committee received a question about mixed marriages.[394] Walter summarized his position in the introduction to his second volume of *responsa*, when he wrote, "It is not our task as liberal Jews to complain about the Orthodox attitude or to be bullied by it, but rather to choose our legitimate path according to the inner logic and development of liberal Judaism."[395]

Another area where traditional Jewish values came into conflict with changing societal norms during the late 20th century was homosexuality. As the gay rights movement gained momentum in America, the Reform movement accommodated it in various ways. The Union of American Hebrew Congregations accepted several gay and lesbian congregations as members in 1974, and the Central Conference of American Rabbis passed a resolution in 1977 condemning legal and societal discrimination against gays and lesbians, but discrimination persisted within the Reform movement in crucial ways. Hebrew Union College continued to refuse rabbinic ordination for openly gay and lesbian students, and few Reform rabbis performed or recognized same-sex marriages.[396]

The Responsa Committee was asked in 1981 whether a congregation should employ a "known homosexual" in a leadership position. Walter started his *responsum* by citing the 1977 resolution against discrimination but soon acknowledged that Jewish tradition was clear about the importance of sexual norms. "Overt heterosexual behavior or overt homosexual behavior which is considered objectionable by the community disqualifies the person involved from leadership positions in the Jewish community," he wrote. "We reject this type of individual as a role model within that Jewish community. We cannot recommend such an individual as a role model nor should he/she be placed in a position of leadership or guidance for children of any age." In the *responsum*, Walter noted that his decision was based partly on the traditional Jewish attitude toward homosexuality and partly on "our contemporary understanding of homosexuality, which understands it as an illness, as a genetically-based dysfunction, or as a sexual preference and lifestyle." For the duration of his time as the chair of the Responsa Committee, Walter continued to base his *responsa* on questions of homosexuality on that "contemporary understanding," even though parts of it were already being challenged by the scientific community.[397]

In 1985, a rabbi and a Hebrew Union College rabbinical student introduced a resolution to the Central Conference of American Rabbis calling for full inclusion of gays and lesbians in the Reform rabbinate.

As chairman of the Responsa Committee, Walter was appointed to an ad hoc committee created in 1986 to consider the resolution. The committee initially expected to reach a decision quickly, but instead debated the matter for more than four years. During that process, the *responsum* Walter wrote in 1981 prohibiting openly gay men and women from holding leadership roles was offered as a precedent against the resolution.[398] In the end, though, the committee recommended full equality for gays and lesbians when it came to admission to Hebrew Union College, rabbinic ordination, membership in the Central Conference of American Rabbis and eventual placement in congregations. Although the committee spoke with one voice, some dissention within its ranks could be felt in certain sections of the report, particularly a section that reaffirmed "heterosexual, monogamous, procreative marriage" as the ideal within Jewish tradition, a position Walter held. By the time the committee presented its final report to the Central Conference of American Rabbis in June 1990, Walter had finished his tenure on the Responsa Committee and joined the leadership of the conference. A year earlier, he had asked to be relieved of his assignment on the ad hoc committee, but his request appears to have been denied.[399]

As with mixed marriage, Walter felt strongly about preserving an ideal and accommodating change in practical ways. When a rabbi asked the committee whether "a known and active homosexual" could be accepted as a convert, Walter wrote that the rabbi should "explain the attitude of traditional Judaism and that of our Reform Movement to him quite clearly. After that, if he continued to show an interest in Judaism and wishes to convert, then we may accept him as any other convert."[400] When the committee was asked whether a lesbian couple should be allowed to participate as parents in the bar mitzvah service of their adopted son, Walter permitted their participation as individuals. "This will indicate to both the congregation and this household that we recognize the love and care given to the child and do not focus on or recognize the lesbian relationship," he wrote.[401] In 1994, Rodef Shalom provided a chapel in the synagogue for a group of Jewish gays, lesbians and bisexuals looking for a permanent place to worship. The prayer group, called Bet Tikvah, became one of the first of its kind in the country to find a home within a large Reform synagogue.[402] Even so, in his *responsa*, Walter consistently denied larger and more meaningful accommodations for gays and lesbians, such as marriage and leadership positions in congregations.

When asked in January 1997 for his thoughts on same-sex marriage, at a time when the Reform movement was actively debating the matter, Walter remained opposed. "My feeling is that homosexuals may live together [and] do whatever they wish. I have no problems with that. But there is no need to call that a marriage," he said. He felt it would be more appropriate for same-sex couples to create a new ceremony, inspired by Jewish tradition. Then he added, "I'm not so sure that we need, as Jews, always to go with the times. There are plenty of issues where we can say and should say, 'No.'"[403]

As he gained expertise in the field of *halakhah*, Walter became increasingly vocal in his call for personal restraint. In lectures and essays throughout his tenure as chair of the Responsa Committee, he made the case for using the Jewish legal process to guide religious practice within the Reform movement. He believed that liberal Judaism had always intended to create its own approach to Jewish law, one that would provide clear expectations to its followers but would also be flexible and open to change. Its failure to do so over its two centuries of existence, even as it had enthusiastically reformed other areas of Jewish life, was a result of its historic circumstances.

Walter often noted that liberal Judaism began with *responsa*, as the first generation of liberal scholars tried to defend their reforms using traditional legal methods. The curricula of the major liberal seminaries in Germany included a strong basis in rabbinic literature. These initial attempts to establish a rabbinic foundation for liberal Judaism had only floundered as the pace of change began to accelerate for Jewish communities in parts of Europe during the 19th century, as Walter explained in a lecture in February 1979. "When thousands were using streetcars on Shabbat, an essay justifying the practice was hardly necessary," he said. "The path then taken was akin to that of all revolutions: it began rather brusquely, pushed much aside, but always with the understanding that these areas were valuable and needed attention after the main struggle was won."[404] The struggle continued even after the revolution ended, as liberal Judaism fought for recognition in Europe and tried to gain steady footing in North America.

By the time Walter became chair of the Responsa Committee in 1977, liberal Judaism had undoubtedly gained steady footing in North America, where a majority of affiliated Jews were associated with the Reform, Conservative and Reconstructionist movements. It was now time, he believed, to revisit those practical aspects of Jewish law that had been abandoned during the early revolutionary days of the movement. In his 1979 speech, titled "The Roots of Reform *Halakhah*," he called on his colleagues to embrace the process of developing standards. He wanted the Reform movement to see *responsa* as more than a source of guidance. It was a step toward crafting a code of practice, just as centuries of oral tradition had preceded the first efforts to codify the law.[405]

Over the next decade, Walter developed this message in various settings. He delivered sermons about personal piety. He gave scholarly lectures analyzing the role Jewish law had played in some of the more radical moments in the history of the Reform movement, such as the creation of the Pittsburgh Platform. He increasingly argued that liberal *halakhah* was becoming less necessary for adapting an ancient religion to modern times than for "strengthening of Jewish ties in a secular age."[406]

Rounding the corner from loose guides to a firm code was beyond the purview of the Responsa Committee, which could only answer the questions it received. After a decade of darting from one question to another, Walter wanted the freedom to consider the entire endeavor of liberal *halakhah* more systematically and to delve more deeply into certain subjects. He began that process in 1987 by organizing a symposium on "Liberal Judaism and *Halakhah*" in honor of Dr. Freehof's ninety-fifth birthday. In a book of lectures collected from the symposium, he described the task ahead. "The nature and basis of Liberal Halakhah remains unclear," he wrote. "How does the *halakhah* influence other areas of Liberal Judaism? What developments can we expect in this field?"[407]

Eager to tackle those questions, Walter decided to form a new committee within the Central Conference of American Rabbis. It would prepare position papers on pressing subjects and would offer practical guidance on questions of modern observance. He ultimately decided it would be easier to work without the restraints inherent in a large institution. Partnering with Rabbi Moshe Zemer, an Israeli expert in liberal *halakhah*, he created an international research center dedicated to establishing an ideological basis for liberal *halakhah* and considering its application in modern life.[408] They initially called their center the Institute of Liberal Halakhah, but, after Dr. Freehof died in 1990, they changed the name to the Freehof Institute of Progressive Halakhah. Given the institutional independence of the Freehof Institute, Walter later grouped this endeavor with Horizon Homes and the Associated American Jewish Museums into the "broader role" of his rabbinate.

The work of the Freehof Institute was the next step for determining the "implicit theology" of liberal Judaism. By holding symposia and publishing essays, the institute encouraged scholars to search for patterns in the history of Jewish law, including its liberal manifestations. By the late 1980s, liberal Judaism had been in existence for nearly two centuries. For nearly half of that time, the Central Conference of American Rabbis had been using the Responsa Committee to consider religious questions from a liberal perspective. And since Dr. Freehof joined the committee after World War II, the committee had been using *responsa* to offer practical guidance for religious observance. The Reform movement in America was increasingly encouraging Jewish practice through recent books such as *Gates of Mitzvah*, which provided a framework for observance. Walter felt it was time to prepare a clear code of liberal Jewish practice.[409]

Walter used the introductions of his two collections of *responsa* to summarize these arguments and to propose some next steps. In *Contemporary American Reform Responsa*, from 1987, he expanded on

Dr. Freehof's famous terms, by claiming, "We are no longer satisfied with guidance but seek governance. It is the duty of liberal Jews to perform *mitzvoth* on a regular basis as a part of their life." He went even further in *New American Reform Responsa*, from 1992, and advocated for the Reform movement to set aside any reservations it had about encroaching on individual autonomy and to embrace a code of practice. Belonging to a community, he noted, involved a commitment to shared values. "We must be willing to give up a certain amount of autonomy to eliminate anarchy," he wrote.[410]

Walter stepped down as chair of the Responsa Committee in 1989, when he was elected vice president of the Central Conference of American Rabbis. He became president two years later. He used his leadership positions to advocate for liberal *halakhah* more broadly. In his acceptance speech as president of the Central Conference of American Rabbis, in June 1991, he challenged his colleagues to create greater unity within the Reform movement by establishing boundaries. He posed a series of questions: "What system of discipline shall we develop for our religious life? Can we redefine ourselves theologically? How can we strengthen the liberal elements in the other American Jewish religious movements?"[411]

In a newspaper interview toward the end of that year, he proposed *halakhah* as a tool for answering those questions. "We have autonomy and therefore we have chaos. We need a greater sense of discipline and sense of direction," he said. He argued that a liberal version of *halakhah* could provide that discipline and direction. The process would be slow and cautious. It might take a century or more to develop a comprehensive system. An important part of that process, he added, would be figuring out how binding any system of liberal *halakhah* should be. "It should be more than guidance and less than governance," he said. "It will be a guide to Reform Jewish life."[412]

Even as president, Walter continued to receive religious questions, although at a much slower pace than he had as chairman of the committee. He now had the luxury of answering those questions he wanted to answer and passing along the rest for the committee to consider. "As the number has diminished from the rather hectic pace of *sheelah* [questions] per week, it has been possible to look at the general nature of the questions and to think a bit more about the whole enterprise of writing Reform *responsa*," he told his colleagues in a Central Conference of American Rabbis newsletter. He had noticed a growing number of questions from professionals, particularly doctors and lawyers. These questions had less to do with ritual matters than with professional ethical dilemmas. He also noticed many questions from congregants who were curious about the origins of certain religious customs. He was heartened by this lay interest in Jewish law, custom and tradition.[413]

In his presidential address to the Central Conference of American Rabbis in June 1992, Walter made an unambiguous call for his rabbinic colleagues to serve that growing interest. The address, called "Standards Now," expanded his long-held belief that the Reform movement had been too lofty and vague in its early days. "We have a wonderful capacity for idealism and have demonstrated that through almost two centuries of Reform Jewish life, but it has been difficult for us to carry it into our daily life and so to make Reform Judaism live day by day. We have emphasized ritual at home and in the synagogue over our daily practice in the ordinary events of our lives," he said. Taking an example from the structure of the Sabbath service, where a reading from the legalistic Torah always preceded a reading from the idealistic Prophets, he called for coupling the prophetic message of the early reformers with a practical message of *halakhah*. In a section of Leviticus scheduled to be read that Saturday, he noted, "ringing statements like, 'love your neighbor as yourself,' have been preceded by specifics, 'you shall not steal,' 'you shall not defraud,' 'you shall not insult the deaf,' 'you shall not place a stumbling block before the blind.'"

The early idealism of the movement had produced loyalty and enthusiasm without direction, he said. The idea of using *responsa* for "guidance, not governance" had been an appropriate attitude when the movement was still debating the value and the purpose of crafting *halakhah* from a liberal perspective. But the time had come to convert those discussions and ideas into actions. "What differentiates a Reform Jewish physician from anyone else? What Reform Jewish path should an engineer, a chemist, a botanist, a geneticist, a homemaker, a lawyer, a business leader, take? Our Judaism needs to be spelled out in detail. We are not talking about *muser* but about *mitzvah*," he said, making a distinction between ethical imperatives and religious obligations. "We should be able to hand each professional a manual and set those kinds of standards for ourselves and for our people. Then we must go further and encompass every aspect of each life—what are the responsibilities of children to aged parents, of a couple to each other? Where are the boundaries between us and the non-Jewish world?" he asked.

Granting each individual total freedom to make all religious decisions was undermining the unity required for a shared vision. "When one joins a community, then a degree of autonomy is surrendered," he said. "In the case of our Reform Jewish communities, we demanded only a minimum of surrender and so received only a minimum of true communal involvement. The unspoken loyalty was present but the expression through action was often totally absent." The results might have been different if every rabbi had enough time to guide each congregant toward educated decisions, he suggested. But that was impossible in most congregations, and so, instead, the movement should provide a clear direction.

Setting standards would eventually lead to a theology, he said, allowing the movement to finally articulate the underlying principles it had struggled to define. The process of developing *halakhah* would reveal the divine principles that had been guiding decision-making all along. "Let 'standards now' be our motto," he concluded.[414]

Aside from a few private responses to Walter over the months that followed, the speech incited neither a groundswell of support nor any strong opposition. To begin the task he had proposed in his speech, he established a new Standards Committee within the Central Conference of American Rabbis and charged the committee with creating ethical standards for a variety of professions. The committee was appointed and met a few times but faded before making progress.[415]

Walter offered a final defense of his position in late 1995, in an article in *Reform Judaism* magazine with the blunt title "Liberal Judaism Needs Standards." He appeared to go one step farther than his earlier call for a code of religious practice. He now suggested that the Reform movement should also attempt to enforce its eventual code by encouraging communities to set expectations. He wrote, "Placing greater emphasis on community does not mean that the rights of individuals to differ and chart new paths ought to be curtailed. The Reform movement will always be open to new ideas, but if we must choose between a Reform Judaism that provides *guidance* or one that provides *governance*, the latter must be our path. Such a path requires that we adopt measurable religious standards for our leaders, board members, and all our congregants. Family as well as professional life should meet the standards we set. Those who wish to remain outside the system will need to work out their own rationale for their actions."[416] In earlier speeches, he had often noted the impossibility of enforcing rabbinic decrees in an open society. He now saw communal standards as a way to mimic the unquestioned authority of earlier generations.

Without the momentum to put these ideas into action through any of the official institutions of the Reform movement, the Freehof Institute became the forum where Walter developed his vision. Over the past twenty-five years, the institute has regularly hosted symposia at the annual meeting of the Central Conference of American Rabbis, collected its papers in book form and published a regular newsletter on Jewish law. From the beginning, Walter invited a variety of rabbis and scholars to contribute to the institute. He wanted to accumulate as wide a variety of learned ideas, opinions and approaches to *halakhah* as he could.

Early on, each symposium and subsequent book focused on subjects with long records in Jewish law to draw upon. These included death, fertility, Israel and the Diaspora, aging, crime and punishment, marriage, gender, the environment, poverty and charity, sexuality, and war and terrorism. As the list of obvious subjects shrank, Walter took the Freehof Institute in an increasingly creative direction. He asked contributors to use ancient Jewish tradition to consider inherently modern subjects such as addiction, new medical frontiers and the Internet. He published a book of essays about the influence of Napoleon on the development of Jewish law and another about the effects of American open society on Judaism.[417]

With this series, Walter has created what is likely the largest and certainly the most varied body of literature on the subject of *halakhah* from a liberal perspective. The influence of his work, though, is hard to measure. Subsequent chairmen of the Responsa Committee have advanced the goal of developing liberal *halakhah*. One even produced a guide to Jewish practice similar to the one Walter proposed in his "Standards Now" speech.[418] Despite these trends, religious obligation is a marginal idea within the American Reform movement. If the movement ever fully embraces liberal *halakhah*, Walter's work on the Responsa Committee and through the Freehof Institute would provide a ready foundation upon which to build. At the moment, his efforts seem to be having a greater influence in Central Europe, where he returned to spend the final decades of his career.

The Jacob family fled Germany
without ever abandoning it. Rabbi
Ernest Jacob maintained close
contact for years with many of
his former Augsburg congregants,
and is seen here with a globe
marking the new homes of his
"congregation in exile."

CHAPTER V

A Little Something

The Jacob family came to America with no expectation of someday returning to Germany. They saw no future for the Jewish people in Europe after the events they personally witnessed and the horrors they later discovered. In the final newsletter Ernest Jacob sent to his dispersed community, in 1949, he analyzed the mood of the country in the wake of its defeat and concluded, "But my own opinion is that the Germans' attitude towards the Jews is one of complete indifference and that now, in its misery, with everything it has coming to it, Germany will, thank God, be just as free of Jews as Hitler always wanted."[419] A revival was beyond his imagination.

Even though Ernest's harsh assessment suggested he was cutting ties with Germany, the Jacob family never lost the great affection it felt for its homeland. Annette continued to read the German poetry and literature she had loved since childhood, and she encouraged her two sons to maintain some fluency in the language, despite the shortage of opportunities to speak German in Missouri. Her appeals worked, and both boys maintained an intellectual interest in their heritage. Walter often steered his studies toward German history, such as his abandoned thesis on rabbis and teachers in Germany after emancipation and his eventual thesis on popular literature by German Jewish authors of that time. His brother Herbert followed a similar path. His first book of political science considered governmental structures in Germany after the chancellorship of Otto von Bismarck.[420] They both focused on the period of history between the unification of the German Empire in 1871 and the election of Hitler in 1933, an era when the prospects for a Jewish-German symbiosis were brightest.

Ernest devoted much of his limited free time to preserving the legacy of Benno Jacob, who had died in London shortly before the end of World War II with his Genesis commentary out of print, his Exodus commentary unpublished and his Leviticus commentary unfinished. Walter increasingly helped his father. Working through the mail and over the phone, they translated several essays into English and advanced to the Genesis commentary. When publishers were hesitant to release a thousand-page work of detailed biblical criticism, Ernest and Walter developed an abridged version. They removed most of the critical invective against the documentary hypothesis to create a small volume of scholarly insights that would be intelligible to lay readers. After more than a decade of work and inquiries to dozens of publishers, they finally convinced KTAV to publish their abridged translation in 1974, returning Benno Jacob's masterpiece to print after a forty-year absence.[421]

The duration of that hiatus was arbitrary but nevertheless meaningful. Forty years is the biblical definition of a generation. It marks the passage of leadership from parents to children. By the mid-1970s, the Jews who had escaped Germany as children were in the prime of their careers. They were leading many of the major institutions of the Reform movement in America, including the Hebrew Union College and the Union of American Hebrew Congregations. They were old enough to remember what had happened across Europe, but they were young enough to see possibilities ahead.

Walter revealed something of this spirit of hopefulness in 1969, in a review of *Legends of Our Time*, Elie Wiesel's memoir about learning to come to terms with the events of the Holocaust by confronting the past. In a Sunday lecture at Rodef Shalom, Walter described the book as "a theology in story," which was his way of distinguishing it from philosophical treatises on the subject of Jewish suffering. "How did Elie

Wiesel break the cycle and move from the desert to the good earth?" Walter asked. "He began by facing the problem intellectually and the situations psychically. He took those difficult trips back to Germany. He returned to the land of the concentration camp to see whether suffering, death and destruction had influenced the world. It was not easy and the disappointments of those journeys were great, for nothing had happened to those who had witnessed death."

Walter was particularly struck by a remarkable encounter described in the book. While riding a bus in Tel Aviv, Wiesel recognized a barracks chief from Auschwitz. He engaged the man, and their brief, tense conversation proved that the barracks chief remained trapped inside the private hell of his wartime experiences. "When Wiesel saw this he realized his own freedom," Walter said. "The confrontation had influenced his own inner being. The old fears were gone and he was able to face the present and future." Walter saw the encounter as an example of the two paths available to victims of tragedy: to stay in the past or to utilize it. When the story of the memoir continued to the Soviet Union, where Wiesel had been inspired to help persecuted Jews gain religious freedom, Walter noted, "He now deals less with the holocaust of the past, than with this oppressed community of our time."[422]

For decades, the only involvement Walter or Irene had with the official institutions of Germany were the compensation claims they filed with the government in the late 1950s.[423] In the mid-1970s, shortly after his parents died, Walter accepted an invitation to attend a rabbinic meeting in Germany, and he returned to the country for the first time since fleeing it in March 1939. He used the trip as an opportunity to revisit some of the places he had known so well in his youth, especially the Great Synagogue of Augsburg. As one of the few synagogues in the country to survive the war, it had passed through several incarnations since he had last seen it. In the summer of 1941, the municipal theater of Augsburg stored sets and backdrops in the main sanctuary. Toward the end of that year, the Nazis turned the holy building into a collection point for the deportation of Jews from throughout the Swabia region. German soldiers later converted the synagogue into a military outpost and attached anti-aircraft artillery on top of its dome. The building fell into disrepair, and when American troops entered the sanctuary after the war, they could see pigeons flying through holes in the shattered stained glass windows high above them.[424]

Augsburg developed two Jewish communities in the immediate aftermath of the war. The first was a small group of Germans who had managed to evade deportation and survived in hiding. The second was a much larger group of Eastern Europeans, mostly Poles, who arrived in the city from a nearby displaced persons camp. Even though the two communities officially merged, each resisted the ways and the customs of the other, and authorities eventually had to force the German contingent to grant full membership privileges and voting rights to the Eastern Europeans in the community. In those years, the Augsburg synagogue also became entangled in a long and precedent-setting lawsuit about the ownership of Jewish communal property in Germany after the war. These internal and external debates kept the Jewish community from being able to make any plans for the future of the synagogue. The building remained mostly unusable until late 1963, when the Jewish community converted the old weekday prayer room and the old wedding chapel into a small synagogue for weekday and Sabbath services.[425] By the mid-1970s, when Walter and Irene visited, the main sanctuary remained in much the same condition as it had been on the morning after Kristallnacht. Stepping into the grand room, Walter found it to be "still beautiful, though burned out and neglected." He was heartened by news that the community had begun an ambitious plan to restore the building and to turn one of the old residential wings into a museum that would tell the story of the Jewish people in Swabia.

Walter and Irene also visited the ancient city of Worms, where one of his ancestors had once served as rabbi. They toured the local synagogue and its Jewish cemetery. Both were the oldest of their kind in the country, built more than nine hundred years earlier. After returning from the trip, Walter delivered a Rosh Hashanah sermon at Rodef Shalom where he described the synagogue and its adjoining cemetery

The Great Synagogue of Augsburg,
designed as a statement of modernity,
is now a solemn and historic symbol
of survival, surrounded by newer
office buildings.

not as relics of a glorious Jewish past but as examples of the persistence of Jewish communities in the face of apparent ruin. "Jews have lived there from the Crusades to the Holocaust, through good and bad years. The names of most of the thousands buried there have lost significance but not the inscriptions. Some praised an individual distinguished for his charity, another for his piety, a third for his learning. Each generation gave the community dozens dedicated to Judaism in these ways," he said.[426] The Crusades or the Holocaust might have seemed at the time like being thrown off a cliff, but, looking back, they could prove to be valleys between great heights.

In the year after his homecoming to Germany, Walter delivered a sermon at Rodef Shalom about the progressive nature of civilizations. He criticized popular literature that ignored the difficult realities of places like small-town America or the Jewish shtetls of Eastern Europe in favor of an idealized and nostalgic tone. He contrasted those stories with the harsh early chapters of Genesis, where the idyll of Eden is brief and quickly undone by expulsion, fratricide and a world-destroying flood. "From the beginning, mankind has faced trouble and aggravation. Is it at all different in our current world? Has mankind improved or gotten worse?" he asked. "Perhaps the only difference lies in our facing those problems better than our ancestors. We are not only more sophisticated but also morally, spiritually better." Those early chapters of Genesis, he continued, described the gradual development of basic human virtues such as remorse, empathy and compassion. Adam and Eve felt only "the slightest twinge of conscience" for their actions in the garden. Ten generations later, Noah saved his family from the flood but made no attempt to appeal for the salvation of humanity. It took another ten generations before Abraham showed a new, higher degree of humanity by bargaining with God for the fate of Sodom and Gomorrah. "For the Bible there was no idealized past, just slow human progress from one generation to the next," Walter said.[427]

Walter offered similar sentiments in sermons and lectures throughout the 1970s and 1980s, as major anniversaries of important moments in the history of the Holocaust gave him opportunities to offer his perspective about those events. In a Sunday lecture at Rodef Shalom on the fortieth anniversary of Kristallnacht, in November 1978, he asked why the Holocaust had made such a deep impression on humanity, when so many other human tragedies were quickly forgotten. The reason, he argued, was that the events of those years had revealed three "key weaknesses of western life." The first was racism, which he described as the tendency of civilized societies to build complex philosophical structures to dignify their basest prejudices. The second was "excessive nationalism," which sought to elevate one group by oppressing other groups within its midst. The third was the failure of Christianity to prevent the catastrophe emerging across the continent, despite the moral imperatives of its teachings and the cultural dominance it enjoyed in Europe. Those three weaknesses seemed to be endemic to western life, Walter said, and the Holocaust had captivated the imagination of the public because it demonstrated "how easily we are led in the wrong direction."

He ended with an optimistic outlook. In the aftermath of World War II, he noted, the Jewish people could have abandoned the religious demands of Judaism entirely, or traded religion for nationalism and fled wholesale to the new Jewish State. They instead developed Israel while also strengthening Jewish life around the world, particularly in America. He even felt hopeful about Europe. "We have not taken up the cry of retribution, nor have we rejected all those who murdered or aided our persecutors," he said. "Now, a generation later, we have been quite willing to work with the Germans, to buy their products, to visit their land. We have considered it wrong to bear the spirit of vengeance into the future."[428]

He elaborated on this idea the following year in a sermon titled "Sympathy, But Not Sorrow." In it, he used the Exodus—the original tale of Jewish suffering at the hands of a cruel nation—to consider the growing trend of Holocaust remembrance, from plans to establish a national Holocaust memorial in Washington, D.C., to a popular Holocaust miniseries on television, to the hundreds of popular and scholarly books about the Holocaust. He worried about the effect of making the Holocaust a "leading motif" of Jewish history. "Despite short-term positive effects, we must wonder about the long-range implication. What will a center for the study of Judaism seen through the Holocaust portray? It will tell of suffering, misery and death. Is that really what we want to remember about the Jews of Poland, the Jews of Germany, and the rest of Europe? Their miserable death was the final chapter of centuries which produced good meaningful lives. We should recall their positive contributions to Judaism and the world; how they succeeded despite persecution for such a long time," he said. A nation was no different than an individual, he added. "If an individual dwells upon the disasters of his or her life, then by middle-age there will be enough to bring despair. Who wants to deal with such a gloomy, defeated individual?" When the Israelites left Egypt, he insisted, they also left behind their anger and bitterness over their slavery and looked toward a brighter future. "We should remember the suffering which has occurred," he concluded, "but only to awaken sympathy."[429]

Every time Walter returned to Augsburg, he first visited the concentration camp at Dachau, where his father and the other men of Augsburg had suffered or died for being Jews.[430] After paying his respects, he left behind any resentment he felt. He made this spirit of forgiveness explicit when he returned to Augsburg in September 1985 to participate in the rededication of the restored synagogue. The Jewish community had spent the previous decade restoring the original splendor of the main sanctuary and converting the street-level apartments into one of the first Jewish museums in the country. They rebuilt the charred pews, replaced the shattered stained glass windows and scrubbed the soot from the dome until its gold tiles sparkled again. They repaired the Jewish symbols affixed to the ledge of the balcony and the arch over the pulpit. They remained faithful to the original design in all but one respect. Where the grand organ originally stood as a symbol of Jewish liberalism, they instead placed a giant brass menorah. The members of the new community came from Poland and Russia and had no desire to hear organ music on the Sabbath.[431]

During the rededication ceremony, Walter stood at the high pulpit where he had presented his *Tora wimpel* as a small boy. He rekindled the eternal light above the ark and watched as the leaders of the community carried a few Torah scrolls into the sanctuary where dozens of scrolls had once been paraded during his youth. He later acknowledged that he "went with mixed emotions, but felt good about it afterwards." In his rededication address to a large audience including members of the Jewish community of Augsburg and dignitaries from the German government, he attributed those feelings to the passage of time. The ceremony was occurring forty years after the end of World War II, the same period that the Israelites had wandered through the desert before they entered the Promised Land. "A whole generation died in the wilderness. They were not spiritually mature enough to take possession of the land that God had promised them. Everything had to wait for the next generation," he said.

Any rabbi could have sensed the relevance of the anniversary. What made the sermon particular to Walter's sensibility was his willingness to include the Germans in his metaphor of a new generation seeking redemption. "Today we celebrate, also one generation later, and that's a good thing looking at it from both sides, the Jewish and the German," he said. "We Jews who have come together here today can look around without alarm. Everyone taking part here was born or grew up after the Nazi period. It's a generation that we feel comfortable with."[432]

These messages of hope and caution were extensions of the message of "personal piety" and religious obligation that Walter was promoting in other areas of his rabbinate. In a Rosh Hashanah sermon at Rodef Shalom, a few weeks after he returned from Augsburg in 1985, he described the rededication as the story of two men. The first was Julius Spokonjy, the president of the Augsburg congregation. Raised in Poland, Spokonjy was imprisoned during the Nazi occupation of his country. He had been shot and left to die in a crowded ditch but crawled to safety and survived the war by hiding in a forest. He arrived in Augsburg from a displaced persons camp, and when he saw the grand, neglected synagogue on a main street of his new city, he resolved to return the building to its original glory. He faced opposition not only from local government officials but also from within the Jewish community. He had succeeded through determination and resourcefulness, organizing a series of deals to finance the project. "A single man was able to make a difference; he could effect change in the community," Walter said. "If he could do this, why can not we? Each of us can accomplish so much, but we provide excuses. They come easily to us."

Walter also described his encounters with Hans Breuer, the mayor of Augsburg. "He dealt very frankly with the past as he reviewed the long Jewish history, all the persecutions which had occurred centuries ago and in our lifetime. He accepted the guilt of Germany and that of the generation of his parents. Nothing was glossed over or left unspoken," Walter said. Breuer felt empathy for Jewish suffering because he and his family had also been forced from their ancestral home, in Czechoslovakia, during the war. It was easy to reconcile with a fellow victim, Walter told his congregation, but what about persecutors? "Can we forgive the Germans?" he asked. "We should not even talk about it in that fashion. We can not discuss 'the Germans,' just as we do not want others to deal with 'the Jews.' Let us talk about individuals. Can we forgive them? Can we ever stretch out our hands honestly and sincerely?" If the answer was no, he reminded the congregation, was there any sense in asking God to forgive us during the High Holidays? "There is only one standard for God, for Jews, for Germans. The magnitude of sin may be different, but the standard remains."[433]

Walter and Irene returned to Germany again in November 1988, to commemorate the fiftieth anniversary of Kristallnacht. They arrived at their hotel to find a letter waiting for them from Walter's childhood maid in Augsburg. "This lady wanted to reestablish some contact and also explain what she and her family had done during the war," Walter explained in a sermon at Rodef Shalom. In a private letter to members of his family, a few days later, he added some details about the meeting. "This lady and her husband live in retirement in a simple apartment. They wanted to avoid discussions of persecution and war, but their daughter, who was visiting from Munich, insisted on covering the subject. The clash of generations was interesting," Walter wrote with his flair for understatement.

Witnessing this "clash of generations" bolstered the sense of openness and opportunity Walter felt as a new generation came of age in Germany. The country was home to only about forty thousand Jews at the time, and yet Walter and Irene saw reminders of the anniversary everywhere they went—in newspaper articles, in bookstore displays, at public commemorations. While attending one of these commemorations, Walter also saw an example of the ways the past could be revised as memories moved into history. In the keynote address, a high-ranking German diplomat spoke of his sorrow for the past, but he blamed the worst evils of those years on economic insecurity, social ills and an overwhelmingly powerful authoritarian regime.[434]

Hearing those excuses inspired Walter to add "some rather sharp remarks" to the speech he had prepared for a commemoration service in Augsburg the following evening.[435] What the events of the Holocaust laid bare, he insisted, were the failings of individual people in a civilized society. "We have learned that many Germans felt shame in 1938. Private feelings of shame are good for the conscience, but otherwise they do not help," he said. Neither did the centuries of culture and philosophy, which were often "a thin veneer, as thin as human skin" and had little to do with basic goodness and humanity. "The greatest Jewish figures of the past who advanced our religion were not philosophers but men and women who bore religion into their daily life," he continued. "That remains one of the grand teachings of the patriarchal tales of Abraham, Isaac and Jacob. They were not saints or prophets but men for whom God and religion existed. They were individuals with problems, with families in which not everything went well. They lived through economical difficulties yet they were open to the word of God. They heard and followed the eternal God. This was not their entire life but a significant portion of it. Such individuals could speak with God and could plead for Sodom and Gomorrah. Abraham was filled with concern for his fellow human beings and he feared no one, so he spoke up. Did such possibilities exist in Germany in 1938? Could anyone have said no to Hitler?"

Shifting from preacher to historian, Walter reviewed the responses to Nazism. Bulgaria and Finland had both resisted the call for deportation, and their Jewish communities largely survived the war. Hungary had also resisted for a time, despite its own deep antagonism toward its Jews. Even in Germany, he continued, individual men and women had resisted Nazism in ways large and small. He recalled the milkman who had slipped through the jeering crowd on the morning after Kristallnacht to make his usual delivery. "That was a simple good man and we must have more of them," he said.[436]

Reaction to the speech was "mixed," Walter acknowledged later. His last-minute additions were "not particularly popular." And he "may have threatened some Christian theological concerns" with the rest of his speech, which insisted that "God's ancient covenant" with the Jewish people remained intact, despite the catastrophe. His forcefulness was an attempt to lift the veil of tragedy from the story of the Jewish people. Walter felt it was important to present a hopeful vision of Judaism, especially for the many younger people in attendance. He was pleased that a march to the Augsburg city square, after the commemoration service, ended not with prayers of mourning but with an old French ghetto song of defiance followed by the Israeli national anthem. "Our commemoration therefore concluded on a positive note which looked toward the future of the people of Israel, of Jews and Judaism," he said.[437]

The Berlin Wall fell exactly one year to the day after Walter delivered his address in Augsburg. In the years that followed, as the Cold War ended and the map of Europe changed, thousands of Soviet Jews immigrated to Germany and joined existing Jewish communities. This migration occurred as Walter was rising through the ranks of the Central Conference of American Rabbis, and he made it one of the themes of his presidency. He wanted his colleagues to pay more attention to the many small liberal Jewish communities outside the United States. The membership of the Conference included dozens of rabbis from Reform congregations across Canada and a smaller but still significant number from congregations throughout Central and South America. By chance, the two conventions during his presidency were in San Antonio and Montreal, which gave him an opportunity to look across the borders. At the Texas convention, he gave the first paragraph of his presidential address in Spanish. In Quebec, he used French. "I didn't translate it," he said. "If you got it, you got it. If not, it's too bad."[438]

Walter devoted a large portion of his second and final presidential address, in June 1993, to the global responsibilities of the Reform movement. He wanted his colleagues to think beyond North America, and also beyond Israel. He challenged the idea that Israel offered a level of Jewish authenticity not found anywhere else in the world. "We need to begin to change this view. We do not really feel that life in the Diaspora is second best and not as productive as Israel," he said. "As we look at the creativity of Jews outside the land, we should begin with the Torah, which came from the desert not Israel, and we may continue with the later books of the Bible and, of course, the Talmud and so much else. Intellectually the Diaspora has been as creative as Israel, perhaps more so." Taking a broader view of Jewish authenticity would also help Israel, he believed. He argued that removing the messianic halo that had surrounded the Jewish State since its establishment in the aftermath of World War II would free the Israeli people to be judged by the same standards applied to every other nation.[439]

Throughout his career, Walter took a measured approach toward Israel. In many ways, he introduced Zionism to Rodef Shalom, not only through symbolic actions such as bringing an Israeli flag onto the pulpit but also through larger activities, such as leading the first congregational visits to the country. Either of those gestures would have been unthinkable under his predecessors.[440] He also regularly addressed the political and spiritual circumstances of Israel. He used the freedom of the pulpit at Rodef Shalom to vigorously defend Israel against charges of racism and to oppose specific American policies toward the country, such as President George H. W. Bush's rejection of a loan guarantee package to Israel in 1991.[441] He also openly challenged certain Israeli policies, often described regional conflicts from both a Jewish and a Palestinian perspective and regularly called for Israeli politicians to make a greater effort toward the cause of peace in the region.[442] From his earliest days as senior rabbi, Walter called for Israel to recognize the Reform movement as an equal branch within Judaism. He asked his congregation to actively support liberal Jewish institutions when they visited the country.[443] He later represented the Reform movement on the Ad Hoc Committee on Gerut and undertook a series of ultimately unsuccessful negotiations with Conservative and Orthodox rabbinic authorities to establish a common standard of conversion in Israeli law.[444]

When he discussed Israel from the pulpit, Walter tried to separate the religious ambitions of the Jewish people from their aspirations for nationhood. He clearly valued the former over the latter. He often described Zionism as a messianic impulse, born from the same cultural ferment responsible for the prophetic impulse within liberal Judaism. Too many Jews used their support for the country as a proxy for religious observance, he believed, when Israel was, in fact, simply a secular state.[445] His position recalled the militantly anti-Zionist stance of his grandfather Benno Jacob in the late-19th century, when the creation of the Jewish State was simply an idea, and arguments against it were entirely intellectual. "The Zionists replace the Temple by Palestine," Benno once wrote.[446] Walter softened that stance to accommodate the successes of the Jewish State, which his grandfather did not live to see. Walter later attributed some of his broadened perspective to Irene, who had eagerly moved to Israel in its earliest years because she admired the courage and energy of its citizens.[447]

The nuanced views Walter held about Israel reflected his ambivalence about nationalism. In a lecture on the subject at the University of Pittsburgh, in 1984, he described nationalism both positively and negatively. It could provide "ethnic identity, an outlet for creativity and for group diversity," and it could also foster "xenophobia with its intense hatred of the outsider." Jews were as susceptible to these dangers as any other group, he noted, and not only in the case of Jewish nationalism. His parents and his grandparents were among the Jews who embraced German and Prussian nationalism during World War I.[448] After watching the movie *Downfall*, a fictional account of the events leading to the military defeat of the Nazis at the end of World War II, Walter posed a troubling hypothetical question in his weekly family letter. "One wonders how we would have reacted to some of this and earlier moves on his part, if Hitler had not been anti-Semitic," he wrote.[449] Walter has often described liberal Judaism as a system for adapting the religion to different settings, which could be seen as his way of enjoying the beneficial qualities of nationalism while avoiding the features he felt were detrimental. His advocacy for the Diaspora was, at its heart, an expression of the idea that Judaism belonged wherever Jews chose to live.

By the early 1990s, Jews were once again choosing to live in Central Europe. In his final presidential address to the Central Conference of American Rabbis, Walter said that the established Reform institutions across North America needed to do more to help these burgeoning Jewish communities in Europe. France had nearly half a million Jewish citizens and only a few liberal congregations. Germany had more than one hundred thousand Jews in its midst, and almost no liberal congregations. The millions of Jews emerging from Communism in the eastern half of the continent had almost no religious infrastructure, liberal or otherwise. "There are no Liberal Jewish communities because our movement in America has not done what it should have done," he said.[450]

The demands of the presidency during a period of budgetary restraint prevented Walter from devoting much energy to that cause during his two-year term, but he took a few practical steps. One was to commission translations of Reform prayer books into Russian and French. His simple idea, involving a small team and a modest budget, had the potential to expand the reach of Reform liturgy to hundreds of thousands of people. But the Russian venture stalled when it came to distribution, and the French translation was never completed. The fate

As he rose through the Central
Conference of American Rabbis,
Walter attended more meetings
than he might have preferred
and found ways to pass the time.

of those two projects, he said, highlighted the risk of taking on a project energetically and unilaterally, without acquiring firm institutional support.[451] That said, he kept doing things unilaterally anyway.

In his address, Walter asked younger rabbis to devote a few years of their apprenticeship and older rabbis to set aside a portion of their retirements to help these growing Jewish communities throughout Europe.[452] His appeal did not inspire his colleagues to travel overseas in large numbers. But when he had the opportunity to do so, he took it, and his actions had a far greater influence than his words.

The opportunity presented itself in November 1995, when Walter and Irene accepted an invitation to attend a meeting of emerging liberal Jewish congregations from German-speaking countries in Central Europe. The World Union of Progressive Judaism had arranged the "study seminar" as a pressure-free way to unite the small but growing collection of liberal-minded groups in Germany, Switzerland and Austria. About one hundred and fifty people from twelve formal congregations and informal prayer groups met at a former palace on the outskirts of Vienna to pray, to study and to discuss the future of liberal Judaism in the section of Europe where it had emerged centuries earlier.[453]

By the early decades of the 20th century, liberal Judaism had become the dominant form of the religion in Central Europe. Most of the Jewish *gemeinde*, or citywide communities, throughout the region had voluntarily chosen liberalism, and they accommodated the smaller traditional segments within their midst. The peaceful coexistence between the large liberal congregation in Augsburg and the smaller traditional congregation in nearby Kriegshaber was a noteworthy example of a situation occurring throughout the region. After the war, Jews arriving in the country from displaced persons camps rebuilt the religion according to the traditional customs they had known from their youth in Eastern Europe, and traditional Judaism once again became dominant across Germany.

The migrations across Europe following the Cold War shifted the balance again. A liberal minority was emerging in response to the traditional establishment. Over the course of the weekend, as Walter listened to people from these communities describe their difficulties navigating governmental bureaucracies, he heard echoes of the original battles liberal Judaism had fought with traditional religious authorities in the early 19th century. The Jewish establishment was reluctant to accept Russian immigrants who could not conclusively prove their Jewish identities and was even more reluctant to approve conversions. The liberal communities were eager to serve Jews who were stuck in religious limbo, as well as those who wanted more social involvement. But the liberal communities were also highly decentralized. Only a few congregations were official state-sanctioned *gemeinde*, eligible for public funds. The majority were *havurot*, or informal religious fellowships working entirely outside of the official system.[454]

As with the initial generation of liberal Jews, the current group was mostly lay-led. They welcomed sporadic visits from itinerant rabbis, but they craved permanent spiritual leadership. The seminar was an opportunity for the international institutions of liberal Judaism to present their best face to potential members. One star of the weekend was Rabbi Tovia Ben Chorin, who was born in Jerusalem in 1936 to recent refugees from Germany. He announced plans to relocate to Zurich and lead the largest of the new liberal congregations. In describing the seminar in a letter to his family, Walter praised Rabbi Ben Chorin and added, "He can provide leadership for this group — they need an Isaac Meyer Wise!"[455]

With this reference to the foremost organizer of the Reform movement in America in the late 19th century, Walter unwittingly predicted the role he himself would play in the region over the coming decades. One of the organizers of the seminar spotted this quality immediately, and later described Walter as "more of an eminence grise" than the other presenters on the agenda. Walter and Irene, he added, "considered themselves on the hustings, and enjoyed it. People enjoyed them too." Walter spent much of the weekend getting to know as many of the participants as he could. His study session on "Progressive Judaism and Halakhah" had the highest attendance of any event that weekend.[456]

By the end of the gathering, the communities felt a sense of common cause and were eager to organize. They made plans to form an umbrella group. Several enthusiastic lay leaders had decided to train for the rabbinate at the Leo Baeck College in London. But those efforts would take years to reach fruition, and Walter believed that the communities needed immediate resources. "From us they need visiting rabbis and the long term loan of Torah," he noted. "I am working on both."[457]

Walter retired from Rodef Shalom at the end of 1996. His good health and high energy led many congregants to question his decision. "Some people have trouble seeing all the other things in which I am involved," he explained in his weekly letter to family.[458] The "other things" included some of the traditional pastimes of retirement. Walter was a new grandfather. Kenney had a son, Zachary, in 1995 and a daughter, Madeleine, in 1997. A third grandchild came into the family in 1999, when Daniel married a woman who had a teenage daughter, Bari, from a previous marriage. At the time Zachary was born, Kenney had recently moved to Ohio to take a position as a synagogue administrator. In a letter to his newborn grandson, Walter wrote, "It is Friday afternoon and time to get ready for Shabbat. That is the day when all Jews except rabbis and Temple Administrators do not work. Work is what you do when you don't sleep—at least most of it. I know this is confusing as you only sleep and eat—you can continue eating on Shabbat. Consider it a *responsum*."[459]

The joke contained a kernel of truth. Walter used the newly acquired free time of his retirement to travel more frequently with Irene and to watch more movies after dinner, but, in general, he treated his retirement as an opportunity to shift the balance of his busy schedule away from the daily responsibilities of leading a congregation and toward the "broader role" of being a rabbi. Those voluntary communal ventures included the temporary exhibits at the Rodef Shalom Gallery and the traveling exhibits of the Associated American Jewish Museums, and also the symposia and books of the Freehof Institute of Progressive Halakhah.

They also included his ongoing effort to preserve Benno Jacob's legacy. After Ernest died in 1974, Walter continued this task alone. Working in a piecemeal fashion over eight years, whenever he had a few minutes to spare, he translated the entire thousand-plus-page Exodus commentary into English. Today he is quick to note that he could have finished it sooner, if not for his congregational responsibilities.[460] He used the momentum surrounding the publication of the translation in 1992 to launch several related ventures, including scholarly symposia and new translation projects.

These projects, and the ongoing work to maintain the Biblical Botanical Garden at Rodef Shalom and his private garden at home, were enough to fill his schedule. But after returning from the seminar in Vienna, he added another project to this list. He began looking for practical ways to advance liberal Judaism throughout Central Europe.

One of the lay leaders at the Vienna seminar was a young man named Walter Homolka. As a West German university student in the early 1980s, Homolka had developed a scholarly interest in Jewish law and sent an inquiry to Walter Jacob, in his capacity as chairman of the Responsa Committee. They first met in person in 1985, when Walter Jacob came to Germany to rededicate the Augsburg synagogue, and they maintained a correspondence over the years, as Homolka focused his university studies on theology, began to organize communal endeavors in Munich and eventually decided to apply to rabbinical schools.[461]

Homolka was a non-traditional candidate for a liberal rabbinical school. He was a recent convert to Judaism, living in a large country with a small Jewish population that, at the time, had almost no liberal element. His youth offered few opportunities for Jewish education before he enrolled in a Jewish Studies program at a German university. He had high marks, but both the Hebrew Union College in Cincinnati and Leo Baeck College in London were reluctant to accept his pre-existing credits and were skeptical of his background and temperament.[462]

Walter Jacob, however, was impressed with Homolka and spent more than two years advocating on his behalf to the heads of liberal

Jewish organizations.[463] He argued that West Germany was unlikely to produce another prospective young liberal rabbinical student as capable and enthusiastic anytime soon, and that the movement would be wise to find a way to accommodate the non-traditional student, rather than to insist on strictly adhering to policy. In a letter to Gerard Daniel, who was then president of the World Union for Progressive Judaism, Walter wrote, "It seems to me that an able young man like this one should be given an opportunity to study for the rabbinate even if it is unclear how he may serve the Jewish people subsequently. You may be perfectly right that he would not be appropriate for the German Jewish community as it is presently constituted. On the other hand, he may develop into just the ideal rabbi for them. I wonder how someone might have judged my abilities at the time when I was entering the Hebrew Union College, and it hardly seems fair to do so with young Homolka now."[464]

The appeal worked, and the Leo Baeck College accepted Homolka as a student in the spring of 1986. But other complications soon emerged. In his first year of rabbinical school in London, Homolka realized he was gay, and his subsequent effort to understand the ramifications of his circumstances led him to the *responsum* that Walter wrote in 1981 against gays and lesbians holding leadership positions within congregations. Taking the message to heart, Homolka quit rabbinical school. At the time, he explained his decision as a simple change of heart about entering the rabbinate. He has since been open about the true nature of his decision but has never discussed the matter with his mentor. "I learned from him also that you don't have to talk about everything all the time," Homolka said.[465]

Instead of entering the rabbinate, Homolka became a committed member of a new liberal congregation in Munich called Beth Shalom. The congregation emerged after the closure of American military installations throughout the country at the end of the Cold War. The withdrawal of the US Army from Munich deprived a group of liberally minded American Jewish ex-pats living in the city of regular religious services and classes led by a military chaplain. To continue their religious pursuits in the manner they preferred, these families

Walter graduated from college the
same year his young brother Herbert
graduated from high school. Their
parents both taught at Drury College,
leading the entire family to be dressed
in academic robes on graduation day.
Walter took the robes out of storage
when he installed Dr. Walter Homolka
as the new rabbi of Beth Shalom, a
liberal congregation in Munich.

started a Sunday School and later a prayer group. It quickly expanded, becoming a new congregation organized outside of the state structure. Several German-born Jews joined, Homolka among them.[466]

At the meeting in Vienna, Homolka asked Walter to help Beth Shalom establish the routines and infrastructure of congregational life. "It soon became apparent that if you wanted to do this, you needed to have some sort of standing in Germany," Walter explained. To gain this standing, Walter agreed to serve as the *Oberrabbiner*, or chief rabbi, of Beth Shalom Congregation.[467] By accepting the position, he unexpectedly and unassumingly became the sixteenth generation in his family to serve in the rabbinate in Central Europe, fulfilling the potential that had seemingly been stolen from him and his family when they fled the country.

Working pro bono, Walter traveled to Munich with Irene every few months to provide spiritual leadership for the congregation. By extension, he also provided practical organizational leadership for the wider movement to re-establish liberal Judaism throughout Central Europe. He led services and taught classes. He secured a Torah scroll for the congregation by borrowing one from Rodef Shalom in Pittsburgh. He also helped the group in Munich establish the basic elements of communal life, from leading conversion classes, to assembling a religious library, to helping create the umbrella association that would allow liberal congregations to petition the government with a single voice.[468]

Walter declined to move to Munich. From the beginning, he saw his position as a temporary solution until the congregation could find a committed liberal rabbi who understood local culture, language and politics. Given the pressing need, Homolka decided to complete the rabbinic training he had started a decade earlier. By 1997, the Reform movement in America was changing its position on questions of homosexuality and leadership. The report of the Ad Hoc Committee on Homosexuality and the Rabbinate in 1990 had recommended that Hebrew Union College both admit and ordain openly gay and lesbian rabbinical students. Over the following decade, other organizations passed resolutions in a similar spirit.

Homolka still represented an unusual case academically. The Hebrew Union College and the Leo Baeck College were both still hesitant to accept his existing credits from German universities, and Homolka thought it was unreasonable to be expected to repeat several years of schooling to satisfy their bureaucratic concerns. Eventually, Leo Baeck College agreed to a compromise. They would endorse his ordination but would not perform it.[469]

To resolve this discrepancy, Walter organized a private ordination. The process of an elder teacher conferring the title of "rabbi" upon a worthy student can be traced to biblical times, when Moses appointed Joshua as his successor by laying his hands upon his protégé before the high priest and the assembly. Over several centuries, rabbinic ordination became an institutional responsibility, and private ordination was increasingly viewed with suspicion. By the late 20th century, most rabbis throughout the world were trained and ordained at rabbinic seminaries, not in private ceremonies.

Walter was open to alternatives. Asked in late 1992 for his thoughts on private ordination, he declined to either approve or reject the practice outright. He instead described rabbinic ordination as a system for maintaining high standards within the profession. Students at the Hebrew Union College and the Leo Baeck College were trained with the needs of liberal Judaism in mind. When graduates of Reconstructionist, Conservative or Orthodox seminaries sought ordination within the Reform movement, he noted, they were examined not only for their Jewish knowledge but also for their particular outlook toward Judaism. "Through this we have sought to retain high standards which we feel are necessary for the rabbinate," he wrote.[470]

After responding to the question privately, Walter passed it along to the Responsa Committee for a more thorough consideration. The committee strongly opposed private ordination, concluding that it "undermines the process by which we educate our rabbis and judge their fitness to serve in that position, endangers the survival of our rabbinical schools, and constitutes an affront to the honor of those who taught us Torah. It cannot be justified within our community, and those rabbis who engage in it do a profound disservice to the Reform rabbinate and to Reform Judaism as a whole."[471]

A few years later, in 1995, the leadership of the Central Conference of American Rabbis asked Walter to consider the matter of private ordination in his role as chairman of the new Standards Committee. They thought it would be useful for the Conference to bolster the advisory decision of the Responsa Committee by officially condemning the practice among its members. Again, Walter remained cautious. "There is, after all, a very long history of private ordination and in essence any modern response to this issue would need to say that we have changed our position due to different circumstances, but that is about as far as one would be able to go," he replied.[472] His nuanced position preserved the authority of rabbinic seminaries while accommodating students like Homolka, who met the standards of the profession but fell short of the expectations of the existing rabbinic seminaries.

Walter understood the usefulness of private ordination in certain situations because of his grandfather Benno Jacob's experience. After the dean of the Jewish Theological Seminary in Breslau had refused to sign his ordination papers, Benno turned to a special council of rabbis. In that case, the complication involved a personal dispute between an administrator and a strong-willed student. The complication for rabbinical students such as Homolka arose from a misalignment of the needs of emerging Jewish communities and the policies of established Jewish institutions. Walter believed that allowing private ordination in special cases could satisfy all parties without degrading the standards of the rabbinate. Thinking back on the debate of those years, Homolka said, "Walter Jacob is, in very inconspicuous terms, a very courageous person. He analyzes a situation and then he just deals with it. He may ask for permission. If he doesn't get the permission, he carries on anyway. He's polite but he's certainly very clear."[473]

Agreeing to serve as the rabbi of Beth Shalom in a part-time capacity allowed Walter to maintain the flexibility of his schedule. His first year of retirement included world travels for professional and personal reasons. On a lark, he agreed to be the chaplain for a luxury cruise liner sailing the seas during the week of Passover. He and Irene departed for the trip two weeks early and used the time to explore corners of the South Pacific that Walter had failed to visit as a freshly ordained rabbi in 1955.[474]

They also traveled across North America, both to visit family and friends and to attend symposia and conferences. Walter used these trips to garner support for the liberal congregations emerging throughout Central Europe. One challenge he had accepted for himself after the Vienna seminar was to find Torah scrolls for those congregations. He did this by asking established Reform congregations across the United States to lend extra Torah scrolls to these new liberal congregations in Central Europe. The European congregation would use the borrowed scroll until it could afford to buy one and would pass it along to another congregation. He presented this system as an inverse of the early days of the American Reform movement. "As you remember, Reform Judaism began in Germany and German congregations were immensely helpful to their American counterparts," he wrote in a request to his cousins in St. Joseph, Missouri. "Many of our Torahs were brought over to new struggling American congregations. It would be wonderful to reciprocate now by helping them get underway."[475]

Walter made similar use of opportunities available to him in Pittsburgh. Rodef Shalom organized a symposium in his honor in June 1997, to mark his recent retirement. The idea came from Herbert Jacob, who thought it would be more appropriate to present a retiring rabbi with scholarship, instead of a gold watch. Herbert was diagnosed with an aggressive form of cancer and died before planning began, but a small group from his congregation in Illinois and from Rodef Shalom took over the project. They asked a group of Walter's friends, family, colleagues and students to deliver lectures on his favorite subjects, including Jewish law, the history of liberal Judaism, Jewish-Christian relations and, of course, gardening.[476]

The symposium brought people to Pittsburgh from around the world, which meant that all the parties needed to ordain Walter Homolka were assembled in one place. And so, after the scheduled events had concluded, Walter and two other rabbis performed a small private ordination service. A few weeks later, Walter Jacob traveled to Germany to install Homolka as his successor as the rabbi of Congregation Beth Shalom in Munich. Before the trip, he went into his attic and found his parents' old academic robes from their days as professors at Drury College. During the installation, he wore his mother's robe and lent his father's to Homolka.[477]

As part of the schedule of events surrounding the installation ceremony, the group of liberal congregations from the Vienna seminar officially formed the Union of Progressive Jews in Germany, Austria and Switzerland. The umbrella organization would oversee religious school curricula, help match rabbis with congregations and advocate for liberal Judaism nationally and internationally. The group had been working informally for months and had already completed a translation of an existing liberal prayer book into German. "The whole thing was done in a year! Usually such projects take a decade," Walter wrote admiringly in his family letter.[478] With the prayer book complete, the group was now translating a liberal Passover haggadah.

Walter appreciated this fortitude. Describing the inaugural meeting of the group, he wrote, "As usual there is the debate between those who wish to move slowly and cautiously and those who want to proceed. I am with the latter and we are going in that direction. My motto and fortunately that of Homolka is proceed while others debate and soon the subject of the debate will be obsolete."[479] Walter returned to Munich toward the end of that year, when the World Union of Progressive Judaism held its biennial conference in the city. It was the first such meeting of the group on the European continent since its inaugural convention in Berlin in 1928—another sign of revitalization in Germany.[480]

This spirit of renewal carried into his personal affairs, too. "It is strange," he wrote to a cousin after he returned to Pittsburgh and contemplated his first year of retirement, "but in this year I have revisited all the places where I have lived—Augsburg, London, St. Joseph and

Springfield—not quite as I did not return to the Philippines. There were also opportunities to see most of the family here and in Israel, plus a host of friends. It was more traveling than at any time since my stint in the chaplaincy."[481]

In addition to all the traveling, Walter had advanced many other interests during the year. He launched a series of projects to make Benno Jacob's work more accessible—publishing the original unabridged German version of the Genesis commentary, translating the Hebrew version of the entire Genesis commentary, and organizing symposia to encourage younger scholars who were just discovering the commentaries. He was also continuing the work of the Freehof Institute of Progressive Halakhah. He organized four symposia and edited two volumes of scholarly essays during his first year of retirement, and he expected to maintain a similar pace going forward. At the same time, he oversaw three nationally touring exhibits and two symposia for the Associated American Jewish Museums and published three issues of its newsletter devoted to Jewish art and architecture.[482]

Walter kept to his usual routines on his stops in Pittsburgh during the course of the year. An unexpected late-spring cold snap forced him and Irene to remove all the plants from the Biblical Botanical Garden and replant them all just a few days later, in time for the garden to open. They did the same thing with their garden at home.[483] Despite their many obligations, Walter and Irene visited just as many museums and attended just as many concerts as they had in calmer years, and Walter still paid regular calls to some of his former congregants, especially the housebound elderly among them. Looking ahead, he expected the coming year to be "a little less hectic, but just as full," adding, "As long as one is blessed with health and energy, one should do a little something."[484]

With the new Union of Progressive Jews in place, Walter Jacob and Walter Homolka turned their attention to addressing the lack of liberal Jewish leadership in the region. About three years after the Vienna seminar, there were some forty liberal Jewish groups in Central Europe.[485] Their lay leaders were largely self-taught and craved training, and all of the groups except those in a few major cities needed permanent rabbis.[486] Walter was reluctant to rely on the existing liberal rabbinic seminaries to provide leadership. Sending prospective rabbinical students to the Leo Baeck College in London or the American campuses of Hebrew Union College would take leaders away from their congregations for years. Some might not return.[487] Beyond those practical considerations and concerns lay a deeper conviction about the nature of the rabbinate. Walter believed that rabbis would serve their congregations best if their training had been specifically designed to address the circumstances of the communities they would be leading. "These people are going to be serving congregations largely in Central and Eastern Europe. So why cart them off to England?" he asked.[488]

Walter assumed it would take a decade to develop a rabbinic training program in Germany. In the interim, he privately appealed to leaders within the Reform movement in America to take an active interest in lay leaders and prospective rabbinical students from Europe. He wanted to create a mentorship program with "philosophical depth," as opposed to the "practical" training these students might receive in an "American para-rabbinic course." In 1998, he asked the Union of American Hebrew Congregations to allow a group of German congregational leaders to spend a month at Jewish summer camps across the United States, where they would have an opportunity to soak up the "intense, self-confident American Reform setting."[489]

When the project failed to come together as he had hoped, he created a "leadership training" program on his own, in Pittsburgh. The program was both scholarly and organizational. Students spent their mornings studying with Reform rabbis from across the Pittsburgh area and their afternoons hearing presentations from many of the major Jewish organizations in the city. They also received an introduction to Jewish liturgical music from Mimi Lerner, a mezzo-soprano who was also a beloved cantorial soloist at Rodef Shalom. Walter called on the entire congregation to help. Rodef Shalom members housed and fed the students. The Junior Congregation arranged social activities. The Sisterhood financed a trip to Washington, D.C., where the group spent time at the Religious Action Center of Reform Judaism and the United States Holocaust Memorial Museum. Other than air travel between Europe and Pittsburgh, all costs were covered.[490]

As planning for the leadership program was underway, Walter Jacob and Walter Homolka also figured out how to create their rabbinic training program in Germany without incurring the expense of developing a new academic institution from scratch. As many as thirty-four public universities throughout the country already offered courses in Jewish studies, and many of those universities also had extensive departments where students could study the basic texts they would encounter at any of the existing liberal rabbinic seminaries. By creating a curriculum within those existing university offerings, they could start training students with minimal overhead. And because the state-owned higher education system was free, students enrolled in the program would not have to pay tuition.[491]

Walter Jacob and Walter Homolka proposed the program as a partnership with the University of Potsdam, which had one of the largest Jewish Studies departments in the country and a good Jewish library. With this solution, they would be able to open their "Seminary Without Walls" for a little more than $25,000.[492] They developed the program together. As rector of the college, Walter Homolka chartered the school, organized the board and negotiated an agreement with the University of Potsdam. As president, Walter Jacob garnered support from major Reform and Reconstructionist institutions in America. To help raise funds and promote the endeavor, he created a tax-exempt charity called the American Friends of the Union of Progressive Jews in Germany, Austria and Switzerland. He assembled an eleven-member advisory board consisting of "virtually all American rabbis who had been educated in pre-war Central Europe," including Hebrew Union College Chancellor Rabbi Alfred Gottschalk, former Union of American Hebrew Congregations President Rabbi Alexander M. Schindler,

Responsa Committee Chairman Rabbi W. Gunther Plaut and Hebrew Union College Professor of Jewish History Michael Meyer.[493] "So that you had stationery you could send out with some impressive names on it," he said.[494] Walter assumed many of the practical responsibilities for this organization. Working either from his home office or from the small study he still kept at Rodef Shalom, he scheduled fundraising meetings and handled administrative tasks such as filing annual reports and writing thank-you notes.

In the final days of the "leadership training" program in Pittsburgh, in August 1999, Walter Jacob and Walter Homolka officially announced their new seminary.[495] They named their school the Abraham Geiger College after the 19th century German rabbi known as "the founding father of the Reform movement." Abraham Geiger helped start the *Jüdisches Theologisches Seminar* in Breslau and led the *Hochschule für Jüdische Wissenschaft* in Berlin. He was an early proponent of social justice, equal rights for women and dialogue with other faiths.[496] He was a radical thinker but a moderate reformer. As a scholar, he applied the scientific methods of the German academy to the study of Jewish history. As a pulpit rabbi, he understood the value of tradition and custom in leading a congregation. He wanted Judaism to adapt to the modern world but was willing to temper this desire in the face of reality. He fostered changes desired by congregants, rather than imposing changes.[497]

Those qualities made Geiger an ideal model for the seminary Walter Jacob and Walter Homolka were trying to create. They wanted their rabbinical school to be rigorous in its scholarship and practical in its outlook. After sending out a press release announcing the founding of the college, they opened a bottle of champagne to accompany their lunch and quickly got back to work.[498] They needed to continue fundraising and to assemble a small administrative staff before they could open their "doors." Soon they rented an office in Berlin. They still use it today. In the main hallway, above a doorway, they hung an illustrated aphorism that read: "The only way to predict the future is to create it."

The Abraham Geiger College officially opened in November 2000 and became the first rabbinic seminary in Central Europe since the Nazis closed the *Hochschule für Jüdische Wissenschaft* back in 1942. Students started taking classes in 2001. In the early years, Walter rented an apartment nearby and spent a month at a time in Germany during the school year. If a professor called off, he picked up the class, often with little notice. He also recruited students, meeting one in the Atlanta airport, where they happened to have overlapping layovers.[499]

The strategy of proceeding while others debated proved to be an effective method of garnering support. As efforts to create the Abraham Geiger College got underway, one former skeptic of the project compared its momentum to a steamroller and refused to stand in its way.[500] The European board of the World Union for Progressive Judaism endorsed the concept of a European rabbinic seminary in principle in 1999. The European Council of Rabbis endorsed the college outright in 2000. The European Union for Progressive Judaism admitted the Abraham Geiger College as a member in 2001. But the college struggled to get support from Jewish institutions in America with interests and activities in the region. "They remained cautious and despite a pluralistic stance in North America, refused to apply it to Europe," Walter wrote.[501]

Endorsements were important, but financial support and official recognition were even greater concerns. The two went hand in hand. Jewish congregations in Germany typically receive funds from two public sources. The first is a "church tax" collected through federal income taxes and disbursed proportionally to all religious groups in the country. The liberal Jewish congregations do not currently benefit from these funds. The second source is a special contract between the federal government and the Central Council of Jews in Germany, an umbrella group known locally as the *Zentralrat*. The *Zentralrat* favored traditional congregations over the emerging liberal ones and refused to distribute any of the funds to liberal groups, including the Abraham Geiger College. As the federal government was renewing its new contract with the *Zentralrat* in 2002, Walter launched an advocacy campaign. He asked American rabbis to appeal to German consuls on behalf of liberal institutions in Germany.[502] The effort failed, and the new federal contract still excluded the Abraham Geiger College and other liberal groups in the country. By early 2004, these groups were threatening to file a lawsuit against the government or to form a second *Zentralrat* for liberal congregations. The two sides eventually reached a compromise in July 2004, when the *Zentralrat* allowed fifteen liberal congregations to apply for some $4 million in federal funds.[503]

Without sufficient public funding, Walter raised money through the American Friends. In retrospect, he said, he wishes he had hired a full-time fundraiser. Instead, he undertook this task almost entirely alone, in a highly personalized fashion. He started by approaching German-born Jews living in the United States. Some were amenable to the idea, but some were still too resentful of Germany to support any endeavor in the country. "So I had a nice cup of tea and went on to the next party," he said.[504] Every time he traveled for any reason, from rabbinic conferences to family functions, he arranged informational sessions with potential donors. By the end of 2000, he had raised approximately $480,000 this way. He maintained close contact with his network of donors, sending individualized thank-you notes and personalized greetings before Jewish holidays. By 2006, he had amassed more than five hundred donors. Writing thank-you notes required several days of work.[505]

Walter also set about building a rabbinic library for the Abraham Geiger College. The effort began early in his retirement, when he decided to clean his study at Rodef Shalom for the first time in more than thirty years. Colleagues his age were doing the same thing, he learned, and he helped them ship their unwanted books to Germany. Walter also decided it would be appropriate to send some of the few remaining volumes in Dr. Freehof's rabbinic library to Germany. Most of the collection had been donated to Hebrew Union College years earlier, but a few worthwhile odds and ends remained on the shelves at Rodef Shalom. And when Dr. Freehof's widow, Lillian Freehof, made Walter an executor of her will, he arranged for many of the more than eighteen hundred volumes in Dr. Freehof's personal library to go to the Abraham

Abraham Geiger Kolleg
Rabbis for Europe

Rabbiner Walter Jacob 13.03 1930

ÖSTERREICH €0.55

21.10.04-11

1014

The success of the Abraham Geiger College brought Walter honors across central Europe, including his face on a postage stamp issued by the Austrian government. "I don't think it's deserved. But there it is. What do you do?" he said at the time.

Geiger College.[506] An observant visitor to the college today can spot the distinctive two-toned bindings of Dr. Freehof's handiwork peeking out from many shelves. Walter also donated some of the *responsa* volumes he had acquired from the Nazi archives when he clerked at the Hebrew Union College library. After a roundabout journey, the books have returned home.

Walter began making public appeals for religious books in early 2004. He encouraged his colleagues to donate volumes from their personal collections and convinced Hebrew Union College to donate hundreds of duplicate volumes from its library to the Abraham Geiger College. Within a few months of starting this campaign, he had collected eight hundred books in his office at Rodef Shalom, which to this day serves as a clearinghouse for books bound for the Abraham Geiger College.[507]

The early success of the college brought attention to Walter, and he began receiving high honors from across Europe. He was made a Knight Commander of the Federal Republic of Germany in 1999. He was elected to the European Academy of Sciences and Art in 2001. Pope John Paul II named him Commander of the Equestrian Order of St. Gregory the Great in 2004. That same year, the Austrian government put his face on a postage stamp. "I don't think it's deserved," Walter said when the *Jewish Chronicle* asked for his thoughts on the stamp. "But there it is. What do you do?"[508]

W alter celebrated his fiftieth anniversary in the rabbinate in 2005, and other career milestones soon followed. Within the span of a few weeks in the summer of 2006, the Biblical Botanical Garden celebrated its twentieth anniversary and Horizon Homes celebrated the thirtieth anniversary of its expansion. After opening the first group home on Negley Avenue with nine children, Horizon Homes purchased other houses throughout the region and later merged into a larger agency. By 2006, the organization cared for two hundred and seventy five residents at fifty-two homes in Allegheny County.

Walter claims to take more pleasure from contemplating the future than remembering the past, and an opportunity to do so came in September 2006, when the inaugural class of Abraham Geiger College completed the five-year program. The college held the ceremony in Dresden, which was the home of one of the first liberal Jewish congregations in the world. The city also offered a story of renewal. The Nazis destroyed the Dresden synagogue during Kristallnacht, and Allied bombers notoriously left much of the city in ruins toward the end of World War II. In the decades after the war, the city lovingly rebuilt many major buildings. A new, ultramodern synagogue was dedicated on the grounds of the original synagogue in 2001.[509]

The commencement began with an academic graduation at the restored Dresden city hall. A procession of guests, dressed in academic robes and decorated with medallions, entered to a fanfare of trumpets. They were seated prominently on a wide stage. As president of the college, Walter was given the tallest chair—"so visible, I had to look interested and alert through all the speeches, not always easy," he admitted in his weekly letter, referring to the many speeches from government and religious officials. He much preferred listening to his three new graduates defending their theses.

The ordination ceremony the following morning was a more intimate affair, held in the Dresden synagogue. Some two hundred and fifty people sat in the small sanctuary, and television cameras delivered a live feed of the event to two and a half million viewers throughout the country. "My biggest congregation ever!" Walter joked. Over the following days, every major news outlet in Germany and the United States covered the ordination, and the stories traveled through wire services all over the world. Walter was amazed that the event had struck "such a responsive chord."

The ceremony began with a prayer service drawn from two centuries of liberal liturgies from Germany, England and America, and was augmented by a cantor and a choir. The actual ordination ritual was relatively simple. Walter laid his hands upon each graduate, one by one, and delivered the traditional words of rabbinic ordination. Describing the occasion in his weekly letter, a few weeks later, Walter revealed that he became privately overwhelmed with emotion during the ceremony. He had started thinking about his parents and grandparents, his wider family and all those many childhood friends who had been killed before they could flee the country. "Fortunately," he added, "the emotions of the moment did not interfere with my German." In a brief address, he spoke about the unlikeliness of the occasion. When his family left Germany in March 1939, they had assumed Judaism would never again have a permanent and growing presence in the region.

The ordination represented the renewal of Jewish religious life on the continent as well as personal continuity for Walter. His family had been rabbis in the region for fifteen generations. He was the sixteenth generation, and now he was ordaining a new generation. What had once seemed like an end was being proven to be merely a brief departure.

When he described these events a few weeks later, in the letter to his family, Walter realized he was writing on his father's birthday. "What would he have thought about this turn of events?" he wondered. "I think he would have been pleased, but also a bit skeptical."[510] Walter allowed himself to revel in the experience. "The moment of ordination was, of course, emotional for me," he wrote in the *Jewish Chronicle* of Pittsburgh, upon his return. "I could not help but think back on how my family left Germany in March of 1939. We were grateful for that opportunity to escape, but it was a journey into the unknown. My young friends and classmates who I left behind and hoped to see again were not as fortunate. None of them survived. Now I was back in Germany after a full life, 60 years after the last ordination in 1942, to help rebuild a rabbinic tradition. Why was I blessed to undertake this task? It was a wistful and joyful moment."[511]

The Abraham Geiger College
awarded its Geiger Prize to German
Chancellor Angela Merkel in 2015,
marking a major milestone for the
small but growing seminary.

The Seventeenth Generation

I n the years since the Abraham Geiger College held its first ordination in 2006, the once-upstart school has become another pillar of support strengthening the worldwide institutional structure of liberal Judaism. Today, it is fully integrated with the two other liberal rabbinic seminaries. Its students now spend their first year of training in Jerusalem, alongside students from Hebrew Union College in America and Leo Baeck College in England. The Central Conference of American Rabbis fully accredited the Abraham Geiger College in 2010, which has allowed graduates to join the American rabbinic organization as well as the General Rabbinic Conference of Germany.[512]

The Abraham Geiger College has also become economically stable. The global financial crash of 2008 put the college approximately $350,000 behind its fundraising goals, prompting public and private donors to take action.[513] By early 2009, the college had raised 600,000 euros from the German federal government and the combined German state governments, 200,000 euros from the *Zentralrat* and the equivalent of 200,000 euros from donors in North America. Of those North American funds, approximately 40 percent came from individuals and institutions in Pittsburgh.[514] Rodef Shalom congregants regularly include the college in their charitable giving, as they have done for decades for Horizon Homes and the Biblical Botanical Garden.

Through this combination of institutional and economic stability, the Abraham Geiger College has been able to achieve its goal of merging religious scholarship with the practical demands of the rabbinate. The college helped the burgeoning Conservative movement in Germany establish the Zacharias Frankel College. Together, the two liberal rabbinic seminaries partnered with their mutual academic sponsor, the University of Potsdam, to establish the School of Jewish Theology in late 2013. In doing so, they fulfilled Abraham Geiger's original 19th-century vision of incorporating rabbinic training into the German academy, thus giving cultural authority to the position of "the rabbi" in an age when religious bodies can no longer enforce their will upon laity.

The Abraham Geiger College has also become more diverse. Its student body and faculty include both men and women and people of various sexual orientations. A cantorial training program provides an alternate path for Jewish leaders to serve their communities. The college has drawn students from Europe, South America, Africa and the Middle East and has placed graduates with liberal congregations in Sweden, France and South Africa, as well as in cities throughout Germany. The college has also recently begun recruiting prospective rabbinical students to lead emerging liberal congregations in Poland and the Czech Republic, two countries with no heritage of liberal Judaism to build upon.

But these administrative milestones of the Abraham Geiger College can overshadow a more profound religious accomplishment. To imbue rabbinical students with the authority to interpret the doctrines of an ancient faith for modern times, a rabbinic training program requires a good reputation, in addition to a rigorous scholarly practice and a framework for providing practical skills. As Walter Homolka said about the early days of the Abraham Geiger College, before it had a record of success, "What is the Abraham Geiger College ordination? If you are an institution that is only two years old, or five years old, what value does [ordination] have? It has only the value of those people who sign." The authority imparted to a new rabbi through the act of ordination is based on the reputation of the one who is doing the ordaining as much as it is based on the achievements of the one who is being ordained. Homolka offered his situation as a useful example. If he had been ordained at one of the existing rabbinic seminaries, his authority as a rabbi would be based on the reputation of that institution within the wider Jewish world. With a private ordination, his authority is instead based on the individual reputation of rabbis such as Walter Jacob. Walter Jacob empowered Walter Homolka by agreeing to vouch for him.[515]

In a similar way, Walter Jacob empowered the entire Abraham Geiger College. Its institutional stability stands upon his personal reputation. The college ordains graduates based on the unanimous consent of its entire faculty, and several people sign each ordination certificate, but Walter performs the actual ritual. By laying his hands upon the shoulders of each graduate, Walter is endorsing their future in the rabbinate. Their religious authority begins as an extension of his reputation, which he established through decades as a congregational rabbi at Rodef Shalom and as a scholar on the international stage.

Although the act of ordination is intended to extend a chain of communally recognized authority stretching back to the days when the Israelites were poised to enter the Promised Land, it is also a highly personal and individualized event. One rabbi is creating another rabbi. During the course of the ordination ceremony, Walter always whispers a message to each graduate. The graduates prize these messages and keep them private. The only reason they know that each message is unique is because some take longer to whisper than others.[516] The intimacy of this gesture reinforces the feeling that Walter is not only granting religious authority but also bequeathing a personal spiritual inheritance.

The students and graduates of the Abraham Geiger College understand that the experiences they are having today in Jewish communities throughout Europe connect them not only to the larger story of Judaism but also to the private story of the Jacob family, with its many generations of rabbis. Walter and Irene lost both of their sons during the years they were establishing the Abraham Geiger College; Kenney died in 1999 and Daniel died in 2007. After those deaths left the Jacobs childless, the students and alumni of the Abraham Geiger

College collectively sent a letter of condolence to Walter and Irene.[517] In the letter, they included a passage from the Talmud, found in the morning prayers. It read: Rabbi Elazar said in the name of Rabbi Haninah: Torah scholars increase peace in the world. As it says, *"All of Your children are students of God; great is the peace of Your children"* (Isaiah 54:13). Read this not *banayich*—meaning, 'Your children'—but rather *bonayich*—'Your builders'.

In the context of the Talmud, this wordplay is intended to illustrate that each generation can build upon the work of previous generations by continuing the task of studying holy texts. But the students and alumni of the Abraham Geiger College were reversing the allusion. They were telling Walter and Irene that if children are like builders, then builders must also be like children. These young rabbis know that they bear the responsibility for rebuilding Jewish life in Europe. They also know that their connection to the Abraham Geiger College personally binds each of them to Walter and to the fifteen rabbinic generations before him.

By teaching and ordaining this new generation of rabbis, Walter has blessed them, and therefore they are, in a spiritual sense, his children. Each one has joined his lineage. They are the seventeenth generation devoted to increasing peace in the world.

Endnotes

Appropriately, given his love of history, Walter Jacob has preserved a large body of material that will allow future generations to research his life and his work. Also appropriately, given his many associations, this body of material is divided across many repositories, both public and private. A guide will prove useful to future researchers.

Walter's professional papers are housed in sixty-five boxes (and counting) at the archives of Rodef Shalom Congregation in Pittsburgh, Pa. These boxes contain correspondence, congregational materials, organizational records and newspaper clippings. In some cases, materials in these boxes are duplicates of materials housed in other repositories, particularly the American Jewish Archives in Cincinnati, Ohio. Many of the newspaper articles cited in this book came from the Pittsburgh Jewish Newspaper Project, found at *http:// digitalcollections.library.cmu.edu/portal/collections/pjn/index.jsp.*

His personal papers are currently kept in his home. Some are stored in printed form, and some are saved onto 3.5-inch floppy disks that occupy a long shelf in his home office. Included among his personal papers are copies of the weekly letters he has written to members of his family. These letters started out as a way to keep in touch with his parents and his younger brother. With the passage of time, and the death of his immediate relatives, he sent these letters to family in the United States, England and Israel. He sent the same letter to everyone, with a few personalized details added when appropriate.

Walter has participated in two oral history interviews. The first was conducted as part of the Oral History Project of the National Council of Jewish Women, Pittsburgh Section. Of the more than five hundreds oral histories included in the pioneering project, Walter's is certainly the longest, running more than seventeen hours. It was conducted in a series of sessions in 1996 and 1997, as Walter was finishing his rabbinate at Rodef Shalom and preparing for his "retirement." All the Oral History Project recordings are kept at the University of Pittsburgh and can also be found online. The second oral history was a much shorter interview conducted in 1998 by the Survivors of the Shoah Visual History Foundation. Irene Jacob also sat for oral histories with both organizations. As part of my research for this book, I conducted a series of interviews with Walter between 2015 and 2017. I used these interviews to discuss recent events in his life, to resolve ambiguities from earlier interviews and to get to know him better as a person. I also conducted interviews with his colleagues, congregants, friends and family members. In December 2015, I accompanied Walter to Germany to attend the Abraham Geiger Award ceremony, to tour the Abraham Geiger College and to meet administrators and graduates.

The sermon booklets Walter produced annually during his thirty-year tenure as senior rabbi of Rodef Shalom were a surprisingly useful source of biographical information. Walter can be reserved in interviews but was unceremoniously revealing in sermons. He shared stories from his past, delivered reports about his current activities and offered clear statements about his beliefs. The sermon books also include loving dedications to family and friends. The sermon booklets were published informally, and their conventions change from year to year. The citations below make no attempt to resolve the incongruities of the books, such as the irregular information about what day of the week or what week of the year a particular sermon was delivered or the evolving spelling of certain Jewish holidays. These inconsistencies are part of the charm of the collection. All of the sermon booklets can be found at the Rodef Shalom Archives.

As part of his effort to preserve the legacies of his grandfathers, Walter donated the papers of both men to the Leo Baeck Institute in New York. The materials from both collections are mostly in German, which is why they do not appear in my citations. Those who wish to review the materials can find them online. The Benno Jacob Collection can be found at *https://archive.org/details/bennojacobf001*, and the Jakob Loewenberg Collection can be found at *https://archive.org/details/jakobloewenberg*.

Finally, as I was writing this book, the Jewish Culture Museum Augsburg-Swabia published a volume about the Jacob family as part of its Lifelines series. The Lifelines series documents the lives of individual Jewish families from Augsburg both before and after World War II. Each book includes illustrations and a section of translated documents, which were exceptionally useful for my purposes. The entire Lifelines series can be purchased through the Jewish Culture Museum website at *http://en.jkmas.de*.

[1]   Walter Jacob Oral History, 1996–1997, National Council of Jewish Women, Pittsburgh Section Records, 1894–2011, AIS.1964.40, Archives Service Center, University of Pittsburgh (also available online at: *Pittsburgh and Beyond: The Experience of the Jewish Community* site, http://images.library.pitt.edu/cgi-bin/i/image/image-idx?view=entry;cc=ncjw;entryid=x-ais196440.207).

[2]   On his academic title, see program for *Akademische Abschlussfeier* (Dresden: Abraham Geiger College, 2006), 1. On his way of answering the telephone, see Debra Pine, "Reflections on Rabbi Walter Jacob," tribute associated with "Golden Jubilee celebrating Dr. Walter Jacob's 50 Years in the Rabbinate," June 18, 2005, Rodef Shalom Congregation, Pittsburgh, Pa. (typescript included in private collection of Walter Jacob).

[3]   "Minutes of Special Meeting of the Board of Trustees of Rodef Shalom Congregation," April 7, 1966, Pittsburgh, Pa., Rodef Shalom Archives.

[4]   The quotations and note about audience laughter come from an incomplete transcript of a lecture Walter delivered to the executive board of the Union of American Hebrew Congregations in March 1993 on "The Role of the Non-Jew in the Synagogue," found in the Rodef Shalom Archives (Box 51, Folder 20). The master of ceremonies who introduced Walter was most likely Rabbi Alfred Gottschalk, then president of the Hebrew Union College-Jewish Institute of Religion. The transcript included introductory remarks and a question and answer session. Walter later published a revised version of his speech in his annual book, see Walter Jacob, "Our Relationships," delivered March 1993, in *A Selection of Sermons and Lectures Delivered by Dr. Walter Jacob to the Rodef Shalom Congregation*, vol. XXV, 21–28, Rodef Shalom Archives (Box 214, Folder 28).

[5]   Walter Jacob to Kate Stern, May 10, 2011, private collection of Walter Jacob.

[6]   Chaim Stern, ed., *Gates of Repentance: The New Union Prayerbook for the Days of Awe* (New York: Central Conference of American Rabbis, 1978, revised 1996), 8.

[7]   Joseph B. Glaser, "Tribute to Outgoing President Walter Jacob," *Central Conference of American Rabbis Yearbook* (1993), 101–102.

[8]   Walter Jacob, "Survival Then and Now," delivered "Shabbat Hannukah," December 7, 1991, in *A Selection of Sermons and Lectures Delivered by Dr. Walter Jacob to the Rodef Shalom Congregation*, vol. XXIV, 29–31, Rodef Shalom Archives (Box 214, Folder 27).

[9]   Walter Jacob, "Advice To The Old," delivered "Shabbat Vay'hi," January 8, 1977, in *A Selection of Sermons Delivered by Doctor Walter Jacob to the Rodef Shalom Congregation*, vol. XI, 36–39, Rodef Shalom Archives (Box 214, Folder 15).

[10]   Ernest I. Jacob, "Installation in Springfield," in *Paths of Faithfulness*, ed. Walter Jacob and Herbert Jacob (Pittsburgh: self-published, 1964), 1.

11 Walter Jacob, "President's Message," *Central Conference of American Rabbis Yearbook* (1993), 3–8.

12 Walter Jacob, "A Toast to the Past or the Future," delivered "Shabbat Matot-Masei," July 9, 1994, in *A Selection of Sermons Delivered by Dr. Walter Jacob to the Rodef Shalom Congregation* Vol. XXVI, 21–24, Rodef Shalom Archives (Box 214, Folder 29).

13 Walter Jacob, interview by Shulamit Bastacky, March 23, 1998, Pittsburgh, Pa., interview 39836, Survivors of the Shoah Visual History Foundation, VHS copy in Rodef Shalom Archives.

14 Walter Jacob, "Introduction," in *Re-examining Progressive Halakhah*, ed. Walter Jacob and Moshe Zemer (New York: Berghahn Books, 2002), viii.

15 Antje Yael Deusel, interview by author, December 3, 2015, Bamberg, Germany.

16 Walter Jacob, "The Pangs of Pacifism," delivered Sunday, February 6, 1966, stand-alone self-published volume, Rodef Shalom Archives (Box 214, Folder 1).

17 Walter Jacob, "Rabbinic Authority-Power Sharing: Old and New Formulas," in *Rabbinic-Lay Relations in Jewish Law*, ed. Walter Jacob and Moshe Zemer (Tel Aviv and Pittsburgh: The Freehof Institute of Progressive Halakhah, 1993), 83–97.

18 Michael A. Meyer, "Adapting Judaism to the Modern World," in *Response to Modernity: A History of the Reform Movement in Judaism* (New York and Oxford: Oxford University Press, 1988), 10–61.

19 On genealogical and biographical information about the Loewenberg family, see Ernst L. Loewenberg, *The Family of Levi and Friederike Lowenberg*, second edition/library edition, ed. F. M. Loewenberg (Jerusalem: self-published, 1999), accessed July 11, 2017, http://swja.arizona.edu/sites/default/files/lowenberg.pdf. In an introduction, Ernst Loewenberg explained the discrepancy in the spelling of the family surname: "The family name was spelled Löwenberg in German. Only Jacob [sic] Loewenberg spelled it with 'oe,' and his descendants continued to do so. The early immigrants dropped the 'Umlaut;' thus the name was written Lowenberg." On the autobiographical novel, see Jakob Loewenberg, *Aus zwei Quellen: Die Geschichte eines deutschen Juden* (Berlin: 1914), as translated and cited in Benigna Schönhagen, *"We think back full of sorrow": The Jacob Family of Augsburg* (Augsburg: Jewish Culture Museum Augsburg-Swabia, 2015), 13.

20 Loewenberg, *The Family of Levi and Friederike Lowenberg.*

21 Walter Jacob, National Council of Jewish Women oral history.

22 Loewenberg, *The Family of Levi and Friederike Lowenberg.*

23 Walter Jacob, "Midsummer Night's Dream or Nightmare?" delivered Sunday, March 17, 1968, in *A Selection of Sermons Delivered by Doctor Walter Jacob to the Rodef Shalom Congregation*, vol. II, 21–29, Rodef Shalom Archives (Box 214, Folder 5).

24 On the history, development and philosophy of the school, see Wilhelm Mosel, "Former Anerkannte Höhere Mädchenschule von Dr. J. Loewenberg (accredited Dr. J. Loewenberg Girls' Grammar School)," accessed July 4, 2016, www.blankgenealogy.com/histories/Biographies/Jaffe/J.%20Loewenberg%20School%20Hamburg.pdf.

25 Walter Jacob to Eli Loewenthal, December 12, 2007, private collection of Walter Jacob.

26 Mosel, "Former Anerkannte Höhere Mädchenschule von Dr. J. Loewenberg."

27 Meyer, *Response to Modernity*, 121–122.

28 Walter Jacob, *Benno Jacob: Scholar and Fighter* (Berlin: Hentrich & Hentrich/ Pittsburgh: Rodef Shalom Press, 2012), 10.

29 Meyer, *Response to Modernity*, 86.

30 Ismar Schorsch, "Catalogues and Critical Scholarship: The Fate of Jewish Collections in 19th-Century Germany," *Tablet Magazine*, December 28, 2015, accessed December 28, 2015, www.tabletmag.com/jewish-arts-and-culture/books/194367/catalogues-and-scholarship.

31 Walter Homolka, "A Vision Come True: Abraham Geiger and the Training of Rabbis and Cantors for Europe," in *Being Jewish in 21st Century Germany*, ed. Olaf Glöckner and Haim Fireberg (Berlin: Walter de Gruyter GmbH & Co, 2015), 244.

32 Walter Jacob, *Benno Jacob: Scholar and Fighter*, 11–12.

33 Schönhagen, *"We think back full of sorrow,"* 16; Kurt Wilhelm, "Benno Jacob, A Militant Rabbi," *Leo Baeck Institute Yearbook* 7, no. 1 (January 1962): 75.

34 Schönhagen, *"We think back full of sorrow,"* 16.

35 Walter Jacob, *Benno Jacob: Scholar and Fighter*, 13.

36 Wilhelm, *Leo Baeck Institute Yearbook* 7:76–77.

37 Walter Jacob, "To Learn, To Teach, To Fight, To Help: A Memorial Address given to Viadrina-K.C., 100th Anniversary," delivered September 22, 1986, Princeton, NJ, in *A Selection of Sermons and Lectures Delivered by Dr. Walter Jacob to the Rodef Shalom Congregation*, vol. XIX, 10–17, Rodef Shalom Archives (Box 214, Folder 22).

38 Walter Jacob, *Christianity Through Jewish Eyes: The Quest for Common Ground,* (United States: Hebrew Union College Press, 1974), 15.

39 Walter Jacob, "The American Sukkah," delivered September 30, 1985, in *A Selection of Sermons and Lectures Delivered by Dr. Walter Jacob to the Rodef Shalom Congregation,* vol. XVIII, 34–40, Rodef Shalom Archives (Box 214, Folder 21).

40 Wilhelm, *Leo Baeck Institute Yearbook* 7:85.

41 On the biographical information about Benno Jacob contained in this section, see Wilhelm, *Leo Baeck Institute Yearbook* 7; Walter Jacob, *Benno Jacob: Scholar and Fighter,* 27–29; Walter Jacob, "The Life and Works of Benno Jacob," in *The Second Book of the Bible: Exodus* (Hoboken: KTAV Publishing House Inc., 1992), xv; Walter Jacob, "Introduction," in *Die Exegese hat das erste Wort,* Walter Jacob and Almuth Jürgensen, eds (Stuttgart: Calwer Verlag, 2002); Walter Jacob, National Council of Jewish Women oral history.

42 Walter Jacob, National Council of Jewish Women oral history.

43 Wilhelm, *Leo Baeck Institute Yearbook* 7:79.

44 Walter Jacob, *Benno Jacob: Scholar and Fighter,* 28.

45 On the scholarly accomplishments of Benno Jacob described in the three preceding paragraphs, see Walter Jacob, "Introduction," in *Die Exegese hat das erste Wort.*

46 Benno Jacob, *The First Book of the Bible: Genesis,* ed. Ernest I. Jacob and Walter Jacob (New York, KTAV Publishing House, Inc., 1974) 223–225.

47 Walter Jacob, "Rabbi in Two Worlds," in *Paths of Faithfulness,* ed. Walter Jacob and Herbert Jacob (Pittsburgh, self-published, 1964), xviii.

48 Walter Jacob, *Benno Jacob: Scholar and Fighter,* 16.

49 "Report of Ernst Jacob's speech in Saarbrücken," in *Judisch-liberale Zeitung,* August 28, 1925, as translated in Schönhagen, *"We think back full of sorrow,"* 90.

50 On the courtship of Ernst Jacob and Annette Loewenberg, see Walter Jacob, National Council of Jewish Women oral history. On Annette's personality, see Jakob Loewenberg, "Our Little Ann," (poem by Jakob Loewenberg for his daughter Annette, Hamburg, April 15, 1915), Jewish Museum of Westphalia, Dorsten, as translated in Schönhagen, *"We think back full of sorrow,"* 82.

51 "Report of Ernst's Jacob's installation as community rabbi," in *Augsburger Neueste Nachrichten,* September 2, 1929, 4, (State and City Library of Augsburg), as translated in Schönhagen, *"We think back full of sorrow,"* 91.

52 On the history of Augsburg, see A. Freimann, "Augsburg," *The Jewish Encyclopedia, Vol. II Apocryphia-Benash* (New York and London: Funk and Wagnall Company, 1925), 306–307; "Augsburg," *The Encyclopedia of Jewish Life Before and During the Holocaust, Volume 1: A-J,* ed. Shmuel Spector et al. (New York: New York University Press, 2001) 61–63; Susanne Rieger and Gerhard Jochem, "Chronology of the History of the Jews in Bavaria 906–1945," trans. H. Peter Sinclair, last modified October 22, 2006, accessed December 3, 2015, www.rijo.homepage.t-online.de/pdf/EN_BY_JU_bye.pdf; "Augsburg," in *Jewish History and Contemporary Life and Culture,* The Holocaust Center of the Jewish Family and Children's Services of San Francisco, the Peninsula, Marin and Sonoma Counties, last modified 2012, accessed November 28, 2015, http://jfcsholocaustcenter.org/wp-content/uploads/2015/06/Augsburg-History-and-Current-NC-2012.pdf.

53 On the Augsburger *hillukim,* see David Katz, "A Case Study in the Formation of a Super-Rabbi: The Early Years of Rabbi Ezekiel Landau, 1713–1754" (PhD diss., University of Maryland, 2004), accessed December 31, 2015, http://hdl.handle.net/1903/245. On the Augsburg Synagogue organ, see Benigna Schönhagen, "The Organ in the Augsburg Synagogue—an Extinguished Tradition," in *The Augsburg Synagogue—A Building and its History,* ed. Benigna Schönhagen (Augsburg: Augsburg Jüdisches Kulturmuseum Augsburg-Schwaben, 2010), 51. On the Augsburg Synod, see "The Augsburg Synod," in W. Gunther Plaut, *The Rise of Reform Judaism* (New York: The World Union for Progressive Judaism Ltd., 1963), 94.

54 Annette Jacob, "The Night of the 9th of November, 1938," National Council of Jewish Women, Pittsburgh Section Records, 1894–2011, AIS.1964.40, Archives Service Center, University of Pittsburgh (Box 103, Folder 6).

55 Walter Jacob, National Council of Jewish Women oral history.

56 Walter Jacob, "My First Purim," undated, Rodef Shalom Archives (A2006.001 Box 1).

57 Schönhagen, "*We think back full of sorrow,*" 35.

58 On youth services, see Ernst Jacob, "Organizing the Sabbath for Jewish Youth—Experiences and Suggestions," in *Bayerische Israelitische Gemeindezeitung,* December 15, 1934 (No. 24) 526ff., in Schönhagen, "*We think back full of sorrow,*" 96. On adult programming in Augsburg, see Schönhagen, "*We think back full of sorrow,*" 29. On visits to the elderly, see Walter Jacob, "Rabbi Dr. Ernest I. Jacob—Leading Augsburg's Jews in Two Worlds," in *The Augsburg Synagogue— A Building and its History,* ed. Benigna Schönhagen (Augsburg Jüdisches Kulturmuseum Augsburg-Schwaben, 2010), 69.

59 Walter Jacob, "Rabbi Dr. Ernest I. Jacob—Leading Augsburg's Jews in Two Worlds."

60 Walter Jacob, interview by author, February 23, 2015, Pittsburgh, Pa.

61 On Ernest Jacob's scholarship, see Walter Jacob, "Rabbi Dr. Ernest I. Jacob—Leading Augsburg's Jews in Two Worlds," 69–75; Walter Jacob, "Rabbi in Two Worlds"; Ernst Jacob, "Judaism and Sexuality," in *Sexual Issues in Jewish Law*, ed. Walter Jacob and Moshe Zemer (Pittsburgh: The Freehof Institute for Progressive Halakhah, 2005), 1–18.

62 The book fell out of print during the Nazi era. The German publisher Hentirch & Hentrich republished the original text, with a new introduction by Walter, in 2015.

63 Ernst Jacob, "The Jewish Community," in *Israelitische Religionslehre* (Munich: 1933), translation in Schönhagen, "*We think back full of sorrow*," 94.

64 Walter Jacob, Survivors of the Shoah oral history.

65 Walter Jacob, *Pittsburgh and Beyond*; Walter Jacob, Survivors of the Shoah oral history.

66 Joseph Gutmann, *The Jewish Life Cycle*, (Leiden: E.J. Brill, 1987), 7.

67 On Purim in Augsburg, see Walter Jacob, "My First Purim." On the celebration of other Jewish holidays in Augsburg, see Walter Jacob, Survivors of the Shoah oral history.

68 On family life, see Walter Jacob, National Council of Jewish Women oral history; Walter Jacob, Survivors of the Shoah oral history; Walter Jacob, interview by author, February 23, 2015, Pittsburgh, Pa. On snooping, see Walter Jacob, "No Gifts Please," delivered "Yom Kippur," September 25, 1993, in *A Selection of Sermons Delivered by Dr. Walter Jacob to the Rodef Shalom Congregation*, vol. XXVI, 9-15, Rodef Shalom Archives, (Box 214, Folder 29). On pulling the chair away, see Walter Jacob, National Council of Jewish Women oral history. On playing over the balcony, see Walter Jacob, Survivors of the Shoah oral history.

69 Walter Jacob, "An Enigmatic Tale," delivered "Rosh Hashanah," September 9, 1992, in *A Selection of Sermons and Lectures Delivered by Dr. Walter Jacob to the Rodef Shalom Congregation*, vol. XXIV, 13–17, Rodef Shalom Archives, (Box 214, Folder 27).

70 Walter Jacob, Survivors of the Shoah oral history.

71 Schönhagen, "*We think back full of sorrow*," 42.

72 Walter Jacob, Survivors of the Shoah oral history.

73 Walter Jacob, "Rabbi Dr. Ernest I. Jacob—Leading Augsburg's Jews in Two Worlds," 72.

74 Walter Jacob, Survivors of the Shoah oral history.

75 Ibid.

76 Schönhagen, "*We think back full of sorrow*," 37–40.

77   Walter Jacob, interview by author, February 23, 2015, Pittsburgh, Pa.

78   Walter Jacob, Survivors of the Shoah oral history.

79   Ibid.

80   Annette Jacob, "The Night of the 9th of November, 1938."

81   On the destruction of the Augsburg Synagogue, see Schönhagen, "*We think back full of sorrow*," 43; Walter Jacob, "Kristallnacht—A 40th Anniversary: Holocaust and History," delivered Sunday, November 12, 1978, in *A Selection of Sermons Delivered by Doctor Walter Jacob to the Rodef Shalom Congregation*, vol. XI, 20–30, Rodef Shalom Archives, (Box 214, Folder 15); Walter Jacob, "Zakhor Al Tishkah, Remember and Do Not Forget," delivered November 9, 1988, Augsburg, Germany, in *A Selection of Sermons and Lectures Delivered by Dr. Walter Jacob to the Rodef Shalom Congregation*, vol. XXI, 27–35, Rodef Shalom Archives (Box 214, Folder 24).

82   Walter Jacob, Survivors of the Shoah oral history.

83   Walter Jacob, National Council of Jewish Women oral history.

84   On Dachau, see Walter Jacob, National Council of Jewish Women oral history; Walter Jacob, Survivors of the Shoah oral history; Schönhagen, "*We think back full of sorrow*," 44.

85   Schönhagen, "*We think back full of sorrow*," 43; Walter Jacob, Survivors of the Shoah oral history.

86   Walter Jacob, Survivors of the Shoah oral history.

87   Walter Jacob, National Council of Jewish Women oral history.

88   Walter Jacob, "Zakhor Al Tishkah, Remember and Do Not Forget."

89   On Kristallnacht, see Walter Jacob, Survivors of the Shoah oral history; Walter Jacob, National Council of Jewish Women oral history; Annette Jacob, "The Night of the 9th of November, 1938."

90   Annette Jacob, "The Night of the 9th of November, 1938."

91   Walter Jacob, National Council of Jewish Women oral history.

92   On Ernst Jacob after Dachau, see Walter Jacob, Survivors of the Shoah oral history; Walter Jacob, National Council of Jewish Women oral history; Annette Jacob, "The Night of the 9th of November, 1938."

93   On the decision to remain in Germany, see Schönhagen, "*We think back full of sorrow*," 44; Walter Jacob, National Council of Jewish Women oral history; Walter Jacob, Survivors of the Shoah oral history; Annette Jacob, "The Night of the 9th of November, 1938."

94   Annette Jacob, "The Night of the 9th of November, 1938."

[95] Walter Jacob to Kate Stern, April 14, 2010, private collection of Walter Jacob.

[96] Annette Jacob, "The Night of the 9th of November, 1938."

[97] Walter Jacob, Survivors of the Shoah oral history.

[98] Walter Jacob, "Pilgrim's Progress," delivered "Succos," October 19, 1967, in *A Selection of Sermons Delivered by Doctor Walter Jacob to the Rodef Shalom Congregation*, vol. II, 30–33, Rodef Shalom Archives (Box 214, Folder 5).

[99] On sharing a house, see Walter Jacob, National Council of Jewish Women oral history. On stripping the bicycle, see Walter Jacob, Survivors of the Shoah oral history.

[100] Walter Jacob, National Council of Jewish Women oral history.

[101] Walter Jacob, Survivors of the Shoah oral history.

[102] Schönhagen, "*We think back full of sorrow*," 50.

[103] Walter Jacob, Survivors of the Shoah oral history.

[104] On Dachau, the early days of World War II in England and emigration troubles, see Walter Jacob, National Council of Jewish Women oral history; Walter Jacob, Survivors of the Shoah oral history.

[105] Walter Jacob, Survivors of the Shoah oral history.

[106] On the final days of the voyage, see Walter Jacob, National Council of Jewish Women oral history; Walter Jacob, Survivors of the Shoah oral history.

[107] Walter Jacob to Eli Loewenthal, January 3, 2001, private collection of Walter Jacob.

[108] Walter Jacob to Kate Stern, January 3, 2011, private collection of Walter Jacob.

[109] Walter Jacob, Survivors of the Shoah oral history.

[110] Walter Jacob, National Council of Jewish Women oral history.

[111] Ibid.

[112] Annette Jacob to Benno Jacob, February 16, 1940, private collection of Walter Jacob. In his NCJW oral history, Walter said that their landlords were Jewish, but the letter his mother wrote at the time explicitly describes the family as being Christian Scientist.

[113] On the mice and the World's Fair, see Walter Jacob, National Council of Jewish Women oral history; Walter Jacob, Survivors of the Shoah oral history.

[114] Walter Jacob to "girls," February 18, 1940, private collection of Walter Jacob.

[115] Walter Jacob, National Council of Jewish Women oral history.

[116] Walter Jacob, Survivors of the Shoah oral history.

[117] Walter Jacob, "My Fifty Years in America," delivered "Shabbat Miketz," December 30, 1989, in *A Selection of Sermons and Lectures Delivered by Dr. Walter Jacob to the Rodef Shalom Congregation*, vol. XXII, 19–23, Rodef Shalom Archives (Box 214, Folder 25).

[118] Lee Shai Weissbach, *Jewish Life in Small-Town America* (New Haven and London: Yale University Press, 2005), 204.

[119] Walter Jacob, interview by author, February 23, 2015, Pittsburgh, Pa.

[120] Ernest Jacob to Benno Jacob, March 22, 1940, private collection of Walter Jacob.

[121] Ibid.

[122] Ernest Jacob to Mr. and Mrs. Ludwig Loewenthal, March 29, 1940, private collection of Walter Jacob.

[123] Karl Richter, "A Refugee Rabbinate," in *The Jewish legacy and the German Conscience: essays in memory of Rabbi Joseph Asher*, ed. Moses Rischin and Raphael Asher (Berkeley: Judah L. Magnes Museum, 1991), 205–218.

[124] Annette Jacob to "Papa," February 23, 1940, private collection of Walter Jacob.

[125] On the train trip, see Ernest Jacob to "my dear ones," May 24, 1940, private collection of Walter Jacob; Ernest Jacob to Benno Jacob, May 3, 1940, private collection of Walter Jacob; Ernest Jacob to Benno Jacob, April 18, 1940, private collection of Walter Jacob; Ernest Jacob to Benno Jacob, May 31, 1940, private collection of Walter Jacob.

[126] Ernest Jacob to Benno Jacob, May 3, 1940, private collection of Walter Jacob.

[127] Ernest Jacob to Benno Jacob, May 16, 1940, private collection of Walter Jacob.

[128] Ernest Jacob to Benno Jacob, May 31, 1940, private collection of Walter Jacob.

[129] On moving to St. Joseph, see Annette Jacob to "Papa," May 20, 1940, private collection of Walter Jacob. On the diagram, see Ernest Jacob to Benno Jacob, July 6, 1940, private collection of Walter Jacob. On the idyllic nature of small-town lift, see Annette Jacob to "My Dear Ones," August 1, 1940, private collection of Walter Jacob.

[130] Walter Jacob, "Harry S. Truman—In Memoriam," delivered December 29, 1972, in *A Selection of Sermons Delivered by Doctor Walter Jacob to the Rodef Shalom Congregation*, vol. VII, 41–43, Rodef Shalom Archives (Box 214, Folder 11).

[131] Annette Jacob to "Claire, Joel and Kenny [sic]," November 11, 1962, private collection of Walter Jacob.

[132] Walter Jacob, "A Tribute to My Parents," delivered Sunday, April 14, 1974, in *A Selection of Sermons Delivered by Doctor Walter Jacob to the Rodef Shalom Congregation*, Vol. VIII, 3–6, Rodef Shalom Archives, (Box 214, Folder 12).

[133] Walter Jacob, interview by author, May 11, 2015, Pittsburgh, Pa.

[134] Walter Jacob, Survivors of the Shoah oral history.

[135] On reactions to the heat, see Ernest Jacob to Benno Jacob, July 19, 1940, private collection of Walter Jacob; Walter Jacob, National Council of Jewish Women oral history.

[136] Walter Jacob, National Council of Jewish Women oral history.

[137] Walter Jacob, interview by author, March 10, 2015, Pittsburgh, Pa.

[138] On the early embarrassments in Missouri, see Walter Jacob, National Council of Jewish Women oral history; Walter Jacob, Survivors of the Shoah oral history.

[139] Walter Jacob, interview by author, March 28, 2017, Pittsburgh, Pa.

[140] On the Jacob family's reactions to the war, see Ernest Jacob to "My dear ones," July 12, 1940, private collection of Walter Jacob; Annette Jacob to "Papa, my dear ones," May 20, 1940, private collection of Walter Jacob; Annette Jacob to "Papa," October 19, 1940, private collection of Walter Jacob.

[141] Walter Jacob, Survivors of the Shoah oral history.

[142] Walter Jacob, National Council of Jewish Women oral history.

[143] On the family friends in Springfield, see Walter Jacob, interview by author, February 23, 2015, Pittsburgh, Pa.; Walter Jacob, National Council of Jewish Women oral history; Walter Jacob to Eli Loewenthal, October 1, 2007, private collection of Walter Jacob.

[144] Walter Jacob, interview by author, February 23, 2015, Pittsburgh, Pa.

[145] Walter Jacob, interview by author, May 11, 2015, Pittsburgh, Pa.

[146] On his graduating class, see Walter Jacob, National Council of Jewish Women oral history; Walter Jacob, Survivors of the Shoah oral history.

[147] Walter Jacob, "The Role of the Non-Jew in the Synagogue."

[148] Walter Jacob, National Council of Jewish Women oral history.

[149] Roger Dryna, "Boots & Paddles," *Antigo Daily Journal*, March 2, 1967 (clipping in Rodef Shalom Archives).

[150] Walter Jacob to Kate Stern, November 30, 2010, private collection of Walter Jacob.

[151] Walter Jacob, informal conversation with author while sharing taxi to the Abraham Geiger Award ceremony at the Jewish Museum, December 2, 2015, Berlin, Germany.

[152] Walter Jacob, National Council of Jewish Women oral history.

[153] Dryna, "Boots & Paddles."

[154] On the kindness of Americans, see Walter Jacob to Kate Stern, January 3, 2007, private collection of Walter Jacob; Walter Jacob, interview by author, February 23, 2015, Pittsburgh, Pa.

[155] Walter Jacob, National Council of Jewish Women oral history.

[156] Walter Jacob, interview by author, March 10, 2015, Pittsburgh, Pa.

[157] *Springfield News-Leader and Press*, May 29, 1947, 16 (clipping in private collection of Walter Jacob).

[158] Walter Jacob, untitled Drury College address, 1950, private collection of Walter Jacob.

[159] Walter Jacob, National Council of Jewish Women oral history.

[160] George Sturm, telephone interview by author, March 31, 2015.

[161] Walter Jacob, interview by author, February 23, 2015, Pittsburgh, Pa.

[162] Walter Jacob, interview by author, April 13, 2015, Pittsburgh, Pa.

[163] On the career of Herbert Jacob, see Graeme Zielinski, "Herbert Jacob, Professor of Political Science at Nu," *Chicago Tribune*, August 30, 1996, accessed March 30, 2017, http://articles.chicagotribune.com/1996-08-30/news/9608300020_1_professor-jacob-scholar-american-political-science-association. On other career details and "trespassing," see Walter Jacob, National Council of Jewish Women oral history.

[164] Walter Jacob, "Installation of New President: Response and Acceptance," *Central Conference of American Rabbis Yearbook* (1991), 70.

[165] In a remarkable coincidence, the first soldier Ernest visited at the Army medical hospital in Springfield was one of his former congregants from Augsburg.

[166] On Ernest Jacob's rabbinate in Missouri, see Walter Jacob, "Rabbi in Two Worlds"; Walter Jacob, "Rabbi Dr. Ernest I. Jacob—Leading Augsburg's Jews in Two Worlds."

[167] Herbert Jacob, "The Rabbi's Role in a Midwestern Community," in *Paths of Faithfulness*, ed. Walter Jacob and Herbert Jacob (Pittsburgh: self-published, 1964), xxxiii.

[168] John Loren Sandford, *Healing the Nations: A Call to Global Intercession* (Baker Books, 2000), e-book version accessed July 12, 2016 through Google Books.

[169] The settlement locations of various exiled members Jewish Community of Augsburg come from a permanent exhibit panel at the Jewish Culture Museum of Augsburg.

170 On the *Rundbriefe*, see Ernst Jacob, "Passover greetings from the Jewish Community of Augsburg, 1937," Jewish Culture Museum of Augsburg, in Schönhagen, "*We think back full of sorrow*," 51–52, 98; Walter Jacob, "Rabbi in Two Worlds"; Walter Jacob, "Rabbi Dr. Ernest I. Jacob—Leading Augsburg's Jews in Two Worlds."

171 Walter Jacob, "The Broader Role of the Rabbi," in *Pursuing Peace Across the Alleghenies: The Rodef Shalom Congregation, Pittsburgh, Pa. 1856–2005*, ed. Walter Jacob (Pittsburgh: Rodef Shalom Press, 2005), 357.

172 Walter Jacob, "Rabbinic Authority-Power Sharing: Old and New Formulas," from *Rabbinic-Lay Relations in Jewish Law*, ed. Walter Jacob and Moshe Zemer (Tel Aviv and Pittsburgh: The Freehof Institute of Progressive Halakhah, 1993), 83.

173 Walter Jacob, Survivors of the Shoah oral history.

174 Ibid.

175 On the state of Reform Judaism after World War II, see W. Gunther Plaut, "Epilogue," in *The Growth of Reform Judaism*, (New York: The World Union for Progressive Judaism Ltd., 1965) 347–362.

176 On his experiences as a Hebrew Union College student, see Walter Jacob, interview by author, April 13, 2015, Pittsburgh, Pa. On his assessment of Prof. Bettan, see Walter Jacob to "My dear ones," November 1, 1961, private collection of Walter Jacob.

177 Walter Jacob, "A Comparison of the Theologies of Isaac Mayer Wise and Kaufmann Kohler," May 1953, (Rodef Shalom Archives; Box 239, Folder 55).

178 Walter Jacob, interview by author, April 13, 2015, Pittsburgh, Pa.

179 Walter Jacob, "Emergency in Talmudic Law" and "The Expression 'to take God's Name in Vain': A History of its Interpretation," May 1953 and May 1954, (Rodef Shalom Archives; Box 239, Folder 55).

180 Walter Jacob to Ellis Rivkin, January 3, 1958, Rodef Shalom Archives (Box 137, Folder 24).

181 Walter Jacob to Ellis Rivkin, May 18, 1958, Rodef Shalom Archives (Box 137, Folder 24); Walter Jacob, "A Bibliography of Novels and Short Stories by German Jewish Authors 1800–1914," offprint from *Studies in Bibliography and Booklore* 6, no. 2 (Winter 1962/1963), found in Rodef Shalom Archives (Box 215, Folder 108).

182 On his experiences as a student rabbi, see Walter Jacob, National Council of Jewish Women oral history.

[183] On the Jewish populations of small American towns, see "Jewish Population Estimates," in *American Jewish Yearbook* 52 (1950). On his expectations and goals as a student rabbi, see Walter Jacob, interview by author, Pittsburgh, Pa., May 11, 2015.

[184] Walter has told this story often. The quotation used here comes from his annual informal Yom Kippur afternoon address at Rodef Shalom on September 23, 2015.

[185] On his interest in small-town Jewish communities, see Records of the Synagogue Documentation Project, 1904–1999, MSS# 317, Rauh Jewish History Program and Archives at the Sen. John Heinz History Center; "The Western Pennsylvania Synagogue Documentation Project," Rodef Shalom Archives (Box 24, Folder 39). On the need for accommodation, see Walter Jacob, interview by author, Pittsburgh, Pa., May 11, 2015.

[186] Walter Jacob et al, "A Layman Officiating at a Jewish Wedding" (1979), in *American Reform Responsa* (New York: CCAR Press, 1983), 401–403.

[187] Walter Jacob, "Our Relationships," 27.

[188] Display advertisement, *The American Israelite*, June 2, 1955, 16.

[189] Walter Jacob, National Council of Jewish Women oral history.

[190] Walter Jacob to "Hillel and Piske," July 3, 1999, private collection of Walter Jacob.

[191] Walter Jacob, interview by author, April 13, 2015, Pittsburgh, Pa.

[192] Walter Jacob, Survivors of the Shoah oral history.

[193] Walter Jacob, National Council of Jewish Women oral history.

[194] On his chaplaincy, see Walter Jacob, interview by author, April 13, 2015, Pittsburgh, Pa. On the "area rabbinate," see Walter Jacob, Survivors of the Shoah oral history.

[195] On his weekly bulletins, see Walter Jacob, "*M'mizrach*—Chapel Bulletin," no. 1–73 (November 18, 1955–April 19, 1957), private collection of Walter Jacob.

[196] Walter Jacob, interview by author, June 9, 2015, Pittsburgh, Pa.

[197] Walter Jacob, "Where Are We Going: As American Jews," delivered Sunday, January 7, 1968, in *A Selection of Sermons Delivered by Doctor Walter Jacob to the Rodef Shalom Congregation*, vol. II, 12–20, Rodef Shalom Archives (Box 214, Folder 5).

[198] Walter Jacob, "*M'mizrach*—Chapel Bulletin."

[199] Walter Jacob, interview by author, April 13, 2015, Pittsburgh, Pa.

[200] Walter Jacob, untitled talk at a public event honoring the 25th anniversary of the death of Dr. Solomon B. Freehof, June 14, 2015, Rodef Shalom Congregation, Pittsburgh, Pa.

[201] Walter Jacob, interview by author, April 13, 2015, Pittsburgh, Pa.

[202] Mark Staitman, interview by author, October 12, 2015, Pittsburgh, Pa.; Danny Schiff, interview by author, October 28, 2015, Pittsburgh, Pa.

[203] On the recollections of his early years at Rodef Shalom under Dr. Freehof, see Walter Jacob, National Council of Jewish Women oral history. The Junior Congregation was a semi-autonomous entity within Rodef Shalom Congregation, allowing singles and young married couples to arrange programming and gain leadership skills at the large congregation. The Junior Congregation was started in 1937 and lasted until 2005.

[204] On the history of Rodef Shalom Congregation, see J. Leonard Levy, "Pittsburg," *The Jewish Encyclopedia, Vol. X Philipson-Samoscz* (New York and London: Funk and Wagnall Company, 1925), 63–64; *Rodef Shalom Congregation: 150 Years of Living by Jewish Values* (Pittsburgh: Rodef Shalom Press, 2005); Martha Berg, "Our Story," Rodef Shalom Congregation, accessed April 6, 2017, https://rodefshalom.org/about/history.

[205] Walter Jacob, National Council of Jewish Women oral history.

[206] Walter Jacob, untitled talk at a public event honoring the 25th anniversary of the death of Dr. Solomon B. Freehof, June 14, 2015, Rodef Shalom Congregation, Pittsburgh, Pa.

[207] Walter Jacob, interview by author, April 13, 2015, Pittsburgh, Pa.

[208] Annette Jacob to Walter Jacob, July 6, 1958, private collection of Walter Jacob.

[209] Herman Krasne to Walter Jacob, September 20, 1966, Rodef Shalom Archives (Box 117, Folder 24).

[210] Rowna Sutin, interview by author, June 5, 2015, Pittsburgh, Pa.

[211] Walter Jacob, "A Tribute to Solomon B. Freehof," delivered June 14, 1990, in *A Selection of Sermons and Lectures Delivered by Dr. Walter Jacob to the Rodef Shalom Congregation*, vol. XXII, 1–7, Rodef Shalom Archives (Box 214, Folder 25).

[212] On responses to compliments, see Walter Jacob to Charles Jay Miller, December 18, 1992, Rodef Shalom Archives (Box 14, Folder 30); Walter Jacob to Henrietta Chotiner [sic], February 19, 1982, Rodef Shalom Archives (Box 4, Folder 8); Walter Jacob to Harold S. Bigler, December 21, 1992, Rodef Shalom Archives (Box 14, Folder 1); Walter Jacob to Martin Goldberg, April 19, 1984, Rodef Shalom Archives (Box 8, Folder 33).

[213] On the letters Walter wrote in response to congratulatory notes received after he announced his retirement, see "Congratulatory Messages," Rodef Shalom Archives (Box 6, Folder 32). On aging in Jewish law, see Walter Jacob, "Beyond Methuselah—Who is Old?" in *Aging and the Aged in Jewish Law*, ed. Walter Jacob and Moshe Zemer (Tel Aviv and Pittsburgh, Freehof Institute of Progressive Halakhah, 1998), 1–20.

214 Walter Jacob, National Council of Jewish Women oral history.

215 Walter Jacob to Morton M Kanter, November 26, 1958, Rodef Shalom Archives (Box 126, Folder 1).

216 On the worship program at Rodef Shalom, see Walter Jacob, "Showing the Way—The Rodef Shalom Pulpit 1854–1998," from *Pursuing Peace Across the Alleghenies: The Rodef Shalom Congregation, Pittsburgh, Pa. 1856–2005*, ed. Walter Jacob (Pittsburgh: Rodef Shalom Press, 2005) 13–92. On his views about the state of homiletics, see Walter Jacob, "The Decline of the Sermon," offprint from *Central Conference of American Rabbis Journal* (January 1964), found in Rodef Shalom Archives (Box 215, Folder 109).

217 Walter Jacob, "Is Judaism Too Staid?" delivered December 11, 1965, typescript, Rodef Shalom Archives (Box 132, Folder 3); Walter Jacob, "Outside Influence," delivered January 31, 1959, typescript, Rodef Shalom Archives (Box 126, Folder 9).

218 Walter Jacob, "The United Jewish Federation: An Appraisal and A Critique," delivered February 28, 1965, typescript, Rodef Shalom Archives (Box 214, Folder 44).

219 On the responses to the retirement of Dr. Freehof, see "Minutes of the Regular Meeting of the Board of Trustees of Rodef Shalom Congregation," January 11, 1966, Pittsburgh, Pa., Rodef Shalom Archives; M. L. Aaron, "To the Members of Rodef Shalom Congregation," January 12, 1966, Rodef Shalom Archives (Box 125, Folder 10).

220 Walter Jacob, National Council of Jewish Women oral history.

221 On the congregational responses to Walter's election, see "Rabbinate Personal, 1966," Rodef Shalom Archives (Box 125, Folders 11–12). On M. L. Aaron's tribute, see M. L. Aaron, "Minutes of the Annual Meeting of Rodef Shalom Congregation: President's Report," February 27, 1966, Pittsburgh, Pa., Rodef Shalom Archives.

222 Louise Marcovsky to Mrs. S. I. Lasner, undated, Rodef Shalom Archives (Box 125, Folder 10).

223 Walter Jacob, interview by author, March 10, 2015, Pittsburgh, Pa.

224 Frederick Pomerantz, telephone interview by author, April 19, 2016.

225 Walter Jacob, National Council of Jewish Women oral history.

226 "Minutes of Special Meeting of the Board of Trustees of Rodef Shalom Congregation," April 3, 1966, Pittsburgh, Pa., Rodef Shalom Archives.

227 "Minutes of Special Meeting of the Board of Trustees of Rodef Shalom Congregation," April 7, 1966, Pittsburgh, Pa., Rodef Shalom Archives.

228 Walter Jacob, "Program for Rodef Shalom Congregation," April 1966, Rodef Shalom Archives (Box 34, Folder 10).

229 "Minutes of Special Meeting of the Board of Trustees of Rodef Shalom Congregation," April 20, 1966, Pittsburgh, Pa., Rodef Shalom Archives.

230 Walter Jacob, National Council of Jewish Women oral history.

231 Rabbi Solomon B. Freehof, "Dear Friends," April 24, 1966, Rodef Shalom Archives (Box 125, Folder 10).

232 On congratulatory letters and his initial plans for Rodef Shalom, see Walter Jacob to Samuel Sandmel, April 21, 1966, Rodef Shalom Archives (Box 117, Folder 24). On the statement issued by the Pulpit Committee, see "To Fellow Members of Rodef Shalom Congregation," April 26, 1966, Rodef Shalom Archives (Box 125, Folder 10).

233 Frederick Pomerantz, telephone interview by author, April 19, 2016.

234 Walter responded to hundreds of congratulatory messages after his election. For the ones cited here, see Walter Jacob to Silas Adelsheim, May 11, 1966, Rodef Shalom Archives (Box 139, Folder 07); Walter Jacob to Mr. and Mrs. Carl Adelsheim, May 20, 1966, Rodef Shalom Archives (Box 125, Folder 11); Walter Jacob to Joseph S. Weizenbaum, May 12, 1966, Rodef Shalom Archives (Box 125, Folder 15); Walter Jacob to Fred Pomerantz, May 27, 1966, Rodef Shalom Archives (Box 125, Folder 15); Walter Jacob to Mrs. S. I. Lasner, May 19, 1966, Rodef Shalom Archives (Box 125, Folder 12).

235 Albert W. Bloom, "Rabbi Jacob Plans Ahead for Temple," *Jewish Chronicle* (Pittsburgh, Pa.), May 6, 1966, 1 and 9.

236 Walter Jacob to Joseph S. Weizenbaum, May 12, 1966, Rodef Shalom Archives (Box 125, Folder 15).

237 On the immediate changes, see Walter Jacob and Stanley Levin, "Dear Parents," June 16, 1966, Rodef Shalom Archives (Box 139, Folder 06); Walter Jacob, "Dear Friends" and "Bar and Bas Mitzvoh at Rodef Shalom," August 4, 1966, Rodef Shalom Archives (Box 139, Folder 06). Rodef Shalom Congregation began offering bat mitzvahs in 1966, when it introduced the bar mitzvah service. The first bat mitzvah ceremony was held on November 11, 1967. On limiting the involvement of the bar and bat mitzvah student in the prayer service, see Walter Jacob, National Council of Jewish Women oral history.

238 Walter Jacob, interview by author, June 9, 2015, Pittsburgh, Pa.

239 "Installation Service for Rabbi Walter Jacob," November 6, 1966 (Rodef Shalom Archives; Box 125, Folder 3).

240 Walter Jacob, interview by author, June 9, 2015, Pittsburgh, Pa.

[241] On the traditions of the pulpit at Rodef Shalom Congregation, see Walter Jacob, "Showing the Way," 14. On his strategies for change, see Walter Jacob, interview by author, June 9, 2015, Pittsburgh, Pa. On combining initiative and common sense, see Walter Jacob, interview by author, February 23, 2015, Pittsburgh, Pa.

[242] On the case of the Israeli flag on the pulpit and the case of the prayer shawls, see Walter Jacob, National Council of Jewish Women oral history.

[243] Walter Jacob, interview by author, June 9, 2015, Pittsburgh, Pa.

[244] Walter Jacob, "One Hundred and Forty Year—A Blessing or a Burden," delivered "High Holidays," 1996, in *A Selection of Sermons and Lectures Delivered by Walter Jacob and Irene Jacob to the Rodef Shalom Congregation*, vol. XXV, 9–18, Rodef Shalom Archives (Box 214, Folder 31).

[245] Mark Staitman, "An American Rabbinate," in *An American Rabbinate: A Festschrift for Walter Jacob*, ed. Mark N. Staitman and Peter S. Knobel (Pittsburgh: Rodef Shalom Press, 2000), 8–9.

[246] On his record of promoting women, see Walter Jacob, "Showing the Way," 69; Tony Norman, "'It doesn't seem like work to me,'" *Pittsburgh Post-Gazette* (*The Gazette* magazine), September 25, 1994, 4–5.

[247] On the formation and goals of the Greater Pittsburgh Rabbinic Fellowship, see "Tri-Wing Rabbinical Fellowship is Formed," *Jewish Chronicle* (Pittsburgh, Pa.), December 7, 1967, 1; "GPRF—A Forward Step," *Jewish Chronicle* (Pittsburgh, Pa.), December 14, 1967, 4.

[248] Walter Jacob, *Christianity Through Jewish Eyes*, ix.

[249] On his tenure at the Pittsburgh Theological Seminary, see "Rodef Shalom's Lectures Set for Presbyterians," *Jewish Chronicle* (Pittsburgh, Pa.), May 16, 1968, 26. On the Milton Harris Interfaith Institute, see "Interfaith Talk Set in Oakland," *Pittsburgh Press*, February 7, 1976, 4. On the long-term effectiveness of his interfaith initiatives, see Mark Staitman, "An American Rabbinate," 6.

[250] Tony LaRussa, "Wuerl honors rabbi for his interfaith efforts," *Pittsburgh Tribune-Review*, June 17, 2005 (clipping in Rodef Shalom Archives).

[251] On his views of the Second Vatican Council and his trip to Rome, see Walter Jacob, "To Rome With Cardinal Wright," delivered Sunday, November 9, 1969, in *A Selection of Sermons Delivered by Doctor Walter Jacob to the Rodef Shalom Congregation*, vol. IV, 3–13, Rodef Shalom Archives (Box 214, Folder 8).

[252] "Conscientious Objectors," Rodef Shalom Archives (Box 139, Folder 19).

[253] Rodef Shalom was one of the first religious congregations in the country to actively support the National Farm Workers Association led by Cesar Chavez. The congregation hosted a lecture by labor organizer Al Rojas, who came to Pittsburgh in 1969. The Rojas family gave birth to a daughter that year and

named her "Shalom," see Susan Ferriss and Ricardo Sandoval, *The Fight in the Fields: Cesar Chavez and the Farmworkers Movement* (San Diego, New York, London: Houghton Mifflin Harcourt, 1997), 147.

254 Walter Jacob, "Project Equality," delivered Saturday, July 17, 1971, in *A Selection of Sermons Delivered by Doctor Walter Jacob to the Rodef Shalom Congregation*, vol. V, 53–57, Rodef Shalom Archives (Box 214, Folder 9).

255 Walter Jacob, "In the Family Circle," delivered "Yom Kippur," October 14, 1967, in *High Holyday Sermons Delivered by Doctor Walter Jacob to the Rodef Shalom Congregation*, vol. II, 17–26, Rodef Shalom Archives (Box 214, Folder 3); Walter Jacob, "Who Won–Who Lost? A Hannukoh Sermon," delivered December 30, 1967, in *A Selection of Sermons Delivered by Doctor Walter Jacob to the Rodef Shalom Congregation*, vol. II, 34–38, Rodef Shalom Archives (Box 214, Folder 5).

256 Walter Jacob, "The Tallit," delivered "Shabbat Va-et-hanan," August 15, 1992, in *A Selection of Sermons and Lectures Delivered by Rabbi Walter Jacob to the Rodef Shalom Congregation*, vol. XXIV, 37–40, Rodef Shalom Archives (Box 214, Folder 27).

257 Walter Jacob, "Revolution Now," delivered "Shabbat Shuvoh," October 10, 1967, in *High Holyday Sermons Delivered by Doctor Walter Jacob to the Rodef Shalom Congregation*, vol. II, 11–16, Rodef Shalom Archives (Box 214, Folder 3).

258 Walter Jacob, "The American Sukkah," delivered September 30, 1985, in *A Selection of Sermons and Lectures Delivered by Dr. Walter Jacob to the Rodef Shalom Congregation*, vol. XVIII, 34–40, Rodef Shalom Archives (Box 214, Folder 21).

259 Walter Jacob, "The Synagogue In Our Life: The Institution and Its Leaders— A Dedication Sermon," delivered Sunday, March 29, 1980, in *A Selection of Sermons Delivered by Doctor Walter Jacob to the Rodef Shalom Congregation*, vol. XII, 17–24, Rodef Shalom Archives (Box 214, Folder 16).

260 Walter Jacob, "Liberal Judaism," delivered "Yom Kippur," October 12, 1986, in *A Selection of Sermons and Lectures Delivered by Dr. Walter Jacob to the Rodef Shalom Congregation*, vol. XIX, 1–9, Rodef Shalom Archives (Box 214, Folder 22).

261 Walter Jacob, interview by author, June 9, 2015, Pittsburgh, Pa.

262 "Minutes of the Annual Meeting of Rodef Shalom Congregation," March 11, 1986, Pittsburgh, Pa., Rodef Shalom Archives.

263 Mark Staitman, "An American Rabbinate," 3.

264 Ibid., 10.

265 Assorted documents, 1957–1958, private collection of Walter Jacob.

266 "Minutes of the Annual Meeting of Rodef Shalom Congregation," March 11, 1986, Pittsburgh, Pa., Rodef Shalom Archives.

[267] Walter Jacob, National Council of Jewish Women oral history.

[268] Irene Jacob Oral History, November 16, 1999, National Council of Jewish Women, Pittsburgh Section Records, 1894–2011, AIS.1964.40, Archives Service Center, University of Pittsburgh (also available online at: *Pittsburgh and Beyond: The Experience of the Jewish Community* site, http://images.library.pitt.edu/cgi-bin/i/image/image-idx?view=entry;cc=ncjw;entryid=x-ais196440.206).

[269] Walter Jacob, Survivors of the Shoah oral history.

[270] Irene Jacob, National Council of Jewish Women oral history.

[271] Walter Jacob, National Council of Jewish Women oral history.

[272] Walter Jacob, Survivors of the Shoah oral history.

[273] Irene Jacob, National Council of Jewish Women oral history.

[274] Walter Jacob to Eli Loewenthal, December 16, 2012, private collection of Walter Jacob.

[275] Hanna Gruen, interview by author, August 25, 2015, Pittsburgh, Pa.

[276] Walter Jacob, "Find Yourself," delivered "Yom Kippur," September 29, 1971, in *A Selection of Sermons Delivered by Doctor Walter Jacob to the Rodef Shalom Congregation*, vol. VI, 9–14, Rodef Shalom Archives (Box 214, Folder 10).

[277] Walter Jacob, "A Tribute to My Parents," delivered Sunday, April 14, 1974, in *A Selection of Sermons Delivered by Doctor Walter Jacob to the Rodef Shalom Congregation*, vol. VIII, 3–6, Rodef Shalom Archives (Box 214, Folder 12).

[278] On Poopsie and her parents, see Susan Caine, interview by author, June 14, 2015, Pittsburgh, Pa. On her enjoyment of walks and her demeanor, see Walter Jacob to "My Dear Ones," October 26, 1961, private collection of Walter Jacob. On breaking glasses, see Walter Jacob to Kate Stern, February 18, 2012, private collection of Walter Jacob.

[279] Walter Jacob, interview by author, October 16, 2015, Pittsburgh, Pa.

[280] Cheryl Moore, interview by author, August 19, 2015, Pittsburgh, Pa.

[281] Walter Jacob, National Council of Jewish Women oral history.

[282] Walter Jacob et al, "Adoption and Adopted Children" (1978), in *American Reform Responsa*, ed. Walter Jacob (New York: Central Conference of American Rabbis, 1983), 203–208.

[283] Walter Jacob, interview by author, July 21, 2015, Pittsburgh, Pa.

[284] Walter Jacob, National Council of Jewish Women oral history.

[285] Kenney Jacob, untitled tribute to Walter Jacob, private collection of Walter Jacob.

[286] Cheryl Moore, interview by author, August 19, 2015, Pittsburgh, Pa.

287 Walter Jacob, "Daniel Benjamin Jacob's Bar Mitzvah," delivered "Shabbat B'ha-a-los-kho," June 16, 1979, in *A Selection of Sermons Delivered by Doctor Walter Jacob to the Rodef Shalom Congregation*, vol. XI, 1–4, Rodef Shalom Archives (Box 214, Folder 15).

288 Walter Jacob, "Kenney Jacob's Bar Mitzvah," delivered "Shabbat Ki Si-soh," March 1, 1975, in *A Selection of Sermons Delivered by Doctor Walter Jacob to the Rodef Shalom Congregation*, vol. IX, 27–30, Rodef Shalom Archives (Box 214, Folder 13).

289 Walter Jacob, National Council of Jewish Women oral history.

290 Walter Jacob, "Out of the Depth," delivered "Rosh Hashanah Eve," September 12, 1969, in *A Selection of Sermons Delivered by Doctor Walter Jacob to the Rodef Shalom Congregation*, vol. IV, 14–22, Rodef Shalom Archives (Box 214, Folder 8).

291 Walter Jacob, "Parental Obligation to a Severely Retarded Child" (February 1984), in *Contemporary American Reform Responsa* (New York: Central Conference of American Rabbis, 1987), 298–300.

292 "Trip to Connecticut Institutions," Rodef Shalom Archives (Box 37, Folder 29).

293 "Horizon Homes Inc. Articles of Incorporation," March 12, 1969, Rodef Shalom Archives (Box 37, Folder 7).

294 "Case For Support," ca. 1969/1970, Rodef Shalom Archives (Box 37, Folder 19); "Horizon Homes Inc.," ca. 1969, Rodef Shalom Archives (Box 37, Folder 29).

295 "Specification for the Horizon Home," May 21, 1969, Rodef Shalom Archives (Box 37, Folder 47).

296 Lawrence W. Kaplan to City of Pittsburgh Planning Commission, July 8, 1971, Rodef Shalom Archives (Box 37, Folder 65).

297 Margie Ann Moeller, "The Blockbuster," *Renaissance Pittsburgh*, July/August 1974, 21 (clipping in Rodef Shalom Archives).

298 On fundraising, see "Minutes of the Horizon Home Meeting," June 9, 1969, Pittsburgh, Pa., Rodef Shalom Archives (Box 37, Folder 12); "Minutes of the Horizon Home Meeting," October 14, 1969, Pittsburgh, Pa., Rodef Shalom Archives (Box 37, Folder 12). On the skepticism of foundations, see Walter Jacob, National Council of Jewish Women oral history.

299 On the results of Horizon Homes fundraising in 1970 and 1971, see "Minutes of the Horizon Home Meeting," July 6, 1970, Pittsburgh, Pa., Rodef Shalom Archives (Box 37, Folder 12); "Minutes of the Horizon Home Meeting," February 16, 1971, Pittsburgh, Pa., Rodef Shalom Archives (Box 37, Folder 12); "Minutes of the Horizon Home Meeting," June 3, 1971, Pittsburgh, Pa., Rodef Shalom Archives (Box 37, Folder 12).

300 Walter Jacob, "God Helps Those Who Help Themselves," delivered "Shabbat Sh'lakh," June 4, 1983, in *A Selection of Sermons and Lectures Delivered by Doctor Walter Jacob to the Rodef Shalom Congregation*, vol. XV, 34–39, Rodef Shalom Archives (Box 214, Folder 19).

301 Walter Jacob, National Council of Jewish Women oral history.

302 On organizing, see "Project Hope-Information Sheet," undated, Rodef Shalom Archives (Box 37, Folder 11). On appeals, see Walter Jacob, National Council of Jewish Women oral history.

303 Walter Jacob, National Council of Jewish Women oral history.

304 Walter and Irene named Horizon Homes in the plural form because they always intended to open multiple facilities. They eventually did, over the following years.

305 Walter Jacob, dedicatory inscription, *A Selection of Sermons Delivered by Doctor Walter Jacob to the Rodef Shalom Congregation*, vol. IX, Rodef Shalom Archives (Box 214, Folder 13).

306 "Rabbi and wife found asphyxiated," *Associated Press* as published in *The Sunday News and Tribune* (Jefferson City, Missouri), April 14, 1974, 24.

307 Walter Jacob, "Kenney Jacob's Bar Mitzvah."

308 Walter Jacob, "Daniel Benjamin Jacob's Bar Mitzvah."

309 Ernst I. Jacob, "Installation in Springfield," in *Paths of Faithfulness*, Walter Jacob and Herbert Jacob, eds (Pittsburgh: self-published, 1964), 1.

310 Hanna Gruen, interview by author, August 25, 2015, Pittsburgh, Pa.

311 "Walter Jacob—biographical sketch," *Temple Beth-El* newsletter, vol. 50, no. 3, (October 10, 1974), accessed November 29, 2016, www.glensfallstemple.com/wp-content/uploads/2016/03/Vol-5-No-3-October-10.pdf.

312 Irene Jacob, National Council of Jewish Women oral history; Carol Stein Bleier, "Irene Loewenthal Jacob," in *Her Deeds Sing Her Praises: Profiles of Pittsburgh Jewish Women*, ed. Eileen Lane, Eric Lidji and Lois Michaels (Tarentum: Word Association Publishers, 2016), 96–105.

313 Walter Jacob, "A Garden Path" and "The Gardens: Design and Philosophy," in *Gardening from the Bible to North America: Essays in Honor of Irene Jacob*," ed. Walter Jacob (Pittsburgh, Rodef Shalom Press, 2003), 1–12, 103–108.

314 On the layout and philosophy of the garden, see Donald Miller, "They envision a 'garden city,'" *Pittsburgh Post-Gazette*, August 2, 1984, 17.

315 On Irene's horticultural work, see Walter Jacob, "A Garden Path" and "The Gardens: Design and Philosophy"; Irene Jacob, National Council of Jewish Women oral history.

316 Irene Jacob, National Council of Jewish Women oral history.

317 Beatrice Paul Hirschl, "The Shelf Life," *Pittsburgh Post-Gazette*, November 20, 1995, C-1.

318 Walter Jacob, interview by author, March 10, 2015, Pittsburgh, Pa.

319 On *Roman Holiday*, see Walter Jacob to Kate Stern, August 12, 2009, private collection of Walter Jacob; On travel destinations, see Walter Jacob, interview by author, July 21, 2015, Pittsburgh, Pa.

320 On travel adventures, see Walter Jacob, interview by author, July 21, 2015, Pittsburgh, Pa.; "Get Well Messages, 1986–1989," Rodef Shalom Archives (Box 7, Folder 2).

321 Walter Jacob, interview by author, July 21, 2015, Pittsburgh, Pa.

322 Walter Jacob, interview by Don Riggs, *Starting Today*, WPXI, 1986, VHS in Rodef Shalom Archives.

323 Irene Jacob and Walter Jacob, "How to Use This Book," in *Gardens of North America and Hawaii—A Traveler's Guide*, (Portland, Ore.: Timber Press, 1985), 3.

324 On the plans for the garden, see Irene Jacob, National Council of Jewish Women oral history; Walter Jacob, National Council of Jewish Women oral history; Walter Jacob, "Our Biblical Garden," delivered at the dedication of the Biblical Botanical Garden, "Shabbat B'har B'hukotai," May 23, 1987, in *A Selection of Sermons and Lectures Delivered by Dr. Walter Jacob to the Rodef Shalom Congregation*, vol. XIX, 22–27, Rodef Shalom Archives (Box 214, Folder 22).

325 Irene Jacob, "Building the Biblical Botanical Garden," in *Pursuing Peace Across the Alleghenies: The Rodef Shalom Congregation, Pittsburgh, Pa. 1856–2005*, ed. Walter Jacob (Pittsburgh: Rodef Shalom Press, 2005), 269–292.

326 Gabi Dinman, interview by author, October 29, 2015, Pittsburgh, Pa.

327 Walter Jacob to Kate Stern, February 17, 1999, private collection of Walter Jacob.

328 Walter Jacob, National Council of Jewish Women oral history.

329 On the full scope of her work and accomplishments in the field of horticulture, see *Gardening from the Bible to North America: Essays in Honor of Irene Jacob*.

330 Walter Jacob, untitled address at the 25th anniversary celebration of the Biblical Botanical Garden, July 15, 2011, Rodef Shalom Congregation, Pittsburgh, Pa. (available online at www.youtube.com/watch?v=Lc4sopDvyUQ).

331 On the philosophy and planning for the Associated American Jewish Museums, see Walter Jacob, National Council of Jewish Women oral history.

332 On the history and publications of the Associated American Jewish Museums, see Rodef Shalom Archives (Box 53, Folder 3 and Box 93, Folders 34–39).

[333] Walter Jacob, "After Munich," delivered "Rosh Hashono," 1972, in *A Selection of Sermons Delivered by Doctor Walter Jacob to the Rodef Shalom Congregation*, vol. VII, 3–7, Rodef Shalom Archives (Box 214, Folder 11).

[334] Walter Jacob, "Introduction," in *Books of Fifty Years*, ed. Walter Jacob, (Pittsburgh: Rodef Shalom Congregation Sisterhood, 1984), ix–x.

[335] Walter Jacob, "Nineteen Eighty Four (book review delivered October 5, 1983)," in *Books of Fifty Years*, ed. Walter Jacob, (Pittsburgh: Rodef Shalom Congregation Sisterhood, 1984), 142–148.

[336] Walter Jacob, "Is It Jewish?" delivered "Shabbat B're-shis," October 12, 1974, in *A Selection of Sermons Delivered by Doctor Walter Jacob to the Rodef Shalom Congregation*, vol. IX, 18–20, Rodef Shalom Archives (Box 214, Folder 13).

[337] Walter Jacob, "Homecoming," delivered "Yom Kippur," September 25, 1985, in *A Selection of Sermons and Lectures Delivered by Dr. Walter Jacob to the Rodef Shalom Congregation*, vol. XVIII, 25–33, Rodef Shalom Archives (Box 214, Folder 21).

[338] Walter Jacob, "Restoration Rosh Hashana," delivered "Rosh Hashanah," September 29, 1989, in *A Selection of Sermons and Lectures Delivered by Dr. Walter Jacob to the Rodef Shalom Congregation*, vol. XXII, 9–17, Rodef Shalom Archives (Box 214, Folder 25).

[339] Walter Jacob, National Council of Jewish Women oral history.

[340] Walter Jacob, interview by author, March 13, 2015, Pittsburgh, Pa.

[341] Wilhelm, *Leo Baeck Institute Yearbook* 7:94.

[342] Ernst Jacob, "The Jewish Community," in *Israelitsche Religionslehre*, in Schönhagen, "*We think back full of sorrow*," 94.

[343] Walter Jacob, "*Pesikah* and American Reform Responsa," in *Dynamic Jewish Law*, ed. Walter Jacob and Moshe Zemer (Tel Aviv and Pittsburgh: The Freehof Institute of Progressive Halakhah, 1991), 87–106.

[344] Meyer, *Response to Modernity*, 6.

[345] Walter Jacob, "Authority in Reform Judaism (draft 1)," November 1979, Rodef Shalom Archives (Box 13 Folder 10).

[346] Walter Jacob, "*Pesikah* and American Reform Responsa," 87–88.

[347] "Descriptive Catalogue of Looted Judaica," Conference on Jewish Material Claims Against Germany, Partially Updated Edition 2016, 18, accessed February 8, 2017, http://art-69bd.kxcdn.com/wp-content/uploads/2013/09/Descriptive-Catalogue-of-Looted-Judaica-3-February-2016.pdf.

[348] Ibid., 238.

i

[349] Walter Jacob, "Writing Responsa: A Personal Journey," in *Beyond the Letter of the Law: Essays on Diversity in the Halakhah in honor of Moshe Zemer*, ed. Walter Jacob (Pittsburgh: Rodef Shalom Press, 2004), 104.

[350] On Guttman and Zafren, see Walter Jacob, "Response and Acceptance," *Central Conference of American Rabbis Yearbook* (1991), 70–71. On Marx and Stone, see Walter Jacob, "Writing Responsa: A Personal Journey," 104.

[351] On Freehof's status within the Reform movement, see Joan S. Friedman, *Guidance Not Governance: Rabbi Solomon B. Freehof and Reform Responsa*, (Cincinnati: Hebrew Union College Press, 2013), 46. On Walter's apprenticeship in *responsa* writing under Freehof, see Walter Jacob, "Writing Responsa: A Personal Journey," 104.

[352] Ernest Jacob to Walter Jacob, September 20, 1962, private collection of Walter Jacob.

[353] On the nearly destroyed rabbinic library and the effort to restore the damaged volumes, see Walter Jacob, "Writing Responsa: A Personal Journey," 105.

[354] Walter Jacob, untitled talk at a public event honoring the 25th anniversary of the death of Dr. Solomon B. Freehof, June 14, 2015, Rodef Shalom Congregation, Pittsburgh, Pa.

[355] Jay Goggin, "Antique Jewish Books Saved," *Pittsburgh Post-Gazette*, June 26, 1965, 6.

[356] Walter Jacob, "Writing Responsa: A Personal Journey," 104.

[357] Friedman, *Guidance Not Governance*, 43.

[358] Ibid., 7–9.

[359] Ibid., 24–46.

[360] Meyer, *Response to Modernity*, 324.

[361] Walter Jacob, "Showing the Way," 66–67.

[362] Walter Jacob, "Writing Responsa: A Personal Journey," 107.

[363] Walter Jacob to Stanford M. Adelstein, November 9, 1978, Rodef Shalom Archives (Box 13, Folder 4).

[364] Walter Jacob, "The Right to Create a New Congregation" (November 1983), in *Contemporary American Reform Responsa* (New York: Central Conference of American Rabbis, 1987), 200–202.

[365] Walter Jacob, "Writing Responsa: A Personal Journey," 106.

366 Walter Jacob to Ely Pilchik, June 27, 1977, Rodef Shalom Archives (Box 13, Folder 2).

367 "Minutes of the Responsa Committee Meeting of Central Conference of American Rabbis," January 6, 1977, New York, NY, Rodef Shalom Archives (Box 13, Folder 01).

368 On his intentions for reforming the committee, see "Summary of meetings held on April 22 and June 26, 1980—Responsa Committee," Rodef Shalom Archives (Box 13, Folder 5); Walter Jacob, "Writing Responsa: A Personal Journey," 106–107.

369 Friedman, *Guidance Not Governance*, 229.

370 Ibid., 230.

371 On the evolving position toward bat mitzvah in Reform *responsa*, see, D. Neumark, "Bat Mitzvah" (1913), in *American Reform Responsa*, ed. Walter Jacob (New York: Central Conference of American Rabbis, 1983), 82; Israel Bettan, "Bat Mitzvah" (1954), in *American Reform Responsa*, ed. Walter Jacob (New York: Central Conference of American Rabbis, 1983), 83; Walter Jacob et al, "Reform Attitude Toward Bar Mitzvah and Bat Mitzvah" (1979), in *American Reform Responsa*, ed. Walter Jacob (New York: Central Conference of American Rabbis, 1983), 86.

372 Walter Jacob, "Introduction," in *American Reform Responsa*, ed. Walter Jacob (New York: Central Conference of American Rabbis, 1983), xvi. Walter used a different transliteration of "halakhah" in this instance, and I have retained his spelling.

373 Walter Jacob, "Writing Responsa: A Personal Journey," 113.

374 Ibid., 113.

375 On social functions, see Walter Jacob, interview by author, February 23, 2015, Pittsburgh, Pa. On visiting the sick, see Debra Pine, telephone interview by author, July 20, 2015.

376 Walter Jacob, "Writing Responsa: A Personal Journey," 107.

377 On the nature of "implicit theology," see Walter Jacob, "Explicit and Implicit Theology: A Response to Eugene Borowitz," Rodef Shalom Archives (Box 13, Folder 2).

378 Walter Jacob, interview by author, February 23, 2015, Pittsburgh, Pa.

379 Mark Washofsky, telephone interview by author, May 8, 2015.

380 Walter Jacob, "The Sources of Reform Halakhic Authority," delivered June 22, 1980 at the Central Conference of American Rabbis meeting in Pittsburgh, Pa., in *A Selection of Sermons and Lectures Delivered by Doctor Walter Jacob to the Rodef Shalom Congregation*, vol. XIII, 38–49, Rodef Shalom Archives (Box 214,

Folder 17). A version of the lecture later appeared in the collection *Rabbinic Authority*, ed. Elliot Stevens (New York: Central Conference of American Rabbis, 1982), 31–36.

381 Walter Jacob, "Writing Responsa: A Personal Journey," 108.

382 Walter Jacob, interview by author, April 13, 2015, Pittsburgh, Pa.

383 Walter Jacob et al, "Israeli Flag On a Synagogue Pulpit" (1977), in *American Reform Responsa*, ed. Walter Jacob (New York: Central Conference of American Rabbis, 1983), 66; Walter Jacob et al, "Fabric Used in a Torah Mantle" (1977), in *American Reform Responsa*, ed. Walter Jacob (New York: Central Conference of American Rabbis, 1983), 110; Walter Jacob et al, "Salting Bread Before the Blessing" (1978), in *American Reform Responsa*, ed. Walter Jacob (New York: Central Conference of American Rabbis, 1983), 113.

384 Walter Jacob, "Dress Code for Religious School" (March 1976), *Contemporary American Reform Responsa* (New York: Central Conference of American Rabbis, 1987), 46.

385 On the initial collection of questions to the Responsa Committee from the Family Life Committee, see Friedman, *Guidance Not Governance*, 233; Walter Jacob et al, "An Inquiry About Virginity" (1979), in *American Reform Responsa*, ed. Walter Jacob (New York: Central Conference of American Rabbis, 1983), 477–478; Walter Jacob et al, "Jewish Attitude Toward Sexual Relations Between Consenting Adults" (1979), in *American Reform Responsa*, ed. Walter Jacob (New York: Central Conference of American Rabbis, 1983), 480–483; Walter Jacob et al, "Marriage After a Sex Change Operation" (undated), in *American Reform Responsa*, ed. Walter Jacob (New York: Central Conference of American Rabbis, 1983), 416–419.

386 Walter Jacob, "Writing Responsa: A Personal Journey," 109–112.

387 Walter Jacob et al, "An Unmarried Couple Joining the Synagogue" (1980), in *American Reform Responsa*, ed. Walter Jacob (New York: Central Conference of American Rabbis, 1983), 47.

388 Friedman, *Guidance Not Governance*, 246.

389 Walter Jacob et al, "Prayer for Couple Contemplating Intermarriage" (1979), in *American Reform Responsa*, ed. Walter Jacob (New York: Central Conference of American Rabbis, 1983), 465.

390 Walter Jacob et al, "Reform Judaism and Mixed Marriage" (1980), in *American Reform Responsa*, ed. Walter Jacob (New York: Central Conference of American Rabbis, 1983), 445.

391 Walter Jacob, et al, "Rabbi Officiating at a Mixed Marriage" (1982), in *American Reform Responsa*, ed. Walter Jacob (New York: Central Conference of American Rabbis, 1983), 467.

392 Walter Jacob, "The Roots of Reform Halakah—A Lecture to the New York Association of Reform Rabbis," delivered February 1979 to the Association of Reform Rabbis of New York City, NY, in *A Selection of Sermons Delivered by Doctor Walter Jacob to the Rodef Shalom Congregation*, vol. XII, 25–48, Rodef Shalom Archives (Box 214, Folder 16).

393 "Report of the Committee on Patrilineal Descent on the Status of Children of Mixed Marriages" in *American Reform Responsa*, ed. Walter Jacob (New York: Central Conference of American Rabbis, 1983), 547–550; Walter Jacob, "Patrilineal Descent and Matrilineal Descent" (October 1983), in *Contemporary American Reform Responsa* (New York: Central Conference of American Rabbis, 1987), 61–68.

394 Walter Jacob, "A Child Raised in Two Religious Traditions" (September 1983), in *Contemporary American Reform Responsa* (New York: Central Conference of American Rabbis, 1987), 98–99.

395 Walter Jacob, "Introduction," in *Contemporary American Reform Responsa* (New York: Central Conference of American Rabbis, 1987), xv–xxii.

396 The terminology used for this section, such as "homosexuality" and "gays and lesbians," is intended to reflect the nature of debate at the time, rather than the lexicon considered appropriate today. On the history of the debate, see Michael Loving, "To Ordain or Not To Ordain: The Tale of the CCAR Committee on Homosexuality and the Rabbinate," in *The Sacred Encounter: Jewish Perspectives on Sexuality*, ed. Lisa J. Grushcow. (New York: Central Conference of American Rabbis, 2014), 271–285.

397 Walter Jacob et al, "Homosexuals in Leadership Positions" (1981), in *American Reform Responsa*, ed. Walter Jacob (New York: Central Conference of American Rabbis, 1983), 52–54.

398 Loving, "To Ordain or Not To Ordain."

399 "Report of the Ad Hoc Committee on Homosexuality and the Rabbinate," June 1990, Rodef Shalom Archives (Box 45, Folder 17).

400 Walter Jacob, "Homosexual Convert" (June 1982), in *Contemporary American Reform Responsa* (New York: Central Conference of American Rabbis, 1987), 88–90.

401 Walter Jacob, "Lesbians and Their Children" (March 1986), in *Contemporary American Reform Responsa* (New York: Central Conference of American Rabbis, 1987), 296–297. The question was submitted by Rabbi Mark Staitman, who was an associate rabbi at Rodef Shalom Congregation at the time.

402 "About," Bet Tikvah, accessed July 18, 2016 and July 18, 2017, www.bettikvah.org/aboutbt.html.

403 Walter Jacob, National Council of Jewish Women oral history.

[404] Walter Jacob, "The Roots of Reform Halakah."

[405] Ibid.

[406] Walter Jacob, "Liberal Judaism," delivered "Yom Kippur," October 12, 1986, in *A Selection of Sermons and Lectures Delivered by Dr. Walter Jacob to the Rodef Shalom Congregation*, vol. XIX, 1–9, Rodef Shalom Archives (Box 214, Folder 22); Walter Jacob, "The Influence of the Pittsburgh Platform on Reform *Halakhah* and Biblical Study," in *The Changing World of Reform Judaism: The Pittsburgh Platform in Retrospect*, ed. Walter Jacob (Pittsburgh: Rodef Shalom Press, 1985), 25–39; Walter Jacob, "Introduction," in *Contemporary American Reform Responsa* (New York: Central Conference of American Rabbis, 1987), xv–xxii.

[407] Walter Jacob, "Introduction," in *Liberal Judaism and Halakhah*, ed. Walter Jacob (Pittsburgh: Rodef Shalom Press, 1988).

[408] Walter Jacob, "*Pesikah* and American Reform Responsa."

[409] Walter Jacob, "The Roots of Reform Halakhah."

[410] Walter Jacob, "Introduction," in *Contemporary American Reform Responsa* (New York: Central Conference of American Rabbis, 1987), xv–xxii. Walter Jacob, "Introduction—Setting Limits in Reform Judaism," in *New American Reform Responsa: Questions and Reform Jewish Answers* (New York: Central Conference of American Rabbis, 1992), xix–xxvi. Walter used a different transliteration of "mitzvoth" in this address, and I have retained his spelling.

[411] Walter Jacob, "Response and Acceptance," in *Central Conference of American Rabbis Yaerbook* (1991), 70–72.

[412] "Reform Calls for Greater Religious Adherence," *JTA*, November 5, 1991, accessed February 18, 2016, www.jta.org/1991/11/05/archive/reform-calls-for-greater-religious-adherence.

[413] Walter Jacob, "Message from the President on Responsa," *CCAR Newsletter*, December 1991, Rodef Shalom Archives (Box 45, Folder 56).

[414] Walter Jacob, "Standards Now," in *Central Conference of American Rabbis Yearbook* (1992), 119–125.

[415] Walter Jacob to Rabbi Peter J. Haas, April 9, 1993, Rodef Shalom Archives (Box 5, Folder 39); Walter Jacob, interview by author, July 6, 2015, Pittsburgh, Pa.

[416] Walter Jacob, "Liberal Judaism Needs Standards," in *Reform Judaism*, December 1995, accessed February 22, 2016, www.bjpa.org/Publications/Details.cfm?PublicationID=12844.

[417] "Books," Freehof Institute for Progressive Halakhah, accessed November 20, 2016, https://freehofinstitute.wordpress.com/books/.

[418] Friedman, *Guidance Not Governance*, 256.

[419] Schönhagen, "*We think back full of sorrow*," 70.

[420] On maintaining German fluency, see Walter Jacob, "Response and Acceptance," in *Central Conference of American Rabbis Yearbook* (1991), 70. On Herbert Jacob, see Walter Jacob, "A Tribute to My Brother," delivered August 29, 1996, in *A Selection of Sermons and Lectures Delivered by Walter Jacob and Irene Jacob to the Rodef Shalom Congregation*, vol. XXV, 5–8, Rodef Shalom Archives (Box 214, Folder 31).

[421] On the scale and scope of their efforts to revive the commentaries, see queries to publishers in "Genesis" and "Exodus," Rodef Shalom Archives (Box 163, Folders 2–3).

[422] Walter Jacob, "Legends Of Our Time," delivered Sunday, January 19, 1969, in *A Selection of Sermons Delivered by Doctor Walter Jacob to the Rodef Shalom Congregation*, vol. III, 15–20, Rodef Shalom Archives (Box 214, Folder 7).

[423] Walter Jacob to "Ass. Dr. Schmuderer, Bayerisches Landesentschadigungsamt," May 6, 1960, Rodef Shalom Archives (Box 126, Folder 1); Walter Jacob to Henry Mindin, March 23, 1965, Rodef Shalom Archives (Box 122, Folder 36).

[424] On the history of the Augsburg synagogue, see "Highlights, The Synagogue from 1912 to 2010," in *The Augsburg Synagogue—A Building and its History,* ed. Benigna Schönhagen (Augsburg: Jüdisches Kulturmuseum Augsburg-Schwaben, 2010), 83–84. On the pigeons, see "Synagogue Memories: Walter Sturm, 1988," in *The Augsburg Synagogue—A Building and its History,* ed. Benigna Schönhagen (Augsburg: Jüdisches Kulturmuseum Augsburg-Schwaben, 2010), 135.

[425] Michael Brenner, "The Postwar Community in Augsburg," in *The Augsburg Synagogue—A Building and its History,* ed. Benigna Schönhagen (Augsburg: Jüdisches Kulturmuseum Augsburg-Schwaben, 2010), 88–90.

[426] On his return to Germany, see Walter Jacob, "A High Holiday Sermon," delivered "Rosh Hashanah," September 5, 1975, in *A Selection of Sermons Delivered by Doctor Walter Jacob to the Rodef Shalom Congregation*, vol. X, 3–9, Rodef Shalom Archives (Box 214, Folder 14).

[427] Walter Jacob, "Good Old Days," delivered "Shabbat Noah," October 30, 1976, in *A Selection of Sermons Delivered by Doctor Walter Jacob to the Rodef Shalom Congregation*, vol. XI, 31–35, Rodef Shalom Archives (Box 214, Folder 15).

[428] Walter Jacob, "Kristallnacht—A 40th Anniversary: Holocaust and History," delivered Sunday, November 12, 1978, in *A Selection of Sermons Delivered by Doctor Walter Jacob to the Rodef Shalom Congregation*, vol. XI, 20–30, Rodef Shalom Archives (Box 214, Folder 15).

[429] Walter Jacob, "Sympathy, But Not Sorrow," delivered "Shabbat Bo," January 26, 1980, in *A Selection of Sermons and Lectures Delivered by Doctor Walter Jacob to the Rodef Shalom Congregation*, vol. XII, 29–33, Rodef Shalom Archives (Box 214, Folder 17).

[430] Walter Jacob, "Our Relationships," 28.

[431] Schönhagen, "The Organ in the Augsburg Synagogue," 54.

[432] On his speech at the rededication ceremony, see Walter Jacob, "Rededication of the Great Synagogue of Augsburg," delivered September 5, 1985, in *A Selection of Sermons and Lectures Delivered by Dr. Walter Jacob to the Rodef Shalom Congregation*, vol. XVIII, 6–10, Rodef Shalom Archives (Box 214, Folder 21). Walter delivered the original speech in German and translated the speech into English for publication in his annual sermon booklet. A different English translation of the sermon appears in Schönhagen, "*We think back full of sorrow*," 111. On his feelings about attending the event, see Walter Jacob, Year in Review letter, September 1985, private collection of Walter Jacob.

[433] Walter Jacob, "Spokojony and Breuer," delivered "Rosh Hashanah," September 15, 1985, in *A Selection of Sermons and Lectures Delivered by Dr. Walter Jacob to the Rodef Shalom Congregation*, vol. XVIII, 17–24, Rodef Shalom Archives (Box 214, Folder 21).

[434] On his visit to Germany in 1988, see Walter Jacob, "A Report From Germany on Kristallnacht," delivered November 27, 1988, in *A Selection of Sermons and Lectures Delivered by Dr. Walter Jacob to the Rodef Shalom Congregation*, vol. XXI, 9–16, Rodef Shalom Archives (Box 214, Folder 24). On his private thoughts about the trip, see Walter Jacob to Kate Stern, November 29, 1988, private collection of Walter Jacob.

[435] Ibid.

[436] Walter Jacob, "Zakhor Al Tishkah—Remember and Do Not Forget," delivered November 9, 1988, in *A Selection of Sermons and Lectures Delivered by Dr. Walter Jacob to the Rodef Shalom Congregation*, vol. XXI, 27–35, Rodef Shalom Archives (Box 214, Folder 24).

[437] Walter Jacob, "A Report From Germany on Kristallnacht."

[438] Walter Jacob, National Council of Jewish Women oral history.

[439] Walter Jacob, "President's Message," in *Central Conference of American Rabbis Yearbook* (1993), 3–12.

[440] Mark Staitman, "An American Rabbinate."

[441] Walter Jacob, "Zionism and Racism," delivered Sunday, November 16, 1975, in *A Selection of Sermons Delivered by Doctor Walter Jacob to the Rodef Shalom Congregation*, vol. X, 10–15, Rodef Shalom Archives (Box 214, Folder 14); Walter Jacob to Jerome Apt, October 14, 1991, Rodef Shalom Archives (Box 8, Folder 11).

[442] Walter Jacob, "Showing the Way," 64–66; Walter Jacob, "Religious Freedom in Israel: 168 B.C.E. and 1968 C.E.," delivered Sunday, December 31, 1967, in *A Selection of Sermons Delivered by Doctor Walter Jacob to the Rodef Shalom Congregation*, vol. II, 3–11, Rodef Shalom Archives (Box 214, Folder 5).

[443] Walter Jacob, "Israel Now," delivered Sunday, April 18, 1971, in *A Selection of Sermons Delivered by Doctor Walter Jacob to the Rodef Shalom Congregation*, vol. II, 40–47, Rodef Shalom Archives (Box 214, Folder 9).

[444] On the conversion meetings, see "Summary of the Meeting of the Ad Hoc Committee on *gerut* held at the Jewish Agency – New York," April 3 and 4, 1989, Rodef Shalom Archives (Box 45, Folder 63); "Meeting of the Ad Hoc Committee on *Gerut*, Schocken Library—Jersualem," July 9–14, 1989, Rodef Shalom Archives (Box 45, Folder 63).

[445] Walter Jacob, "Israel at Twenty Five: Toward a New Zionist Ideology," delivered Sunday, April 1, 1973, in *A Selection of Sermons Delivered by Doctor Walter Jacob to the Rodef Shalom Congregation*, vol. VII, 27–33, Rodef Shalom Archives (Box 214, Folder 11); Walter Jacob, "America and Israel," delivered "High Holidays," September 26, 1974, in *A Selection of Sermons Delivered by Doctor Walter Jacob to the Rodef Shalom Congregation*, vol. IX, 3–10, Rodef Shalom Archives (Box 214, Folder 13).

[446] Wilhelm, *Leo Baeck Institute Yearbook* 7:85.

[447] Walter Jacob, speech at Pursuer of Peace Award ceremony, June 5, 2016, Rodef Shalom Congregation, Pittsburgh, Pa.

[448] Walter Jacob, "German Nationalism-Jewish Nationalism," delivered at the University of Pittsburgh exhibition on Jews in Germany under Prussian Rule, June 25, 1984, in *A Selection of Sermons and Lectures delivered by Dr. Walter Jacob to the Rodef Shalom Congregation*, vol. XVI, 1–12, Rodef Shalom Archives (Box 214, Folder 20).

[449] Walter Jacob to Eli Loewenthal, March 24, 2005, private collection of Walter Jacob.

[450] Walter Jacob, "President's Message," in *Central Conference of American Rabbis Yearbook* (1993), 3–12.

[451] On the Russian and French translation projects, see Walter Jacob to Susan Trivers, March 19, 1991, Rodef Shalom Archives (Box 4, Folder 25); Walter Jacob to Leigh Lerner, November 15, 1991, Rodef Shalom Archives (Box 6, Folder 26). On the fate of those projects, see Walter Jacob, interview by author, October 30, 2015, Pittsburgh, Pa.

[452] Walter Jacob, "President's Message," in *Central Conference of American Rabbis Yearbook* (1993), 3–12.

[453] On the details of the conference in Vienna, see Walter Jacob to Kate Stern, November 22, 1995, private collection of Walter Jacob; Irene Jacob to "Piske and Hillel," December 17, 1995, private collection of Walter Jacob; Walter Jacob, National Council of Jewish Women oral history; Clifford M. Kulwin to Jeffery Rose and Rabbi Richard G. Hirsch, World Union for Progressive Judaism Records, MS–16, Box G27, Folder 30. American Jewish Archives, Cincinnati, Ohio.

[454] Walter Jacob to Kate Stern, November 22, 1995, private collection of Walter Jacob; Clifford M. Kulwin report.

[455] Walter Jacob to Kate Stern, November 22, 1995, private collection of Walter Jacob.

[456] Clifford M. Kulwin report.

[457] Walter Jacob to Kate Stern, November 22, 1995, private collection of Walter Jacob.

[458] Walter Jacob to Eli Loewenthal, February 27, 1996, private collection of Walter Jacob.

[459] Walter Jacob to Zachary Jacob, September 1, 1995, private collection of Walter Jacob.

[460] Walter Jacob, interview by author, March 10, 2015, Pittsburgh, Pa.

[461] Walter Homolka to Walter Jacob, December 23, 1983, Rodef Shalom Archives (Box 98, Folder 18); Walter Homolka to Walter Jacob, March 3, 1984, Rodef Shalom Archives (Box 98, Folder 18); Walter Homolka to Walter Jacob, May 27, 1984, Rodef Shalom Archives (Box 98, Folder 18); Walter Homolka to Walter Jacob, September 1, 1985, Rodef Shalom Archives (Box 98, Folder 17); Walter Homolka to Walter Jacob, September 10, 1985, Rodef Shalom Archives (Box 98, Folder 17); Walter Homolka to Walter Jacob, November 20, 1985, Rodef Shalom Archives (Box 98, Folder 17).

[462] Walter Jacob to Gary Zola, March 6, 1984, Rodef Shalom Archives (Box 8, Folder 33); Gerard Daniel to Walter Jacob, January 6, 1986, Rodef Shalom Archives (Box 98, Folder 17); Jonathon Magonet to Gerard Daniel, January 14, 1986, Rodef Shalom Archives (Box 98, Folder 18); Gerard Daniel to Eleanor Schwartz, February 19, 1986, Rodef Shalom Archives (Box 98, Folder 17).

[463] Walter Jacob to Benjamin Kamin, February 21, 1984, Rodef Shalom Archives (Box 98, Folder 18); Walter Jacob to Jakob Petuchowski, October 3, 1985, Rodef Shalom Archives (Box 98, Folder 17); Walter Jacob recommendation for Walter Homolka, November 19, 1985, Rodef Shalom Archives (Box 98, Folder 17).

[464] Walter Jacob to Gerard Daniel, January 14, 1986, Rodef Shalom Archives (Box 98, Folder 17).

[465] On his explanation at the time, see Walter Homolka to Walter Jacob, July 10, 1987, Rodef Shalom Archives (Box 98, Folder 18). On his private feelings and later revelation, see Walter Homolka, interview by author, December 7, 2015, Berlin, Germany.

[466] Walter Homolka, interview by author, December 7, 2015, Berlin, Germany; Jan Mühlstein, "The Return of Liberal Judaism to Germany," *European Judaism: A Journal for the New Europe*, vol. 49, vo. 1 (Spring 2016), 45–48.

[467] Walter Jacob, National Council of Jewish Women oral history.

[468] Ibid.

[469] Walter Homolka, interview by author, December 7, 2015, Berlin, Germany.

[470] Walter Jacob to Alton Meyer Winters, November 17, 1992, Rodef Shalom Archives (Box 45, Folder 29).

[471] "Private Ordination," Central Conference of American Rabbis Responsa Committee, accessed July 19, 2016, http://ccarnet.org/responsa/tfn-no-5753-4-133-140/.

[472] Paul J. Menitoff to Walter Jacob, June 24, 1995, Rodef Shalom Archives (Box 16, Folder 12); Walter Jacob to Paul J. Menitoff, June 29, 1995, Rodef Shalom Archives (Box 16, Folder 12). Walter eventually wrote a historical analysis of private ordination for the *CCAR Journal*, see Walter Jacob, "Private Ordination—Need We Be Concerned," *CCAR Journal* (Winter 1997), 3–8, Rodef Shalom Archives (Box 15, Folder 120).

[473] Walter Homolka, interview by author, December 7, 2015, Berlin, Germany.

[474] Walter Jacob, National Council of Jewish Women oral history.

[475] Walter Jacob to Mr. and Mrs. Allan Lowenberg, June 17, 1997, private collection of Walter Jacob.

[476] Peter S. Knobel, "Introduction, in *An American Rabbinate: A Festschrift for Walter Jacob*, ed. Mark N. Staitman and Peter S. Knobel (Pittsburgh: Rodef Shalom Press, 2000), ix–xiv.

[477] Walter Jacob to "Piske and Hillel," June 3, 1997, private collection of Walter Jacob; Walter Jacob, National Council of Jewish Women oral history.

[478] Walter Jacob to Kate Stern, July 9, 1997, private collection of Walter Jacob.

[479] Walter Jacob to Kate Stern, July 27, 1997, private collection of Walter Jacob.

[480] Walter Jacob to Kate Stern, December 3, 1997, private collection of Walter Jacob.

[481] Walter Jacob to Kate Stern, January 14, 1998, private collection of Walter Jacob.

[482] Walter Jacob to Kate Stern, January 14, 1998, private collection of Walter Jacob.

[483] Walter Jacob, National Council of Jewish Women oral history.

[484] Walter Jacob to Kate Stern, January 14, 1998, private collection of Walter Jacob.

[485] "The Abraham Geiger College: A Seminary Without Walls," Rodef Shalom Archives (Box 93, Folder 34).

[486] Walter Jacob, "The Broader Role of the Rabbi," 363.

[487] Walter Jacob, "The Broader Role of the Rabbi," 364.

[488] Walter Jacob, interview by author, October 30, 2015, Pittsburgh, Pa.

[489] Walter Jacob to Eric Yoffie, August 9, 1998, Rodef Shalom Archives (Box 93, Folder 48); Walter Jacob to Alan L. Smith, August 23, 1998, Rodef Shalom Archives (Box 93, Folder 48).

[490] Walter Jacob, "The Broader Role of the Rabbi," 363–364; Marylynne Pitz, "Germans get a crash course in Jewish heritage," *Pittsburgh-Post-Gazette*, August 25, 1999, 20.

[491] Walter Jacob to Eli Loewenthal, February 4, 1999, private collection of Walter Jacob.

[492] Ibid.

[493] Walter Jacob, "The Broader Role of the Rabbi," 365.

[494] Walter Jacob, interview by author, October 30, 2015, Pittsburgh, Pa.

[495] "The Abraham Geiger College: A Seminary Without Walls."

[496] "Why Abraham Geiger?" ca. 1999, Rodef Shalom Archives (Box 52, Folder 12).

[497] Meyer, *Response to Modernity*, 89–92.

[498] "First Post-War Rabbinic Seminary in Germany," press release, August 18, 1999, Rodef Shalom Archives (Box 52, Folder 12); Walter Jacob to Eli Loewenthal, August 19, 1999, personal collection of Walter Jacob.

[499] On the opening of the college, see Steve Levin, "Local rabbi to take part in dedication ceremony," *Pittsburgh Post-Gazette*, November 4, 2000, 51; Iris M. Samson, "Central Europe gets its seminary," *Jewish Chronicle* (Pittsburgh, Pa.), November 9, 2000, 6. On his teaching regimen, see Walter Jacob, interview by author, October 30, 2015, Pittsburgh, Pa. On recruiting, see Tom Kucera, interview by author, December 4, 2015, Munich, Germany.

[500] Walter Jacob to Eli Loewenthal, July 19, 1999, private collection of Walter Jacob.

[501] Walter Jacob, "The Broader Role of the Rabbi," 365.

[502] Walter Jacob to Eli Loewenthal, December 8, 2002, private collection of Walter Jacob.

[503] "Germany's Liberal Jewish Community Celebrates Anniversary, Acceptance," *Jewish Telegraphic Agency*, July 16, 2003, accessed November 28, 2015, www.jta.org/2003/07/16/archive/germanys-liberal-jewish-community-celebrates-anniversary-acceptance; "Reform Jews in Germany Closer to Earning a Place at the Table," *Jewish Telegraphic Agency*, July 5, 2004, accessed November 28, 2015, www.jta.org/2004/07/06/archive/reform-jews-in-germany-closer-to-earning-a-place-at-the-table; Martin Dommer and Sebastian Knauer, "Many Rooms Under One Roof," *Der Spiegel*, March 5, 2004, accessed November 16, 2015, www.spiegel.de/international/spiegel/religion-many-rooms-under-one-roof-a-298303-druck.html.

[504] Walter Jacob, interview by author, October 30, 2015, Pittsburgh, Pa. On his approach to fundraising and donor relations for his activities in Europe, see Walter Jacob to Eli Loewenthal, January 3, 2001, private collection of Walter Jacob; Walter Jacob to Kate Stern, August 30, 2006, private collection of Walter Jacob.

[505] On his library initiative, see Walter Jacob to Kate Stern, January 6, 1999, private collection of Walter Jacob; Walter Jacob to Kate Stern, August 22, 2001, private collection of Walter Jacob; Walter Jacob to Kate Stern, November 3, 2003, private collection of Walter Jacob; Walter Jacob to Kate Stern, December 29, 2004, private collection of Walter Jacob.

[506] Walter Jacob to Kate Stern, February 2, 2004, private collection of Walter Jacob; Angela Leibowicz, "Jacob organizes book drive for German rabbinical school," *Jewish Chronicle* (Pittsburgh, Pa.), September 9, 2004, 2.

[507] Lee Chottiner, "Rabbi honored with face on postage stamp," *Jewish Chronicle* (Pittsburgh, Pa.), November 4, 2004, 1.

[508] *Akademische Abschlussfeier.*

[509] On his remarks at the ordination and his subsequent thoughts about the event, see Walter Jacob to Kate Stern, September 24, 2006, private collection of Walter Jacob.

[510] Walter Jacob, "The first ordination in Germany since the Shoah won't be the last," *Jewish Chronicle* (Pittsburgh, Pa.), October 5, 2006, 8.

[511] Walter Homolka, "A Vision Come True," 244.

[512] Mike Zoller, "Abraham Geiger College to stay open despite economic woes," *Jewish Chronicle* (Pittsburgh, Pa.), October 30, 2008, 12.

[513] Lee Chottiner, "Officials: German rabbinical school stays afloat with Pittsburgh aid," *Jewish Chronicle* (Pittsburgh, Pa.), April 30, 2009, 4.

[514] Walter Homolka, interview by author, December 7, 2015, Berlin, Germany.

[515] Jona Simon, interview by author, December 8, 2015, Oldenburg, Germany.

[516] Ibid.

Bibliography
Compiled by Martha Berg, Archivist, Rodef Shalom Congregation

This bibliography includes selected books, essays, articles, and reviews written or edited by Walter Jacob. The arrangement is chronological, with books for each year listed before other writings. Individual Responsa and most articles from local publications are not included. When Rabbi Jacob both edited and contributed an essay for a volume, the essay is given as a separate entry immediately below the main entry for the volume. A comprehensive bibliography for the years 1955–2001 may be found in *An American Rabbinate: A Festschrift for Walter Jacob*, edited by Peter Knobel and Mark N. Staitman (Pittsburgh: Rodef Shalom Press, 2000). A complete list of additional publications for the years 2001–2015 is available at the Rodef Shalom Congregation Archives.

Jacob, Walter. "Jews in the Philippines." *Congress Weekly: A Review of Jewish Interests*, no. 1 (January 7, 1957): 10,11.

"Even in Manila." *World Jewish Affairs News and Feature Service*, January 21, 1957: 1, 2.

"A Visit to the Orient." *Reconstructionist*, June 14, 1957: 23–25.

"The New Synagogue: Success or Failure." *Jewish Spectator*, April 1961: 26.

"The Tin Menorah: A Symbol of Neglect." *Congress Bi-Weekly* 28 (November 27, 1961): 17.

"Let's Get Rid of the Tin Menorah: A Symbol of Neglect." *Jewish Digest*, December 1962: 21–23.

"Education and the Jew: A German View." *Religious Education* 58, no. 3 (1963): 269–275.

"The Jewish Retreat." *Jewish Spectator*, June 1963: 25–26.

"The Inter-Religious Dialogue." *Jewish Heritage*, Fall 1963: 31–35.

"A Bibliography of Novels & Short Stories by German Jewish Authors, 1800–1914." *Studies in Bibliography & Booklore* 6, no. 2 (Winter 1963): 75–92.

Jacob, Ernest I. *Paths of Faithfulness: A Collection of Sermons.* Edited by Walter Jacob and Herbert Jacob. Pittsburgh: 1964.

Jacob, Walter, Frederick C. Schwartz, and Vigdor W. Kavaler, eds. *Essays in Honor of Solomon B. Freehof.* Pittsburgh: Rodef Shalom Congregation, 1964.

Jacob, Walter. "The Pulpit Lecture." In *Essays in Honor of Solomon B. Freehof,* edited by Walter Jacob, Frederick C. Schwartz, and Vigdor W. Kavaler, 33–52. Pittsburgh: Rodef Shalom Congregation, 1964.

"Has the Jewish Retreat Failed?" *Jewish Digest,* May 1964: 58–60.

Review of *The New Germany and the Old Nazis,* by T. H. Tetens. *Jewish Social Studies: A Quarterly Journal Devoted to Contemporary and Historical Aspects of Jewish Life* 24, no. 4 (October 1964): 255–256.

"Hitler and Christianity." *Jewish Spectator* 29 (October 1964).

Jacob, Benno. "'The First and Second Commandments': An Excerpt from the *Commentary on Exodus.*" Translated by Walter Jacob. *Judaism* 13, no. 1 (Winter, 1964): 318ff.

Jacob, Walter. *Our Biblical Heritage.* New York: Department of Adult Jewish Education, Union of American Hebrew Congregations, 1965.

"World Union Leaders: Solomon B. Freehof." *Reform Review, Monthly Journal of Modern Judaism, South Africa* 1, no. 3 (May 1965): 8–9.

"Leo Baeck on Christianity." *Jewish Quarterly Review* 56, no. 2 (October 1965): 195–211.

"Moses Mendelssohn and the Jewish-Christian Dialogue." *CCAR Journal* 13, no. 3 (October 1965): 45–51.

"The Tower of Babel, A Fable for Adults." In *Best Jewish Sermons of 5725–5726,* edited by Saul I. Teplitz, 128–134. New York: Jonathan David, 1966.

"Bored? Lonely?" In *Sermonic Talks on Jewish Ideas and Ideals, for Lay Leaders in the Armed Forces of the United States,* 35–36. National Jewish Welfare Board, 1967.

"Sorrow in Time of Joy, A Succot Sermon." In *Sermonic Talks on the Jewish Holidays and Festivals,* 15–16. National Jewish Welfare Board, 1967.

"The Interreligious Dialogue: Three Jewish Pioneers." *Face to Face,* 1967: 13–18.

"Success: Sweet or Sour." *American Rabbi* 2, no. 5 (January 1967): 30–33.

"Where Are We Going as American Jews?" In *Best Jewish Sermons of 5729–5730,* edited by Saul I. Teplitz, 62–71. New York: Jonathan David, 1970.

Jacob, Benno. "'Hear, O Israel.'" Translated by Ernest I. Jacob and Walter Jacob. *Jewish Spectator*, April 1971: 5–7.

Jacob, Walter. "Max Brod's Critique of Christianity." *CCAR Journal* 18, no. 2 (April 1971): 19–28.

"The World of Nature." In *Best Jewish Sermons of 5731–5732*, 72–79. New York: Jonathan David, 1972.

Freehof, Solomon B. *Spoken and Heard: Sermons and Addresses*. Introduction by Walter Jacob. Pittsburgh, PA: Rodef Shalom Congregation, 1972.

Jacob, Walter. *Christianity Through Jewish Eyes: The Quest for Common Ground*. [Cincinnati]: Hebrew Union College Press, 1974.

Jacob, Benno. *The First Book of the Bible: Genesis*. Interpreted by Benno Jacob. His commentary abridged, edited, and translated by Ernest I. Jacob and Walter Jacob. New York: KTAV Publishing House, 1974.

Jacob, Walter. "An Assessment of Christianity, The Historical Setting." *CCAR Journal* 21, no. 5 (Winter 1974): 47–54.

"The Right Question." In *Best Jewish Sermons of 5732–5733*, edited by Saul I. Teplitz, 51–57. New York: 1974.

Review of *Jesus the Jew: A Historian's Reading of the Gospels*, by Geza Vermes. *CCAR Journal*, Spring 1976: 84–87.

Review of *Modern Jewish Ethics: Theory and Practice*, by Marvin Fox. *Religious Education*, September 1976.

"The Tower of Babel." *Pastoral Services,* September 1976: 25–29.

"Success Sweet or Sour." In *Speak to the Children of Israel*, edited by Samuel M. Sliver and Morton M. Applebaum, 64–69. New York: KTAV Publishing House, 1976.

"Bored? Lonely?" In *Speak to the Children of Israel*, edited by Samuel M. Sliver and Morton M. Applebaum, 70–73. New York: KTAV Publishing House, 1976.

"Solomon B. Freehof and the Halachah: An Appreciation." In *Reform Responsa for our Time*, by Solomon B. Freehof, 1–27. [Cincinnati]: Hebrew Union College Press, 1977.

Review of *Jewish Philosophical Polemics Against Christianity*, by Daniel S. Lasker. *Religious Education* 73, no. 3 (May/June 1978): 371.

Review of *Contemporary Halakhic Problems*, by David Bleich, and *Biblical and Post-Biblical Defilement and Mourning: Law as Theology*, by Emanuel Feldman. *Journal of Reform Judaism* 25, no. 3 (Summer 1978): 93–96.

Review of *The Struggle over Reform Judaism*, by Alexander Guttman. *Journal of Reform Judaism*, September 1978: 13.

Review of *Anti-Judaism in Christian Theology*, by Charlotte Klein. *Religious Education* 58, no. 6 (Nov–Dec 1978): 27.

"Dialogue in Europe Today." *Sonderheft Zeitschrift für Religions–und Geistesgeschichte* 31, no. 1 (January 1979): 48–61.

"Conservative Judaism and Halachah." *Journal of Reform Judaism* 26, no. 1 (Winter 1979): 17–24.

"Prophetic Judaism: The History of a Term." *Journal of Reform Judaism* 26, no. 2 (Spring 1979): 33–45.

"Initiation into Judaism." *Religious Education* 74, no. 6 (November/December 1979): 597–602.

"An Interview with Solomon B. Freehof." *Journal of Reform Judaism* 27, no. 3 (Summer 1980): 16–21.

Jacob, Benno. "The Gifts of the Egyptians: A Critical Commentary." Translated by Walter Jacob. *Journal of Reform Judaism* 27, no. 3 (Summer 1980): 59–69.

Jacob, Walter. "Dialogue and Conflict: Jewish-Christian Relations Today." *Religious Education* 76, no. 6 (1981): 587–597.

"Presidential Address: A View from the Bottom." *Religious Education* 77, no. 5 (September/October 1982): 468–471.

"Interview: Solomon B. Freehof: Pioneer—Jewish Educator." *Reach* 12, no. 2 (Summer 1982): 4ff.

Review of *The Middle East: Abstract and Index*, by Amy C. Lowenstein. *Journal of Reform Judaism*, Winter, 1982: 59–60.

"Building a Caring Community." *Sh'ma: A Journal of Jewish Ideas* 13 (November 1982): 3–4.

———, ed. *American Reform Responsa: Collected Responsa of the Central Conference of American Rabbis 1889–1983*. The Preface, Introduction, and many of the Responsa were written by Walter Jacob. New York: Central Conference of American Rabbis (CCAR), 1983.

"Pittsburgh and the Synagogue Tradition." *Carnegie Magazine* 56, no. 8 (May/June 1983): 16–18.

"Resources for Teaching the Holocaust: A Review Essay." *Religious Education* 78, no. 3 (Summer 1983): 444–446.

"Pursuing Justice and Peace—Why is it so Difficult?" *Religious Education* 78, no. 4 (Fall 1983): 487–490.

———, ed. *Books of Fifty Years*. Pittsburgh: 1984. The introduction and six book reviews are by Walter Jacob. Pittsburgh: Rodef Shalom Congregation, 1984.

"Education." *Religious Education* 79, no. 1 (1984): 75–78.

Freehof, Solomon B. *The Sermon Continues*. Edited by Vigdor Kavaler, with introductions by Walter Jacob. Pittsburgh: Rodef Shalom Congregation, [1984].

Jacob, Walter. "On Teaching the Holocaust: A Review Essay." *Journal of Reform Judaism* 31, no. 1 (Winter 1984): 81–85.

———, ed. *The Changing World of Reform Judaism: The Pittsburgh Platform in Retrospect*. Pittsburgh: Rodef Shalom Congregation, 1985.

"The Influence of the Pittsburgh Platform on Reform *Halakhah* and Biblical Study." In *The Changing World of Reform Judaism: The Pittsburgh Platform in Retrospect*, edited by Walter Jacob, 25–39. Pittsburgh: Rodef Shalom Congregation, 1985.

Jacob, Irene, and Walter Jacob. *Gardens of North America and Hawaii: A Traveler's Guide*. Portland, OR: Timber Press, 1985.

Jacob, Walter. "Worte des Rabbiners." *Festzeitung der Israelitischen Kultusgemeinde Schwaben-Augsburg zur Wiedereinweihung der Synagoge*. Augsburg: September 1985: 8–9.

"A Response to Dykstra." *Religious Education* 81, no. 2 (1986): 185–187.

Cohen, Samuel S. *Essays in Jewish Theology*. Edited by Walter Jacob, Stanley Dreyfus, and Sidney Brooks. Cincinnati: Hebrew Union College Press, 1987.

Jacob, Walter. *Contemporary American Reform Responsa*. New York: Central Conference of American Rabbis, 1987.

———, ed. *Liberal Judaism and Halakhah: A Symposium in Honor of Solomon B. Freehof*. Pittsburgh: Rodef Shalom Press, 1988.

"Philosopher and Poseq: Some Views of Modern Jewish Law." In *Liberal Judaism and Halakhah: A Symposium in Honor of Solomon B. Freehof*, edited by Walter Jacob. Pittsburgh: Rodef Shalom Press, 1988.

———, and Irene Jacob. *Forgotten Immigrants: Plant Immigrants to Israel through Three Thousand Years*. Pittsburgh: Rodef Shalom Press, 1988.

———, and Irene Jacob. "A Garden Celebration of Israel's Fortieth Anniversary." *Jewish Spectator* 53: no. 2 (Summer 1988): 36–37.

"The First Violent Step Towards the Holocaust." *Aufbau Sonderbeilage zum 50 Jahrestag des November Pogroms.* November 1988: 29.

_____ et al. "The Greatest American Jewish Leaders." *American Jewish History* 78, no. 2 (December 1988): 169–200.

"The German Jew in America—The Last Wave of Immigrants." In *The German-Jewish Legacy in America, 1938–1988: From Bildung to the Bill of Rights,* edited by Abraham Peck, 351–353. Detroit: Wayne State University Press, 1989.

Freehof, Solomon B. *Today's Reform Responsa.* Introduction by Walter Jacob. Cincinnati: Hebrew Union College Press, 1990.

Jacob, Walter. "The Never Ending Debate." *Reform Judaism* 18, no. 3 (Spring 1990): 23–25.

"Rabbi Akiba" and "Rabbi as Educator." In *Harper's Encyclopedia of Religious Education.* San Francisco: Harper & Row, 1990.

"Community Fellowship and Care (Jewish)." In *Dictionary of Pastoral Care and Counseling.* Nashville: Abington Press, 1990.

"Writing the Rules." *Manna* 29 (Autumn 1990): 8ff.

_____, and Moshe Zemer, eds. *Dynamic Jewish Law: Progressive Halakhah, Essence and Application.* Tel Aviv and Pittsburgh: Freehof Institute of Progressive Halakhah, Rodef Shalom Press, 1991.

"Pesikah and American Reform Responsa." In *Dynamic Jewish Law: Progressive Halakhah, Essence and Application,* edited by Walter Jacob and Moshe Zemer. Tel Aviv and Pittsburgh: Freehof Institute of Progressive Halakhah, Rodef Shalom Press, 1991.

"Organ Transplants—A Reform Jewish Perspective." In *New Harvest: Transplanting Body Parts and Reaping the Benefits,* edited by C. Don Keyes, 196–197. Clifton, NJ: Humana Press, 1991.

"The Judeo-Christian Dialogue in the Twentieth Century: The Jewish Response." In *Toward a Theological Encounter: Jewish Understanding of Christianity,* edited by Leon Klenicki. New York: Paulist Press, 1991.

Jacob, Benno. *The Second Book of the Bible: Exodus.* Interpreted by Benno Jacob. Translated with an introduction by Walter Jacob in association with Yaakov Elman. Hoboken, NJ: KTAV Publishing House, 1992.

Jacob, Walter. *Questions and Reform Jewish Answers: New American Reform Responsa.* New York: Central Conference of American Rabbis, 1992.

_____, and Irene Jacob. "Flora." In *Anchor Bible Dictionary.* New York: Doubleday, 1992.

"Standards Now." *Reform Judaism* 21, no. 1 (Fall 1992): 64.

Jacob, Irene, and Walter Jacob, eds. *The Healing Past: Pharmaceuticals in the Biblical and Rabbinic World*. Leiden: E. J. Brill, 1993.

Jacob, Walter. "Medicinal Plants of the Bible—Another View." In *The Healing Past: Pharmaceuticals in the Biblical and Rabbinic World*, edited by Irene and Walter Jacob, 27–46. Leiden: E. J. Brill, 1993.

_____, and Moshe Zemer, eds. *Rabbinic-Lay Relations in Jewish Law*. Tel Aviv and Pittsburgh: Freehof Institute of Progressive Halakhah, Rodef Shalom Press, 1993.

"Rabbinic Authority—Power-Sharing: Old and New Formulas." In *Rabbinic-Lay Relations in Jewish Law*, edited by Walter Jacob and Moshe Zemer. Tel Aviv and Pittsburgh: Freehof Institute of Progressive Halakhah, Rodef Shalom Press, 1993.

_____, and Moshe Zemer, eds. *Conversion to Judaism in Jewish Law: Essays and Responsa*. Tel Aviv and Pittsburgh: Freehof Institute of Progressive Halakhah, Rodef Shalom Press, 1994.

"Conversion and the Developing Reform Halakhah." In *Conversion to Judaism in Jewish Law: Essays and Responsa*, edited by Walter Jacob and Moshe Zemer, 115ff. Tel Aviv and Pittsburgh: Freehof Institute of Progressive Halakhah, Rodef Shalom Press, 1994.

_____, and Irene Jacob. "Building a Biblical Garden." *Herb Quarterly* 63 (Fall 1994): 26–31.

_____, and Moshe Zemer, eds. *Death and Euthanasia in Jewish Law: Essays and Responsa*. Tel Aviv and Pittsburgh: Freehof Institute of Progressive Halakhah, Rodef Shalom Press, 1995.

"Endstage Euthanasia: Some Other Considerations." In *Death and Euthanasia in Jewish Law: Essays and Responsa*, edited by Walter Jacob and Moshe Zemer. Tel Aviv and Pittsburgh: Freehof Institute of Progressive Halakhah, Rodef Shalom Press, 1995.

_____, and Moshe Zemer, eds. *The Fetus and Fertility in Jewish Law: Essays and Responsa*. Tel Aviv and Pittsburgh: Freehof Institute of Progressive Halakhah, Rodef Shalom Press, 1995.

"'Be Fruitful and Multiply.'" In *The Fetus and Fertility: Essays and Responsa*, edited by Walter Jacob and Moshe Zemer. Tel Aviv and Pittsburgh: Freehof Institute of Progressive Halakhah, Rodef Shalom Press, 1995.

"Von der Duldung zum aktiven Entgegenkommen—Übertritt in den Vereinigten Staaten." In *Nicht durch Geburt allein*, edited by Walter Homolka and Esther Seidel. Munich: Knesebeck, 1995.

"Proefdieren en halacha (Experimental Animals and the Halakhah)." *Leven Joods Geloof* 42, no. 9 (July 1996): 34–37.

"The Interreligious Dialogue, a Personal Jewish View." In *It Takes a Congregation: A Festschrift for Boardman Wright Kathan*. Philadelphia: NLK Publishing, 1996.

———, and Moshe Zemer, eds. *Israel and the Diaspora in Jewish Law: Essays and Responsa*. Tel Aviv and Pittsburgh: Freehof Institute of Progressive Halakhah, Rodef Shalom Press, 1997.

"The Primacy of the Diaspora." In *Israel and the Diaspora in Jewish Law: Essays and Responsa*, edited by Walter Jacob and Moshe Zemer, 141–163. Tel Aviv and Pittsburgh: Freehof Institute of Progressive Halakhah, Rodef Shalom Press, 1997.

Homolka, Walter, Walter Jacob, and Esther Seidel, eds. *Not by Birth Alone: Conversion to Judaism*. Herndon, VA: Cassell, 1997.

Jacob, Walter. "Conversion and Outreach in the United States." In *Not by Birth Alone: Conversion to Judaism*, edited by Walter Homolka, Walter Jacob, and Esther Seidel, 74–82. Herndon, VA: Cassell, 1997.

"Private Ordination—Need We Be Concerned?" *CCAR Journal* 44, no. 1 (Winter 1997): 3ff.

Review of *Reform Jewish Ethics and the Halakhah: An Experiment in Decision Making*, edited by Eugene B. Borowitz. *CCAR Journal* 44, no. 1 (Winter 1997): 83–85.

Moch, Theodor. *Das Judentum: wie es wirklich ist*. Vienna, 1997. Vorwort (Foreword) by Walter Jacob.

Jacob, Walter. "Leo Baeck und Claude Montefiore — Die Evangelien aus jüdischer Sicht." In *Leo Baeck — Zwischen Geheimnis und Gebot*, 185–192. Karslruhe: Bertelsmann Buch AG, 1997.

———, and Moshe Zemer, eds. *Aging and the Aged in Jewish Law: Essays and Responsa*. Tel Aviv and Pittsburgh: Freehof Institute of Progressive Halakhah, Rodef Shalom Press, 1998.

"Beyond Methuselah—Who Is Old?" In *Aging and the Aged in Jewish Law: Essays and Responsa*, edited by Walter Jacob and Moshe Zemer, 1–14. Tel Aviv and Pittsburgh: Freehof Institute of Progressive Halakhah, Rodef Shalom Press, 1998.

Randall, Marga. *How Beautiful We Once Were*. Introduction by Walter Jacob. Pittsburgh: Cathedral Publishing, 1998.

Jacob, Walter. "Benno Jacob." In *Dictionary of Biblical Interpretation*. Nashville: Abingdon Press, 1999.

———, and Moshe Zemer, eds. *Crime and Punishment in Jewish Law: Essays and Responsa*. New York and Oxford: Berghahn Press, 1999.

"Punishment: Its Method and Purpose." In *Crime and Punishment in Jewish Law: Essays and Responsa*, edited by Walter Jacob and Moshe Zemer. New York and Oxford: Berghahn Press, 1999.

———, and Moshe Zemer, eds. *Marriage and its Obstacles in Jewish Law: Essays and Responsa*. Tel Aviv and Pittsburgh: Freehof Institute of Progressive Halakhah, Rodef Shalom Press, 1999.

"The Slow Road to Monogamy." In *Marriage and its Obstacles in Jewish Law: Essays and Responsa*, edited by Walter Jacob and Moshe Zemer. Tel Aviv and Pittsburgh: Freehof Institute of Progressive Halakhah, Rodef Shalom Press, 1999.

Homolka, Walter, ed. *Die Lehren des Judentums nach den Quellen*. Nachwort (Afterword) by Walter Jacob. Berlin: Jüdische Verlagsanstalt, 1999.

Jacob, Walter, and Irene Jacob. "Flora in the Dead Sea Scrolls." In *Encyclopedia of the Dead Sea Scrolls*. Oxford and New York: Oxford University Press, 2000.

"Springtime for Liberal Judaism." *Aufbau* 66, no. 8 (April 2000): 1–2.

"Rabbi Alexander Schindler—In Memoriam." *Aufbau* 66 (September 2000): 14.

———, and Moshe Zemer, eds. *Gender Issues in Jewish Law: Essays and Responsa*. New York and Oxford: Berghahn Press, 2001.

"The Woman in Reform Judaism: Facing or Avoiding the Issues." In *Gender Issues in Jewish Law: Essays and Responsa*, edited by Walter Jacob and Moshe Zemer. New York and Oxford: Berghahn Press, 2001.

"Rabbi Alexander Schindler." *Keschet* 6, no. 4 (January–March 2001): 17.

"Halachische Traditionen." In *Handbuch der Juden in Europa II*, edited by J. Schoeps. Darmstadt: Wissenschaftliche Buchgesellschaft, 2001.

———, and Moshe Zemer, eds. *Re-examining Progressive Halakhah*. New York and Oxford: Berghahn Books, 2002.

"The Law of the Land and Jewish Law." In *Re-examining Progressive Halakhah*, edited by Walter Jacob and Moshe Zemer, 71ff. New York and Oxford: Berghahn Books, 2002.

———, and Almuth Jürgensen, eds. *Die Exegese hat das erste Wort*. Stuttgart: Calwer, 2002.

"The Life and Work of Benno Jacob" and "Benno Jacob on Leviticus." In *Die Exegese hat das erste Wort*, edited by Walter Jacob and Moshe Zemer. Stuttgart: Calwer, 2002.

Geiger, Ludwig. *Abraham Geiger: Leben und Werk für ein Judentum in der Moderne*. Nachwort (Afterword) by Walter Jacob. Berlin: Jüdische Verlagsanstalt, 2002.

Jacob, Walter. "Renewing Reform Judaism: From Pittsburgh to Pittsburgh." In *Platforms and Prayer Books: Theological and Liturgical Perspectives on Reform Judaism*, edited by Dana Evan Kaplan, 81–92. Lanham, MD: Rowan & Littlefield, 2002.

———, and Moshe Zemer, eds. *The Environment in Jewish Law—Essays and Responsa.* New York and Oxford: Berghahn Books, 2003.

"Eco-Judaism—Does It Exist?" In *The Environment in Jewish Law—Essays and Responsa*, edited by Walter Jacob, and Moshe Zemer, 1–23. New York and Oxford: Berghahn Books, 2003.

———, ed. *Gardening from the Bible to North America: Essays in Honor of Irene Jacob.* Pittsburgh: Rodef Shalom Press, 2004.

"A Garden Path," "The Mysterious Lulav and Etrog," and "The Gardens—Design and Philosophy." In *Gardening from the Bible to North America: Essays in Honor of Irene Jacob*, edited by Walter Jacob. Pittsburgh: Rodef Shalom Press, 2004.

———, ed. *Beyond the Letter of the Law: Essays on Diversity in the Halakhah, in Honor of Moshe Zemer.* Pittsburgh: Rodef Shalom Press, 2004.

"Writing Responsa—A Personal Journey" and "Moshe Zemer: An Appreciation." In *Beyond the Letter of the Law: Essays on Diversity in the Halakhah in Honor of Moshe Zemer*, edited by Walter Jacob. Pittsburgh: Rodef Shalom Press, 2004.

"'The Law of the Lord is Perfect'—Halakhah and Antinomianism in Reform Judaism." *CCAR Journal: A Reform Jewish Quarterly*, Autumn 2004: 72–84.

———, ed. *Pursuing Peace Across the Alleghenies: The Rodef Shalom Congregation, Pittsburgh, Pennsylvania, 1856–2005.* Pittsburgh: Rodef Shalom Press, 2005.

"Pittsburgh and the Jewish Community," "Showing the Way—The Rodef Shalom Pulpit, 1854–1998," "An interview with Solomon B. Freehof," and "The Broader Role of the Rabbi." In *Pursuing Peace Across the Alleghenies: The Rodef Shalom Congregation, Pittsburgh, Pennsylvania, 1856–2005*, edited by Walter Jacob. Pittsburgh: Rodef Shalom Press, 2005.

———, and Moshe Zemer, eds. *Sexual Issues in Jewish Law: Essays and Responsa.* Pittsburgh: Rodef Shalom Press, 2006.

"Controlling Passions—Mixed Results." In *Sexual Issues in Jewish Law: Essays and Responsa*, edited by Walter Jacob and Moshe Zemer, 93–118. Pittsburgh: Rodef Shalom Press, 2006.

———, and Walter Homolka, eds. *Hesed and Tzedakah: From Bible to Modernity.* Berlin: Frank & Timme, 2006.

"Hasid and Tzadik—The People's Choice." In *Hesed and Tzedakah: From Bible to Modernity*, edited by Walter Jacob and Walter Homolka, 11–27. Berlin: Frank & Timme, 2006.

_____, and Moshe Zemer, eds. *Poverty and Tzedakah in Jewish Law: Essays and Responsa*. Pittsburgh: Rodef Shalom Press, 2006.

"Against Poverty—From Torah to Secular Judaism." In *Poverty and Tzedakah in Jewish Law: Essays and Responsa*, edited by Walter Jacob and Moshe Zemer, 1–47. Pittsburgh: Rodef Shalom Press, 2006.

_____, ed., in association with Moshe Zemer. *Napoleon's Influence on Jewish Law: The Sanhedrin of 1807 and its Modern Consequences*. Pittsburgh: Rodef Shalom Press, 2007.

"Napoleon's Sanhedrin and the Halakhah." In *Napoleon's Influence on Jewish Law: The Sanhedrin of 1807 and its Modern Consequences*, edited by Walter Jacob in association with Moshe Zemer, 1–64. Pittsburgh: Rodef Shalom Press, 2007.

Jacob, Benno. *Genesis: The First Book of the Bible*. Augmented edition. Interpreted by Benno Jacob. His commentary abridged, edited, and translated by Ernest I. Jacob and Walter Jacob. New introduction by Walter Jacob. New York: KTAV Publishing House, 2007.

Jacob, Walter. "Benno Jacob as Biblical Scholar—A Biographical Sketch." In *Genesis: The First Book of the Bible*. Augmented edition. Interpreted by Benno Jacob. His commentary abridged, edited, and translated by Ernest I. Jacob and Walter Jacob. New introduction by Walter Jacob. New York: KTAV Publishing House, 2007.

"Ein Rabbinat in dunklen Stunden—Ernst L. Jacob, 1899–1974." In *An Meine Gemeinde in der Zerstreuung: Die Rundbriefe des Augsberger Rabbiners, Ernst Jacob, 1941–1949*, edited by Gernot Römer, 5–19. Augsburg: Wilner Verlag, 2007.

"Juden zwischen Peripherie und Zentrum." *Aufbau—Das Jüdische Monatsmagazin* 72 (April 2008): 6–8.

_____, ed., in association with Moshe Zemer. *Only in America: The Open Society and Jewish Law*. Pittsburgh: Rodef Shalom Press, 2009.

"The Case of Feminism—Mechanisms of Change from Europe to America." In *Only in America: The Open Society and Jewish Law*, edited by Walter Jacob, in association with Moshe Zemer, 43–90. Pittsburgh: Rodef Shalom Press, 2009.

_____, ed. *War and Terrorism in Jewish Law: Essays and Responsa*. Introduction by Walter Jacob. Pittsburgh: Rodef Shalom Press, 2010.

"Fighting in National Armies" and "Fighting in the Israeli Army" In *War and Terrorism in Jewish Law: Essays and Responsa*, edited by Walter Jacob. Pittsburgh: Rodef Shalom Press, 2010.

Benno Jacob: Kämpfer und Gelehrter. Berlin: Hentrich & Hentrich, 2011.

Benno Jacob: Scholar and Fighter. Berlin: Hentrich & Hentrich, 2012.

———, ed. *Medical Frontiers and Jewish Law: Essays and Responsa.* Introduction by Walter Jacob. Pittsburgh: Rodef Shalom Press, 2012.

"Changing Views of Health Care Delivery." In *Medical Frontiers and Jewish Law: Essays and Responsa,* edited by Walter Jacob, 103–119. Pittsburgh: Rodef Shalom Press, 2012.

———, ed. *The Internet Revolution and Jewish Law.* Pittsburgh: Rodef Shalom Press, 2014.

"Intellectual Property in the Digital Age: Protect or Share." In *The Internet Revolution and Jewish Law,* edited by Walter Jacob. Pittsburgh: Rodef Shalom Press, 2014.

———, ed. *Addiction and Its Consequences in Jewish Law.* Pittsburgh: Rodef Shalom Press, 2015.

"The Jewish Alcohol Puzzle." In *Addiction and Its Consequences in Jewish Law,* edited by Walter Jacob. Pittsburgh: Rodef Shalom Press, 2015.

Index

Ordination is granted by institutions but rests upon the reputations of individuals. Walter Jacob lays his hands on every graduate of the Abraham Geiger College and delivers a private, personalized message to each new rabbi during the ceremony.